accounting

a smart approach

Mary Carey

Cathy Knowles

Jane Towers-Clark

OXFORD
UNIVERSITY PRESS

OXFORD
UNIVERSITY PRESS
Great Clarendon Street, Oxford OX2 6DP
Oxford University Press is a department of the University of Oxford.
It furthers the University's objective of excellence in research, scholarship, and education by publishing worldwide in
Oxford New York
Auckland Cape Town Dar es Salaam Hong Kong Karachi
Kuala Lumpur Madrid Melbourne Mexico City Nairobi
New Delhi Shanghai Taipei Toronto
With offices in
Argentina Austria Brazil Chile Czech Republic France Greece
Guatemala Hungary Italy Japan Poland Portugal Singapore
South Korea Switzerland Thailand Turkey Ukraine Vietnam
Oxford is a registered trade mark of Oxford University Press in the UK and in certain other countries
Published in the United States
by Oxford University Press Inc., New York

British Library Cataloguing in Publication Data
Data available
Library of Congress Cataloging in Publication Data
Data available
Typeset by Graphicraft Limited, Hong Kong
Printed in Great Britain on acid-free paper by Ashford Colour Press Ltd, Gosport, Hampshire
ISBN 978–0–19–958741–4
5 7 9 10 8 6 4

To T-C, Emily, and Hugh with love, my parents for their never-ending support, my brothers Mark, James, and John, and to my Australian friends, without whom I would never have started on this adventure.

Jane Towers-Clark

For Adrian, Sarah, and Christopher with love.

Mary Carey

To Tim, Chris, Ben, and Becky for their patience.

Cathy Knowles

Preface

This book is aimed at introducing non-accounting students to the fundamentals of financial and management accounting in a clear and practical way. It is particularly suitable for degree courses, both at undergraduate and master's level, where students are being introduced to accounting for the first time. It could be used to support a year-long course or, in part, to accompany one which runs for a semester.

This book brings accounting to life through the provision of a fully integrated case study that runs throughout. It follows the experiences of Sam Smart from the point at which he is considering starting his own business, printing sports kits for local football teams, through to managing a global sports business, manufacturing and distributing a wide range of equipment and clothing. As his business expands, Sam faces key business decisions such as how to manage his cash, price his products, assess new product launches, and evaluate the viability of the business's international retail outlets.

As the Smart business grows and develops, each chapter explains the issues and problems it is facing. In order to explore and resolve the problems posed, relevant accounting techniques are introduced. In this way, the techniques are not studied in isolation but are used immediately to inform the accounting and finance decisions that the business faces. As a result, the use and understanding of various techniques are immediately applied to a practical scenario. In the early planning stages, students consider how profit is measured and the key financial statements are explained. As the business grows, management accounting areas are then covered, including the areas of planning and controlling the business.

By using an integrated case study throughout, students will be able to see the implications of decisions made across a range of financial and management accounting issues. The demonstration exercises in each chapter mainly focus on the Smart case and occasionally introduce other business scenarios, thereby encouraging students to make connections between topics that are usually taught as apparently disparate subject areas. This is a far more coherent approach than that offered by more conventional texts.

This book is written from the perspective of business students, rather than adapting an accounting textbook. As each topic is covered, the focus is on equipping students to understand the main principles such that they are able to analyse, interpret, and question the accounting information that they may well encounter in a business context. As far as possible, unnecessary jargon is avoided and the focus is on meeting the needs of business and management students who do not necessarily plan to become accountants, but who will need a sound appreciation of accounting and finance in order to communicate and succeed in the business world.

The book has been specifically written with the needs of non-accountants in mind. Not only is it based on a teaching method employed at Oxford Brookes University for the past ten years, but business students have also been involved in reviewing the chapters and have found the approach to be very accessible, as the case study approach brings the subject to life.

For lecturers choosing to adopt this book, you will find that each chapter lends itself to providing an interactive teaching session with appropriate demonstration exercises and ponder points throughout. PowerPoint slides are available to accompany each chapter, as well as detailed solutions to all demonstration exercises and practice questions. Two additional case studies are included, one which tests students' understanding of financial accounting and one which tests their understanding of management accounting. These can be used as assessments or as extended seminar tasks. Taken with the assessment guide for the module, this text and its supporting materials will provide you with a complete 'off-the-shelf' package with which to deliver a course.

Brief contents

Contents

Contents

Acknowledgements

We would like to thank the many people who helped us in writing this book, especially our colleagues at Oxford Brookes University. In particular, we are grateful to John Playle for his contributions to the development of this book and to Richard Jeffs for his lasting inspiration. We wish to thank Howard Brown for allowing us the opportunity to build upon a teaching approach adopted by Oxford Brookes over the years. We also would like to acknowledge 'On-hand Sports', a business set-up by one of our former students, which provided the idea for the case study theme.

The authors and publishers would like to thank the following people, for their comments and reviews throughout the process of developing the text and the Online Resource Centre:

Dr Hafez Abdo, *Nottingham Trent University*
Dr Mary Bishop, *University of West of England*
Ian Crawford, *University of Bath*
Martin Kelly, *Queen's University Management School, Belfast*
Chou Chee Ling, *INTI University, Malaysia*
Dr David McAree, *University of Ulster*
Dr Emmanuil Noikokyris, *Univerity of Essex*
Jim O'Hare, *University of Leicester*
Shirley Powell, *Oxford Brookes University*
Rennie Tjerkstra, *University of Kent*
Prof. Dr. Thomas Vogler, *Ingolstadt University of Applied Sciences, Germany*
Iain Ward-Campbell, *Bradford University*

Thanks also to those reviewers who chose to remain anonymous.

How to use this book

Running Case Study

Each chapter opens with our running case study, following Sam Smart as he sets up his own business and considers the financial information needed to make this venture succeed. Applying accounting techniques to Sam's business throughout the textbook truly brings the subject to life and allows you to understand the relevance of accounting within a business context.

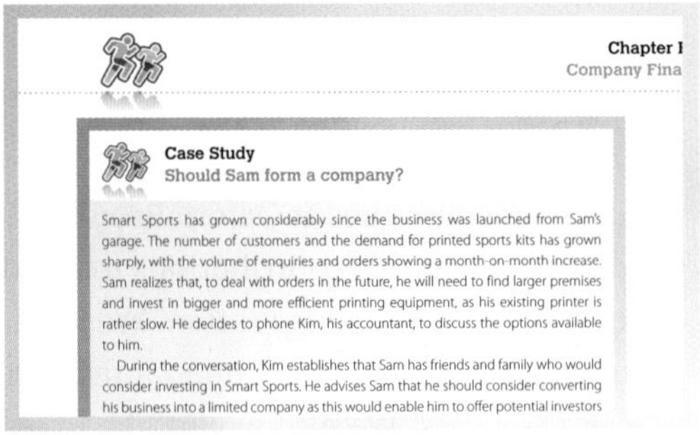
Chapter I
Company Fina

Case Study
Should Sam form a company?

Smart Sports has grown considerably since the business was launched from Sam's garage. The number of customers and the demand for printed sports kits has grown sharply, with the volume of enquiries and orders showing a month-on-month increase. Sam realizes that, to deal with orders in the future, he will need to find larger premises and invest in bigger and more efficient printing equipment, as his existing printer is rather slow. He decides to phone Kim, his accountant, to discuss the options available to him.

During the conversation, Kim establishes that Sam has friends and family who would consider investing in Smart Sports. He advises Sam that he should consider converting his business into a limited company as this would enable him to offer potential investors

Learning Objectives

A bulleted outline of the main concepts and ideas indicates what you can expect to learn from each chapter.

Summary of Key Points

Linked to the learning objectives, each chapter concludes with a summary of the most important concepts you need to take away.

Ponder Points

Regular Ponder Points encourage you to stop, think, and check your understanding of the central themes being covered within each chapter.

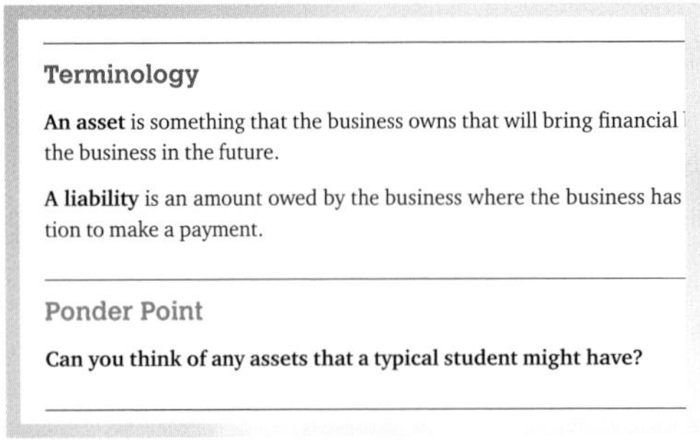
Terminology

An asset is something that the business owns that will bring financial
the business in the future.

A liability is an amount owed by the business where the business has
tion to make a payment.

Ponder Point

Can you think of any assets that a typical student might have?

Terminology

Accounting terms are regularly explained throughout the chapters, and collated to form a convenient glossary at the back of the book.

Wider Reading

Annotated suggestions for wider reading at the end of each chapter signpost where you can find further information to allow you to broaden your understanding of the chapter topics.

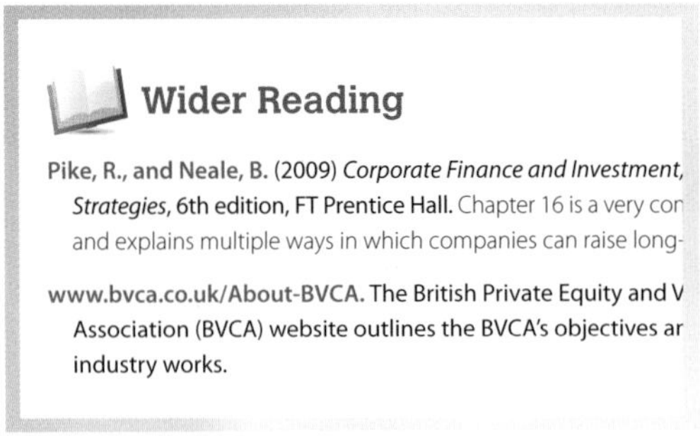
Wider Reading

Pike, R., and Neale, B. (2009) *Corporate Finance and Investment, Strategies*, 6th edition, FT Prentice Hall. Chapter 16 is a very cor
and explains multiple ways in which companies can raise long-

www.bvca.co.uk/About-BVCA. The British Private Equity and V
Association (BVCA) website outlines the BVCA's objectives ar
industry works.

Demonstration Exercises

Regular exercises—focusing on the running case study, but also introducing other business scenarios too—offer you the opportunity to test your understanding of the concepts you have just learned. Answers to these are either demonstrated within the chapter, or given at the end of the book to enable you to check your progress.

For added convenience, templates of the tables you need to complete are available on the Online Resource Centre for you to download and print off.

> l Accounting
>
> **Demonstration Exercise 3.3**
>
> Smart Sports has paid electricity bills totalling £1,920 during its first year of trading, which is the amount on the trial balance. However, this amount covers only electricity used up to 31 October 2011. Sam estimates that the cost of electricity used during November and December 2011 will amount to £240 per month.
>
> a) What is the amount of the accrual?
>
> b) What is the full cost of electricity consumed by Smart Sports during the year ended 31 December 2011?
>
> c) If this figure (from (b) above) for electricity consumed is used in the income statement, what effect will this have on the profit for the year?

Smart Questions: a wider perspective

Carefully devised questions at the end of each chapter allow you to reflect more widely on the topic covered, and enhance your critical thinking skills through considering the assumptions made, or explore the practical implications of using the accounting techniques you have just encountered.

Practice Questions

Detailed questions provided at the end of each chapter present you with the opportunity to check your ability to use the techniques covered, and to interpret your findings. Answers are provided at the back of the textbook to enable you to check your progress before moving on to the next topic. Further practice questions are also provided on the Online Resource Centre.

> **Practice Questions**
>
> **10.1 Pippa**
>
> Pippa runs a photographic studio specializing in black and white portrait photography. Clients book a one hour studio session and are entitled to receive two large photographs of their choice from the sitting.
>
> The following outgoings are associated with Pippa's business:
>
> - Pippa rents the photographic studio for £12,000 per annum.
> - Pippa employs two full-time photographers, each paid a salary of £22,000 per annum.
> - She employs one photographic technician for one day a week. He is paid £120 per day, £6,240 per annum.
> - Advertising costs are £550 per annum.
> - Electricity costs are £1,100 per annum plus £4 per client hour. Each sitting takes two hours.
> - Pippa acts as receptionist and general manager of the business and is paid £16,000 per annum.

Financial and Management Accounting Case Studies

Test your understanding of financial or management accounting concepts by attempting these end of part case studies, provided to consolidate all the material you've learned in the previous chapters.

> Case St
>
> **Management Accounting: Case Study**
> **Orchid Products**
>
> Orchid is a personal products company manufacturing shampoo, conditioner, and liquid soap. As it faces tough competition in a static market with no price inflation, the managing director and his team are considering how best to improve its financial performance. They are considering a number of options. A review of the product profitability suggests that they should not be selling liquid soap, but the sales director is concerned that the management accounting information is misleading. He would prefer to increase sales volume by reducing the selling prices or by running a major advertising campaign. The operations director wishes to use the spare capacity on the manufacturing line by producing a shampoo for a supermarket chain under the supermarket's own label, while the marketing director would like to launch a new shower gel product.

How to use the Online Resource Centre

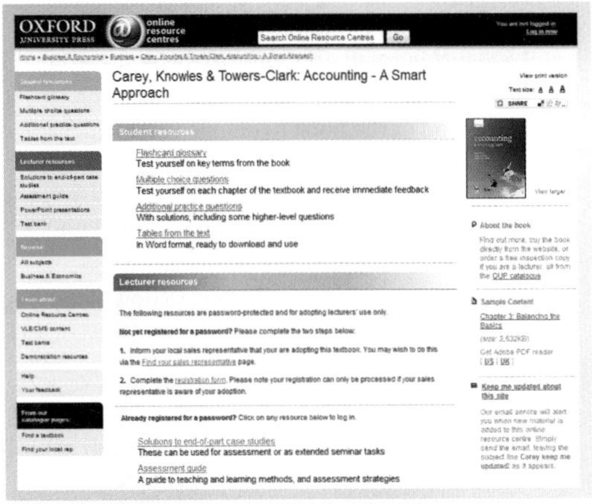

www.oxfordtextbooks.co.uk/orc/carey/
The Online Resource Centre (ORC) comprises resources for both lecturers and students, including:

Student Resources

Free and open-access material available:

Additional practice questions

The provision of additional questions and solutions, allows you more opportunity to apply the techniques learned in the textbook. Higher-level questions are also provided for you to attempt once you feel you have mastered a topic.

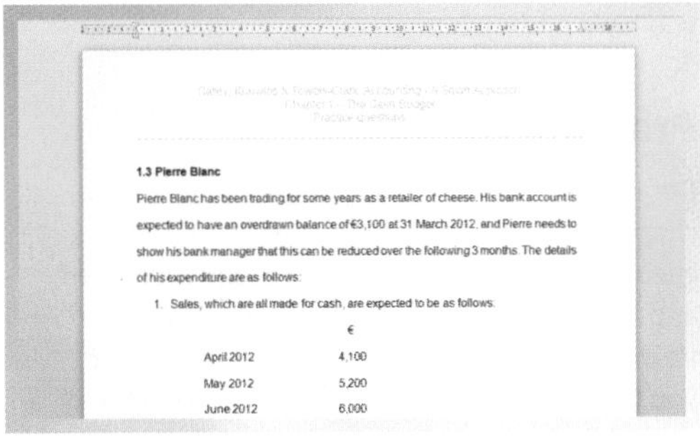

Flashcard glossary

Key glossary terms are available in an interactive flashcard format, and can be downloaded to an MP3 player, allowing you to check your understanding of important key concepts on the go.

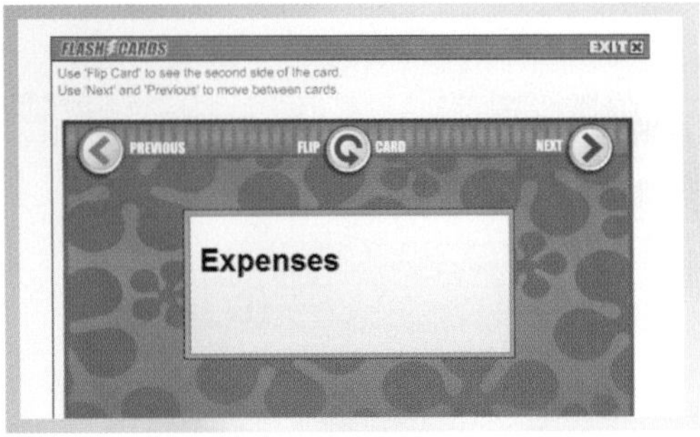

Multiple Choice Questions

A bank of self-marking multiple choice questions is available for each chapter providing instant feedback and page references, ideal for you to test your understanding of a topic before progressing to the next stage.

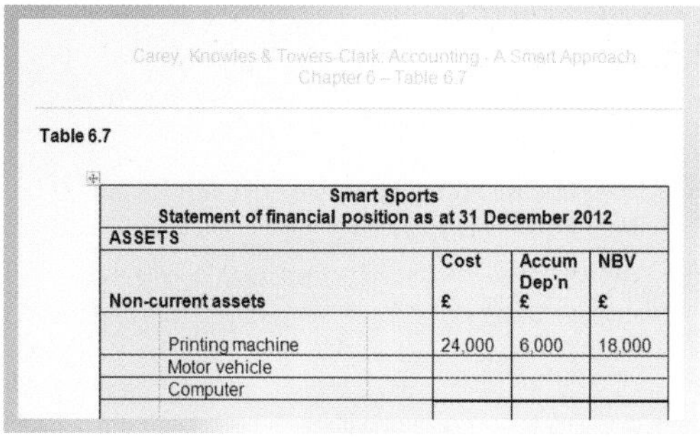

Smart Sports Statement of financial position as at 31 December 2012				
ASSETS				
Non-current assets		Cost £	Accum Dep'n £	NBV £
Printing machine		24,000	6,000	18,000
Motor vehicle				
Computer				

Tables from the text in electronic form

Linked to the demonstration exercises in the textbook, and organized by chapter, the tables you are required to complete are available here to download and print off for convenience.

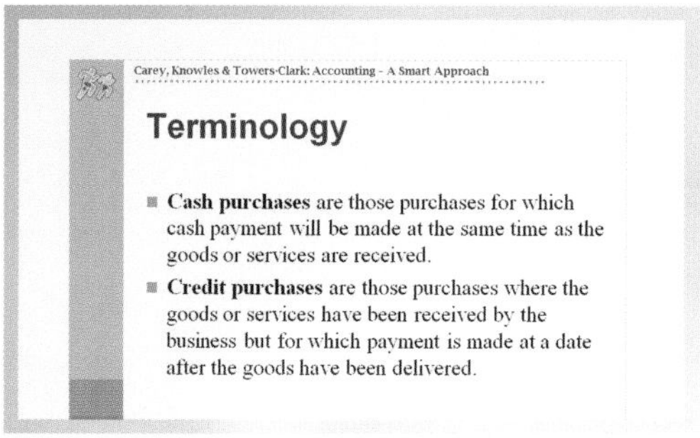

Lecturer Resources

Free for all registered adopters of the textbook:

PowerPoint slides

Accompanying each chapter is a suite of customizable slides, with notes, fully integrated with the textbook, to be used in lecture presentations.

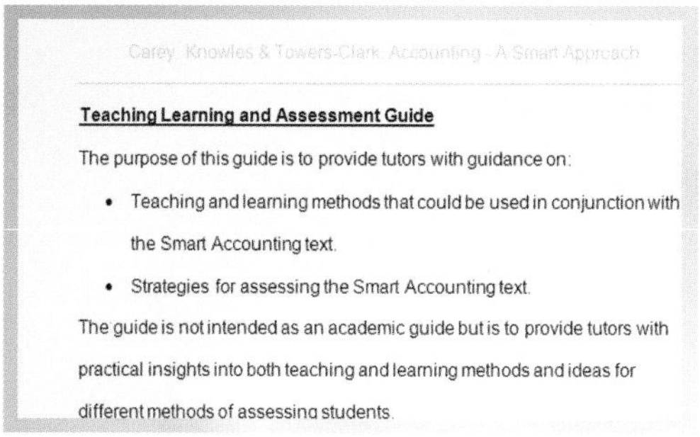

Assessment guide

This comprehensive resource provides you with guidance on how to get the most out of the textbook and online resources within your teaching, as well as offering examples for suggested methods of assessment

Solutions to the financial and management accounting case studies

Solutions to the financial accounting and management accounting case studies in the book are available here, allowing these to be used as assessments or extended seminar tasks.

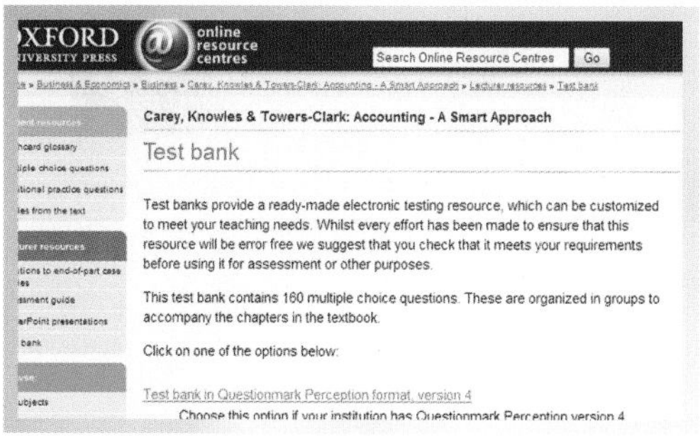

Test bank

This ready-made electronic testing resource, which is fully customizable and contains feedback for students, will help you to save time creating assessments.

Don't forget that all of these resources can be uploaded to your institution's Virtual Learning Environment to allow students to access them directly!

Part One
Financial Accounting

Chapter One
The Cash Budget
Sam has a Smart idea

Learning Objectives

At the end of this topic, you should be able to:

- explain the purpose of accounting
- appreciate why non-accountants need to understand accounting
- understand the basic terminology of business transactions
- prepare a cash budget
- calculate the gross profit margin of a product and business.

Introduction

Accounting is about the information needed to run a business or organization. Accountants consider what information is required and then communicate it in a meaningful way. This involves providing information to those outside the business or organization, such as investors and government authorities, usually about past events. Managers and employees inside the business or organization will need different information to plan strategies, make decisions, and control performance, often about the future.

Case Study
Smart Sports

Sam Smart is 25 years old and a keen sportsman. He is rather frustrated by the future prospects offered by his current job and is tired of working in a large office. He has started to wonder if he could set-up his own business and ideally would like to combine his passion for sport with earning an income. He coaches a football team every week-end and has recently purchased a new team kit for them. Because the service he received from the supplier was rather poor, this has given Sam the idea of setting up a business to supply local teams with their kits individually printed and in their team colours. He would need to invest his own savings and would be prepared to sell his car. His mother, Betty, has made it clear that she would be prepared to make a loan to him.

Sam is confident about running the business, but he is worried about the accounting. He has an old university friend, Kim, who is an accountant and will be able to help. But should Sam understand some accounting himself?

Why should managers understand accounting?

Managers of any business or organization will have to make key decisions, based on accounting information. To make good decisions, they need to be sure that the information makes sense and is reliable. They will want to understand how well the business is doing, so need to be able to interpret the financial and non-financial information properly.

Ponder Point

What key business decisions will Sam need to make, and what accounting information will he need to do this?

Managers need to present clear financial information to people outside the business, which will be difficult to do if they are unsure how the financial plans and actual results have been put together. As they are often legally responsible for reporting profit for organizations, they need to be able to ask the right questions about how the information was collected.

Ponder Point

Who else might need accounting information about Sam's business, and why?

The cash budget

A good example of internal information needed to make financial decisions is the cash budget. It sets out all the cash receipts and payments that a business expects to make over a period of time. This is usually on a month-to-month basis so that the owners can see what their bank balance is likely to be at the end of each month. This will not only provide information for the managers of the business but also for the bank to assess the overdraft facilities that may be necessary.

The cash budget will reflect the receipts and payments Sam expects to make for his business transactions and should not include his personal cash receipts and expenses. His business will be treated as a separate entity. A separate bank account should be used to make payments and receive monies relating to the business.

Terminology

Accounting is the recording and communicating of financial information for both internal and external users.

Capital is the amount the owner has invested in a business.

Drawings are the amount taken out of the business for the owner's personal use.

The entity concept recognizes that the transactions of a business should be recorded separately from the transactions of its owner. This principle should be followed even if the business is not a separate legal entity.

Financial accounting is the provision of financial information to external users.

Purchases are the costs incurred by the business or organization in buying the goods it plans to sell to its customers. A purchase is made when the goods or services are received from the supplier.

Sales are the income earned from selling goods or services. A sale is made when the goods or services are invoiced to the customer, which is usually at the point the goods or services are delivered to the customer.

Expenses are the costs incurred by the business or organization to enable the business to trade.

In the cash budget, all receipts and payments are recorded in the period during which they are expected to actually be received or paid.

Demonstration Exercise 1.1

Sam and Kim begin to draw up the cash budget for the first three months of trading. Sam plans to call the business Smart Sports and he will invest his savings of £10,000 to get it started. His mother has offered to provide a loan if it is needed. Initially, he plans to use his garage to store purchases, print the team kits, and do all the office work necessary for the business. Research, and a good deal of negotiation, has led him to anticipate that the following sales can be made and what the likely costs will be.

a) In January 2011, Sam will purchase a personal computer and software for £2,900, payable on delivery.

b) Sam expects to sell the following football kits:

January	£6,000 to Superstars
February	£2,000 to United
March	£3,000 to the University team

c) Sam expects to make the following purchases of football kits over the next three months:

January	£4,200 for Superstars' kits
February	£1,200 for United's kits
March	£1,650 for the University team's kits

d) All sales and purchases will be made for cash.

e) Sam has decided to buy the team kits from a supplier but will print them with team logos and team names himself. He will need to hire a fabric printing machine at a cost of £100 per month, payable each month. The cost includes all the colour dyes he will need.

f) Sam has agreed to pay Kim £125 per month for his advice and preparation of accounts.

g) Other expenses have been estimated as follows:

£75 on delivery costs per month, payable at the end of each month.
£375 on telephone costs per quarter, payable at the end of the quarter.

£300 on other expenses, such as electricity and insurance, payable at the end of each month.

h) Sam will need to withdraw £600 per month to cover his personal expenses.

Using Table 1.1, complete the cash budget for Sam's first three months of trading from January to March 2011. The cash budget for January has been completed.

Table 1.1

Smart Sports				
Cash budget for the three months ended 31 March 2011				
	Jan £	**Feb** £	**Mar** £	**Total** £
Receipts				
Capital	10,000			
Receipts from customers	6,000			
Total receipts	**16,000**			
Payments				
Computer	2,900			
Payments to suppliers	4,200			
Printer costs	100			
Accountant's fees	125			
Delivery costs	75			
Telephone				
Other expenses (electricity, insurance)	300			
Drawings	600			
Total payments	8,300			
Net receipts/(payments)	**7,700**			
Balance brought forward	–	7,700		
Balance carried forward	**7,700**			

The balance brought forward is the balance at the beginning of the period.

The balance carried forward is the balance at the end of the period.

To calculate cash balances

Cash balance brought forward + total receipts – total payments
= cash balance carried forward

Demonstration Exercise 1.1 – solution

The solution is given in Table 1.2.

Table 1.2

Smart Sports				
Cash budget for the three months ended 31 March 2011				
	Jan 2011 £	**Feb 2011 £**	**Mar 2011 £**	**Total 1st quarter 2011 £**
Receipts				
Capital	10,000			10,000
Receipts from customers	6,000	2,000	3,000	11,000
Total receipts	**16,000**	**2,000**	**3,000**	**21,000**
Payments				
Computer	2,900			2,900
Payments to suppliers	4,200	1,200	1,650	7,050
Printer hire	100	100	100	300
Accountant's fees	125	125	125	375
Delivery costs	75	75	75	225
Telephone			375	375
Other expenses (electricity, insurance)	300	300	300	900
Drawings	600	600	600	1,800
Total payments	**8,300**	**2,400**	**3,225**	**13,925**
Net receipts/(payments)	**7,700**	**(400)**	**(225)**	**7,075**
Balance brought forward	–	7,700	7,300	–
Balance carried forward	**7,700**	**7,300**	**7,075**	**7,075**

Timings of receipts and payments

In the first three months, Sam received cash when he sold his customers their team kits, and he paid cash for his purchases as soon as he received goods from his suppliers.

Once businesses become more established, cash sales will occur more rarely, as customers usually negotiate credit terms that mean sales are made before the resulting monies are received. Conversely, businesses will expect to be allowed credit terms for purchases made so that goods will be received before the resulting payment has to be made. It is vital that the cash budget reflects the timings of cash movements as accurately as possible so that the overall cash position of the business can be estimated.

Terminology

Cash sales are made when the cash is received at the same time as the goods or services are delivered.

Credit sales are made when the payment is received after the goods or services have been delivered.

Cash purchases are those purchases for which cash payment will be made at the same time as the goods or services are received.

Credit purchases are those purchases where the goods or services have been received by the business but for which payment is made at a date after the goods of services have been delivered.

Demonstration Exercise 1.2

Sam sets about planning the cash receipts and payments for the next three months, taking into account the different timings that will arise from sales and purchases being made on credit.

a) Sam expects to sell the following hockey kits:

April	£2,400 to Rovers
May	£4,000 to Tigers
June	£5,000 to Panther Cubs.

He has agreed that Rovers and Tigers will pay for their kits at the end of the month following the sale, but the Panther Cubs will pay cash on receipt of the kits.

b) Sam expects to make the following purchases, still payable in the month in which he takes delivery:

April	£1,500 for Rover's kits
May	£2,000 for Tiger's kits
June	£4,000 for Panther Cub's kits.

c) Sam intends to buy a second-hand printing machine for £5,500 in May so that he can save printing costs in the second half of the year. He will continue to pay £100 per month for April, May, and June for the hire of the old machine.

d) Kim will receive the same fee of £125 each month, and Sam will continue to pay the telephone costs as for the first quarter. He expects delivery costs to increase to £100 per month from May and other expenses to rise by £100 per month from May.

e) Sam will need to withdraw £600 per month to cover his personal expenses.

Using Table 1.3, prepare Sam's cash budget for his second three months of trading from April to June 2011. Using this information, does Sam need to ask his mother, Betty, for a loan or should he arrange an overdraft? If so, what size loan or overdraft should he request, and by when does he need it?

Overdraft facility

When a business anticipates that its bank balance will be in overdraft in the next year, then it needs to arrange an overdraft facility with its bank. The overdraft facility is a limit set in advance by the bank. If the business exceeds that limit, then the bank can choose not to honour any further payments made by the business and/or to charge significant fees and a higher rate of interest.

Ponder Point

In order to agree an overdraft facility, what sort of information might a bank require from a business?

Table 1.3

Smart Sports				
Cash budget for the three months ended 30 June 2011				
	Apr 2011 £	**May 2011 £**	**Jun 2011 £**	**Total 2nd quarter 2011 £**
Receipts				
Capital				
Receipts from cash sales				
Receipts from credit sales				
Total receipts				
Payments				
Printing machine				
Payments to suppliers				
Printer hire				
Accountant's fees				
Delivery				
Telephone costs				
Other expenses				
Drawings				
Total payments				
Net receipts/(payments)				
Balance brought forward				
Balance carried forward				

Calculation of the gross profit and gross profit margin

The cash budget provides key financial information for managing the cash flows of a business. As can be seen in later chapters, cash is different from profit, and it is lack of cash that causes businesses to fail. While it is important for sufficient cash to be generated within the business, it does not provide much useful management information about the profitability of its products. One simple method of assessing profitability is to calculate gross profit margin. The gross profit is the difference between the selling price and the cost of goods sold. The gross profit margin is the relationship between the gross profit and selling price of the goods or services sold, expressed as a percentage.

$$\text{Gross profit margin} = \frac{\text{Gross profit}}{\text{Sales}} \times 100$$

In January, Sam hopes to sell Superstars team kits for £6,000, which will have cost him £4,200. The gross profit made on this transaction would be £6,000 – £4,200 = £1,800, and a gross profit margin of 30% would be made.

$$\text{Gross profit margin} = \frac{1{,}800}{6{,}000} \times 100 = 30\%$$

Demonstration Exercise 1.3

a) Calculate the gross profit margin on each of the football kits that Sam plans to sell between January and March 2011.

b) Calculate the overall gross profit margin that would be made on the three football kits.

c) Calculate the gross profit margin on each of the hockey kits that Sam plans to sell between April and June 2011.

d) Calculate the overall gross profit margin on the three hockey kits.

e) Comment on your findings.

Demonstration Exercise 1.4

During the first six months of the business, Sam is confident of making a large sale each month to a football or hockey club with whom he has already been negotiating. From then on, Sam hopes that sales will start to come in as a result of recommendations and advertisements he plans to place in match programmes.

a) He anticipates that sales during the six months to 31 December 2011 will be made at a gross profit margin of 40%. He estimates they will be as follows:

Forecast sales

	£
July	2,400
August	2,400
September	3,000
October	3,000
November	3,400
December	3,800

b) In addition to making purchases to meet sales, Sam plans to purchase a stock of shirts for £2,000 in July 2011, so that he can meet any unexpected one-off orders.

c) Sales and purchases will be made on one month's credit.

d) Costs payable in cash will be as follows:

Telephone costs: £400 per quarter, payable in arrears.
Electricity: £650 per quarter, payable in arrears.
Accountant's fees: £125 each month.

Other expenses will amount to £110 each month.

e) Sam plans to make drawings of £600 each month.

f) Sam's mother, Betty, will make a loan to the business of £12,000 in July 2011. The loan will carry interest at 6%, which will be payable annually in arrears. Sam plans to use £10,000 of the loan to buy a van later in the year, probably in October. Delivery costs will continue at £100 per month for July to September.

Prepare the cash budget for Smart Sports for the six months ended 31 December 2011.

Summary of Key Points

- Every business and organization needs accounting information to plan, control, and make decisions. Different users will require information for a variety of purposes, both internally and externally.
- All managers should appreciate the fundamentals of accounting as they will need to use the information and be able to interpret its meaning.

- A cash budget is a forecast of all the cash receipts and payments that the organization expects to make.
- A cash budget is a tool for identifying cash shortfalls or surpluses so that managers can make decisions about arranging financing for future needs or investing surplus cash.
- The gross profit margin is a method of assessing the profitability of products sold by a business.

Smart Questions: a wider perspective

1. What assumptions have to be made to prepare a cash budget? Will they be based on judgements or facts?
2. What risks might affect the accuracy of these numbers?
3. What are the consequences if these judgements and assumptions turn out to be unrealistic?
4. Where might a business find additional funding if needed?

Wider Reading

www.cimaglobal.com/Documents/ImportedDocuments/article_web_nov02.pdf. Follow this link to read an article on preparing cash budgets on the Chartered Institute of Management Accountants (CIMA) website.

Practice Questions

1.1 Maris

Maris is preparing a cash budget for her new business. She expects her sales for the first six months to be:

January	February	March	April	May	June
€4,000	€4,400	€5,000	€5,400	€5,600	€6,000

Maris expects that 25% of the sales will be paid for immediately, while 50% will be paid for in the month following the sale, with the remainder paid for two months after.

There is no inventory, as Maris expects to purchase what she sells in the same month, but she makes her purchases on one month's credit. Maris makes a 25% gross profit margin on sales.

REQUIRED:

a) Calculate the purchases Maris will need to make each month.

b) Calculate how much cash she will receive from sales each month from January to June.

c) Calculate how much cash she will pay out for purchases each month from January to June.

1.2 Sue

Sue runs a business called Oxford Cycles, selling fold-up bicycles. She set this up in 2010 and is now looking to expand by taking on two extra members of staff to help meet a recent sharp increase in demand. This is as a result of a contract with the local council, who have given their staff the option of free fold-up bicycles, paid for by the council, if they cycle to work. There has been good take-up from staff in relation to this offer. The contract will be fulfilled over the next year, and the estimated sales figure for Oxford Cycles includes the council's contracted amounts.

Details of the business are as follows:

- Oxford Cycles expects to have a bank balance of £3,500 at 31 December 2011. At that date, the business will owe £1,600 to suppliers for goods supplied in December 2011.
- Sue has negotiated a bank overdraft facility of £2,000 for the next two years to 31 December 2013.
- The shop rental is £900 per quarter, payable in January, April, July, and October.
- All sales are made for cash. Purchases are made on one month's credit.
- Sue's sales income for January to June 2012 is predicted to be as follows:

Income from bicycle sales

	£
January	8,000
February	6,000
March	5,000
April	5,000
May	5,000
June	8,000

Sue makes a 33.33% gross profit margin on each bicycle sold.

- Sue is planning to buy a van at the beginning of January. The cost of the van will be £4,200. Petrol for the van will be paid in cash and is estimated as £200 per month.
- Sue plans to take £700 out of the business each month to cover her personal living expenses.
- The cost of the two new members of staff means that the total monthly wage bill paid in cash will be £1,200 from January 2012.
- Sue spends £400 per month on electricity costs.

REQUIRED:

a) Prepare a cash budget for Oxford Cycles for the six months ending 30 June 2012.

b) What advice would you give to Sue?

Chapter Two
Introduction to the Income Statement
The business starts trading

Learning Objectives

At the end of this topic, you should be able to:

- understand the difference between cash and the profits of a business
- appreciate that a set of accounts is produced from data included in a trial balance
- differentiate between revenue and capital expenditure and understand the significance of the distinction
- prepare a simple income statement for a sole-trader business.

Introduction

Many people assume that a profitable business will also be a business that is generating cash and is therefore able to pay its bills. This is not always the case. In order to establish whether a business has made a profit, an income statement needs to be prepared.

Ponder Point

Do you think that cash and profits are the same? Can you think of any examples where you may not get cash in straightaway?

Case Study
Is there a difference between cash and profits?

Sam Smart, a keen sportsman, has invested £10,000 from his savings and has received a loan of £12,000 from his mother, Betty, to set-up his business, Smart Sports, on 1 January 2011. The business buys in team kits from a local supplier, prints logos on them, and sells them on to local sports teams and clubs. Sam bought a second-hand printing machine and operates this from his garage.

After his first year of trading, Sam turns up to a local football match where the team is wearing the new football shirts purchased from Smart Sports. Dot Linnet, the football coach and a friend of Sam, comes over to ask whether he has made a profit in his first year, as Dot is aware that the business has made numerous sales. She is expecting that Sam would have made good profits, although Sam is unable to answer the question and replies only that he is working on it.

After the match, in which his team lost 4–0, Sam meets Kim, his accountant, in an internet café to find out whether he has made a profit this year. Sam asks Kim if he can see the bank statement for Smart Sports. Kim explains that the bank statement will not tell Sam how much profit he has made, as profits and cash are not the same.

Demonstration Exercise 2.1

A friend of Sam, Danni, sells canned drinks from a van in the centre of Berlin each night. Danni sold 500 drinks during one week. Each drink sold for €3, and each one cost Danni €2 to buy.

1. How much profit did Danni make that week?
2. If Danni had bought 550 cans to sell during that week, how much would Danni's bank balance have increased or decreased in that week?

3. If, during that week, Danni bought a fridge for €280, how would that affect his bank balance?
4. Would the purchase of the fridge affect his profits?

Demonstration Exercise 2.1 – solution

1.

Sales	€1,500
Purchases	€1,000
Profit	€500

2.

Cash in from sales	€1,500
Cash paid for goods	€1,100
Increase in bank balance	€400

3. It would further reduce the bank balance by €280.
4. No. The purchase of the fridge does not affect profits, but does affect the cash balance.

Demonstration Exercise 2.2

If one of Danni's customers, who bought drinks worth €30 during January, was allowed not to pay immediately but was given one month's credit, then:

1. What would be the effect on Danni's profit for January?
2. What would be the effect on Danni's cash balance for January?

For accounting purposes, it is important to understand when the actual transaction has taken place.

When are sales and purchases made?

Sales and purchases can be made for cash or on credit. For accounting purposes, a sale is made when the customer takes delivery of the goods, and a purchase is made when the business receives goods from a supplier. If sales and purchases are made for cash, the cash effect will be recorded immediately.

If a sale is made on credit, then a trade receivable is created until the amount owed by the customer is received. Likewise, if a purchase is made on credit, then a trade payable is created until the amount owed to the supplier is paid.

The cash effect of the credit sale or credit purchase will be recorded when the customer pays the business for goods received or when the business pays the supplier for goods supplied. At this point the trade receivable or trade payable will disappear.

By making sure transactions are accounted for in the period in which they arise, we are taking account of the matching concept in practice.

Terminology

The matching concept requires expenses to be matched to the revenue that they have generated, in order to arrive at the profit for the year.

Trade receivables are the amounts owed by customers of the business who, having been sold goods or services on credit, have not yet paid the business.

Trade payables are the amounts owed to suppliers of the business who, having supplied goods or services on credit, have not yet been paid by the business.

Measuring profit

Sam understands why profits and cash are different, but he explains to Kim that he does not know how to find his profit figure. Kim explains that in order to find out how much profit he has made this year, he will need to prepare an income statement for the business's first year of trading.

Kim has kept a record of all Sam's transactions for his first year of trading and has drawn up a summary of the list of balances as at 31 December 2011. This is called the trial balance.

In order to be able to understand what a trial balance reveals and how it can be converted into an income statement, we need to understand the basic principle behind double-entry book-keeping.

Double-entry book-keeping

Any transaction that the business undertakes will have two effects on the business:

Example 1

When Sam first put money into the new business, the business then:

- had an asset in the form of the business bank account
- had received his investment in the business, which is recorded in the capital account.

Example 2

When Sam first purchased the printing machine, the business then:

- had a new asset, the printing machine
- had reduced the business bank account by the cost of the printing machine.

Example 3

If Sam paid an electricity bill for the garage he is working from, the effect on the business will be:

- a reduction in the bank account
- an expense of the business will have been paid.

The double-entry system is the recording of the two entries for each and every transaction.

Ponder Point

What would be the double-entry effect of Sam taking some money out of the business for his own personal use? Do you know what this is known as?

Although double-entry book-keeping is outside the scope of this book, it is still useful to understand how different accounts will appear in the trial balance.

Terminology

The trial balance is a record of all account balances at a point in time and is used to prepare the final accounts.

The double-entry book-keeping system is the method of recording the two entries for each and every transaction.

Types of account

Kim explains that all of Sam's transactions will be recorded in accounts. There will be six different types of account: asset, liability, income, expense, capital, and drawings. Sam needs to know for each transaction which two accounts will be affected. A simple description of each type of account is as follows:

ASSETS	Items owned by the business. For example, the printing machine and computer will be recorded as an asset.
LIABILITIES	An amount owed by the business. For example, someone who is owed for goods supplied by the business.
CAPITAL	The amount of money that the owner put into the business.
INCOME	The amount earned by the business. For example, the main source will often be sales.
EXPENSES	Amounts incurred by the business to allow it to operate on a day-to-day basis. For example, the rent of a warehouse or salaries paid by the business.
DRAWINGS	Amounts withdrawn by the owners for their own personal use.

From our earlier discussion of double-entry book-keeping, we know that all transactions have a twofold effect and give rise to debit and credit balances.
Debit balance accounts include:

- expense accounts, e.g. rent, wages, electricity
- asset accounts, e.g. property, trade receivables
- drawings.

Credit balance accounts include:

- income accounts, e.g. sales
- liability accounts, e.g. trade payables or loans
- capital account.

Demonstration Exercise 2.3

Consider the Smart Sports business, and for each type of account listed above write down at least one example of an item that might be included under that heading.

The trial balance

A trial balance is drawn up at the end of a financial period, usually at the end of each financial year. It is a record of all the account balances at that point in time and is used to prepare the final accounts.

The trial balance lists the account balances, showing whether there is a debit or a credit balance on each account. The trial balance should always balance. That is, the total of the debit balances should equal the total of the credit balances.

Ponder Point

If the trial balance does not balance, what is this telling you?

Table 2.1 is a simple trial balance. Note:

- All accounts have a debit or credit balance.
- The totals at the bottom of the trial balance are the same.
- The trial balance is prepared at a set point in time.

Table 2.1

Danni's Drinks		
Trial balance as at 31 December 2011		
	Debit €	**Credit €**
Sales		15,000
Purchases	10,000	
Insurance	400	
Petrol	2,000	
Van	10,500	
Bank and cash	6,600	
Trade payables		500
Capital		14,000
	29,500	**29,500**

Smart Sports: the trial balance

Kim has drawn up the trial balance at the end of the first year of trading, as shown in Table 2.2.

Table 2.2

Smart Sports		
Trial balance as at 31 December 2011		
	Debit £	**Credit £**
Capital		10,000
Loan		12,000
Sales		51,000
Purchases	34,500	
Electricity	1,920	
Insurance	1,750	
Telephone	1,500	
Sundry expenses	1,650	
Drawings	7,200	
Accountant's fees	1,500	
Printing machine	5,500	
Delivery costs	1,200	
Computer	3,500	
Bank balance	11,080	
Trade receivables	4,100	
Trade payables		2,400
	75,400	**75,400**

In order to be able to understand what profit Sam has made, we need to first understand how accountants measure the profit or loss that a business has made.

Financial statements are usually prepared on an annual basis, and therefore the accounting period is usually one year.

Capital versus revenue expenditure

Terminology

Capital expenditure refers to expenditure where the business will benefit from it for more than one accounting period; for example, the purchase of a delivery van or building.

Revenue expenditure relates to expenditure on day-to-day expenses; for example, telephone or staff salary costs.

Demonstration Exercise 2.4

Table 2.3 shows the payments that Smart Sports made during the year ended 31 December 2011. Categorize each payment into capital or revenue expenses. The first two have been completed.

Table 2.3

	Capital or revenue expense
Printing machine	Capital
Computer	Capital
Purchases of goods for resale	
Accountant's fees	
Electricity	
Insurance	
Telephone	
Delivery expenses	
Sundry expenses (including postage, stationery)	
Drawings	

Ponder Point

In which category—capital or revenue expense—do you think the purchase of paper clips would fall?

Capital versus revenue income

Income can also be categorized into capital and revenue income.

Terminology

Revenue income will be mainly income from sales. Other examples are rent received and interest received.

Capital income includes money invested by the owner of the business and loans from third parties.

The profit or loss of the business is calculated by comparing revenue income with revenue expenditure. This comparison is made in the income statement.

Capital expenditure that will benefit the business over a number of years is not included in the income statement; it is shown on the statement of financial position. The owner's capital and loans provide long-term funding for the business and are shown in the statement of financial position.

The income statement

Terminology

The **income statement** shows the revenue income less the revenue expenditure for a financial period and computes the profit or loss generated.

The first part of the income statement shows the sales that a business has made and the cost of those goods sold. The cost of sales is deducted from the sales figure to give the gross profit figure:

Gross profit = **Sales** less **the cost of sales**

The cost of sales will be the same as the purchases figure where all of the goods purchased have been sold; that is, where there were no items in inventories, either at the beginning or the end of the year.

Where there are inventories of goods for resale remaining unsold at the end of the year or inventories of goods at the beginning of the year, these have to be taken into account in computing the cost of goods actually sold.

Calculating the cost of goods sold

As revenue and expenses need to be matched, the cost of sales should not include the value of any goods that have not yet been sold. The value of the inventory at the end of the period needs to be deducted in arriving at the cost of sales. Any inventory held at the beginning of the year must also be taken into account. This will enable us to find the cost of the goods actually sold.

Terminology

Inventories (stock) are goods for resale held in stock by the business.

The cost of sales can therefore be calculated as follows:

Cost of sales	
Opening inventories	x
Add: purchases	x
Less: closing inventories	(x)
Cost of sales	x

This ensures that expenses are matched with revenue, such that sales can be compared with the cost of the goods that were sold. The first part of the income statement calculates the gross profit for the year.

Extract from income statement	
Sales	**X**
Less: Cost of sales	
Opening inventories	x
Add: purchases	x
Less: closing inventories	(x)
Cost of goods sold	x
Gross profit	**X**

Ponder Point

If capital expenditure is incorrectly recorded as revenue expenditure, what effect will this have on the profit for the year?

Demonstration Exercise 2.5

Danni sells drinks cans from his van in Berlin. On Monday he started the day with 30 cans in his fridge. He bought 50 more cans during the day, and he finished the day with 20 cans.

1. How many cans did Danni sell on Monday?
2. If Danni sells the cans for €3 and they cost him €2 each, what will his gross profit be? (Hint: You will need to calculate the cost of goods sold.)

Preparing the income statement

After cost of goods sold and the gross profit figure have been computed, the remainder of the income statement can be prepared.

Net profit = Gross profit less all other revenue expenses

Demonstration Exercise 2.6

The revenue income and expenditure for Smart Sports is given in Table 2.4. From this information, prepare the income statement (Table 2.5) for the year ended 31 December 2011.

Table 2.4

	£
Revenue income	
Sales	51,000
Revenue expenses	
Purchases	34,500
Electricity	1,920
Insurance	1,750
Telephone	1,500
Sundry expenses	1,650
Accountant's fees	1,500
Delivery costs	1,200

Note: The amount of purchases that remained unsold at the year end and are therefore included in the inventory amounted to £2,700. As this is a new business, the opening inventories are £nil.

Table 2.5

Smart Sports		
Income statement for the year ended 31 December 2011 *(first draft—without any adjusting entries)*		
	£	£
Income (Sales)		**51,000**
Less: Cost of sales		
Opening inventories		
Purchases		
Less: closing inventories		
Gross profit		
Less: Expenses		
Electricity		
Insurance		
Telephone		
Sundry expenses		
Accountant's fees		
Delivery costs		
Net profit		

Summary of Key Points

- Cash and profits are not the same.
- Transactions are accounted for in the period in which they occur.
- The double-entry system is the recording of the two entries for each and every transaction.
- Accounts can be categorized into six types:
  - income
  - expenditure

  - assets
  - liabilities
  - capital
  - drawings.
- Financial statements are prepared for a period of time, usually one year.
- The profit or loss for the business is calculated by comparing revenue income with revenue expenditure. This is shown in the income statement.
- A trial balance is usually drawn up at the end of the financial year. It is a record of all the account balances at that point in time and is used to prepare the income statement and statement of financial position.
- Cost of sales is made up of opening inventories plus purchases less closing inventories.
- Gross profit equals sales less cost of sales.
- Net profit equals gross profit less all other revenue expenses.

Smart Questions: a wider perspective

1. If a business makes a profit in its first year of trading, can you be sure that it will have a positive bank balance at the year-end?
2. If a business bought a large quantity of extra inventory just before the year-end and planned to sell it at a later date, what effect would this have on the profit for the year?
3. Do you think that it is always straightforward to distinguish capital expenditure from revenue expenditure?
4. Why are drawings taken out by the owner not treated like employees' wages, which are shown as expenses in the income statement?

Wider Reading

Weetman, P. (2006) ***Financial and Management Accounting*****, 4th edition, FT Prentice Hall.** Chapters 5 and 6 of this book are dedicated to looking at accounting information for service businesses and trading businesses.

Practice Questions

2.1 Jo

Jo recently set-up as a satay man along Bukit Timah Road in Singapore providing satay at parties. Jo bought-in 1,700 chicken satays at 50 cents per satay and had 700 satays at the end of the month. He is able to sell each satay for S$1.20 and works on a pay-for-what-you-eat basis.

REQUIRED:

a) Calculate Jo's cost of sales.

b) What gross profit did Jo make in his first month?

2.2 Sophie

Sophie has a hairdressing business and has produced the trial balance in Table 2.6.

Table 2.6

Sophie		
Trial balance as at 31 December 2012		
	Debit €	**Credit €**
Capital		15,000
Sales		35,000
Wages	15,000	
Hair products purchased	5,000	
Rent of salon	6,000	
Light and heat	1,500	
Drawings	6,500	
Fixtures and fittings	7,000	
Trade payables		250
Bank account	9,250	
	50,250	**50,250**

REQUIRED:

Categorize each of the items in Sophie's trial balance into one of the following types:

- income
- expenditure
- assets
- liabilities
- capital
- drawings.

2.3 Helga

Helga's trial balance, drawn up at the end of the first year of trading, is shown in Table 2.7.

Table 2.7

Helga		
Trial balance as at 30 November 2012		
	Debit €	**Credit €**
Capital		50,000
Loan (interest at 5%)		10,000
Sales		235,700
Wages	25,200	
Purchases	182,400	
Rent and rates	15,900	
Motor expenses	3,600	
Sundry expenses	2,000	
Interest on loan	500	
Light and heat	1,800	
Office expenses	3,100	
Drawings	12,000	
Motor vehicles	25,000	
Fixtures and fittings	18,000	
Trade receivables	11,800	
Trade payables		10,500
Bank account	4,900	
	306,200	**306,200**

Note: Closing inventories at 30 November 2012 were valued at €15,000.

REQUIRED:

a) Identify the entries in Helga's trial balance that represent revenue income and revenue expenses.

b) Prepare the income statement for Helga for the year ended 30 November 2012.

c) There are two entries on the trial balance that Helga does not understand: **trade receivables** and **trade payables**. Explain briefly how these accounts have arisen.

Chapter Three
Balancing the Basics
Getting a 'snapshot' of Smart Sports

Learning Objectives

At the end of this topic, you should be able to:

- appreciate the purpose of a statement of financial position
- recognize the assets and liabilities in a business
- understand what an accrual and a prepayment are and how to account for them
- prepare a statement of financial position for a simple business.

Introduction

There are three main financial statements that make up a set of accounts. These are the income statement, which reveals the profit or loss for the year, the statement of financial position, and the statement of cash flows. The statement of financial position shows the assets and liabilities of a business on a particular date and how the business has been financed.

Case Study
The bank wants more information

Sam Smart has been trading for one year as a supplier of printed team kits to local sports clubs. He is in the process of drawing up accounts for his first year of trading and understands the basics of measuring the profit for the year.

Until now, Sam has not needed a bank overdraft, but he has plans to expand the business and is aware that he will need an overdraft facility in the near future. To be considered for one, the bank has asked to see the income statement and the statement of financial position for the business. Sam does not understand why the bank needs to see more than just the income statement, and he decides to ask Kim to explain exactly what a statement of financial position is and what information it contains.

Kim explains that the statement of financial position has until recently been known as the balance sheet and that it is often described as giving a 'snapshot' of a business. It shows the assets and liabilities that a business has at one particular date and how the business has been financed.

Assets and liabilities

Terminology

An asset is something that the business owns that will bring financial benefits to the business in the future.

A liability is an amount owed by the business where the business has an obligation to make a payment.

Ponder Point

Can you think of any assets that a typical student might have?

Demonstration Exercise 3.1

Danni runs a business selling soft drinks from a van that trades outside sporting events and concerts. Which of the following would be assets of Danni's Drinks business?

a) The fridges bought by Danni that are used to keep the drinks cold.
b) Bottles and cans of drinks held for sale.
c) Two boxes of crisps that are out of date and could not be sold.
d) The van that Danni bought from Veni Vans.
e) The till used to record the takings and store the cash taken.
f) The amount owed by a customer who buys drinks on credit.
g) The business's bank overdraft.

Demonstration Exercise 3.1—solution

Items (a), (b), (d), (e), and (f) are assets of the business.

Items (a), (d), and (e) are assets as they will be used by the business to enable it to trade.

Item (b) is an asset as the cans and bottles will result is sales for the business.

Item (c) is not an asset, because the crisps will not bring any future income to the business, as they cannot be sold.

Item (f) is an asset, as the amount owed will result in cash being received by the business in the future.

Item (g) is a liability of the business as an overdraft is an amount owed to the bank.

The statement of financial position

This primary financial statement shows the assets and liabilities which a business has at a given date and how these net assets have been financed.

Layout of the statement of financial position

There is more than one possible way to prepare a statement of financial position; an example of a common format is given in Table 3.1.

There are certain points to note:

- The statement of financial position always has a heading to show the name of the business and the date for which it is being prepared.

Table 3. 1

The Business Name	
Statement of financial position as at the end of the reporting period	
ASSETS	
Non-current assets	
Long-term assets (for example, a car)	xxx
Current assets	
Short-term assets (for example, inventory)	xxx
Total assets	xxx
CAPITAL AND LIABILITIES	
Capital at the beginning of the period	xxx
Profit for the year	xxx
Less: drawings	xxx
Capital at the end of the period	xxx
Non-current liabilities	
Long-term liabilities (for example, a loan)	xxx
Current liabilities	
Short-term liabilities (for example, trade payables)	xxx
Total capital and liabilities	xxx

- The statement of financial position can be thought of as having two halves:
  - **the top half**, which lists all the assets;
  - **the bottom half**, which shows the capital (the owner's investment in the business), and all the liabilities.
- Assets are divided between those that are long-term, known as non-current assets, and those that are short-term, known as current assets. Non-current assets are also known as fixed assets.
- Assets are listed in the statement in order of decreasing liquidity. For example, this means that for current assets the inventory is listed first because it will take the longest to turn into cash. It will be followed by trade receivables and then the bank balance.

- Liabilities are divided between those that are long-term, known as non-current liabilities, and those that are short-term, known as current liabilities.
- Profit is created by the efforts of the owner and hence is added to the capital account, increasing the owner's investment in the business.
- The total assets of the business will equal the closing capital balance plus the liabilities of the business. That is, the total of the top half should equal the total of the bottom half of the statement of financial position. This is why this statement was, and often still is, known as the balance sheet.
- Hence, **Assets = Capital + Liabilities**. This is known as the accounting equation and always holds true for any business.

Terminology

Non-current assets are assets intended for long-term use in the business.

Current assets are assets that will be held by the business for less than one year, including inventory held for resale and cash balances.

Current liabilities are amounts that are due to be paid within a year, including amounts owed to suppliers.

Non-current liabilities are amounts that are due to be paid after a year, including long-term loans.

Demonstration Exercise 3.2

Sam has prepared his income statement for the year ended 31 December 2011, and the balances shown in Table 3.2 remain on his trial balance.

Note that, because the trial balance in Table 3.2 has been prepared after the income statement has been produced, all of the accounts used in preparing the income statement are no longer included on the trial balance. Instead, you will see that the profit for the year is shown. (This profit is the same as the one calculated in Chapter 2.) In addition, the closing inventory figure is shown on this trial balance because it has been adjusted for in preparing the income statement.

Table 3.2

Smart Sports		
Trial balance as at 31 December 2011 (after the income statement has been prepared)		
	Debit £	**Credit** £
Capital		10,000
Loan		12,000
Drawings	7,200	
Printing machine	5,500	
Computer	3,500	
Bank balance	11,080	
Trade receivables	4,100	
Inventory at 31 December 2011	2,700	
Trade payables		2,400
Draft profit for the year		9,680
	34,080	34,080

Using Smart Sports' trial balance given above:

a) Identify the business's non-current assets.

b) Identify the business's current assets and current liabilities.

c) Determine whether the business has any non-current liabilities.

d) Prepare the statement of financial position as at 31 December 2011, using the pro-forma given in Table 3.3.

Table 3.3

Smart Sports		
Statement of financial position as at 31 December 2011 *(first draft without any adjusting entries)*		
ASSETS		
Non-current assets		
--		----------
--		----------

Current assets		
--	----------	
--	----------	
--	----------	

Total assets		==========
CAPITAL AND LIABILITIES		
Capital at the beginning of the year		----------
Add: --		----------
Less: --		----------
Capital at the end of the year		----------
Non-current liabilities		
--		----------
Current liabilities		
--		----------
Total capital and liabilities		==========

Ponder Point

Can you explain why the accounting equation will always work?

Assets = Capital + Liabilities

Case Study
What to do about the electricity bill?

Sam is pleased that he has nearly completed his accounts for his first year of trading, and so far everything balances! When Kim happens to meet Sam at a football game, they spend time chatting about the accounts as they stand on the touchline.

Sam noticed recently that there are amounts the business owed at the year-end that have so far been left out of the financial statements. In particular, he received an electricity bill that covered the last two months of the financial year. It did not seem right to him to just ignore it.

Kim explains to Sam that he will need to adjust for this electricity bill and that he should review all his expense accounts to ensure that they cover the whole financial year. The business may have had the benefit of certain services but not yet paid for them, or it could have paid for some services in advance of receiving the benefit.

Accruals and prepayments

The expenses actually paid by a business will be recorded on the trial balance, but sometimes expenses will have been incurred but not paid for during the financial year. Where this has occurred, the amount owing is known as an accrual and needs to be adjusted for in preparing the accounts.

Terminology

An accrual arises where an expense has been incurred but not paid for by the date when the statement of financial position is prepared.

A prepayment arises where an expense has been paid before the statement of financial position date but the benefit of that expense will be obtained in the following financial year.

Demonstration Exercise 3.3

Smart Sports has paid electricity bills totalling £1,920 during its first year of trading, which is the amount on the trial balance. However, this amount covers only electricity used up to 31 October 2011. Sam estimates that the cost of electricity used during November and December 2011 will amount to £240 per month.

a) What is the amount of the accrual?

b) What is the full cost of electricity consumed by Smart Sports during the year ended 31 December 2011?

c) If this figure (from (b) above) for electricity consumed is used in the income statement, what effect will this have on the profit for the year?

Demonstration Exercise 3.3 – solution

a) The accrual would be for the two months' electricity that had not been paid for. This will amount to £480.

b) The full cost of electricity consumed by Smart Sports during the year ended 31 December 2011 will be £1,920 + £480 = £2,400.

c) By adjusting for this accrual, the profit for the year will be reduced.

In order to account for an accrual, it is necessary to:

- calculate the expense to be included in the income statement by taking the trial balance figure for the expense concerned and adding on the amount of the accrual
- include the accrual as a current liability on the statement of financial position.

Ponder Point

In adjusting for accruals, which accounting concept is being applied?

Just as a business may have accruals where the benefit of an expense has been enjoyed but not yet paid for, so too can a business have prepaid expenses. This will occur where a business has paid for an expense for which it has not yet received the benefit.

Demonstration Exercise 3.4

Smart Sports has paid insurance premiums totalling £1,750 during its first year of trading, which is the amount on the trial balance at the year-end, 31 December 2011. However, this amount provides insurance cover up to 31 March 2012. Sam has calculated that the cost of insurance is £117 per month.

a) How much of the £1,750 trial balance figure represents insurance cover that the business has not yet had the benefit of?

   (In other words, what is the amount of the insurance prepayment?)

b) What is the true cost of insurance cover provided for Smart Sports during the year ended 31 December 2011?

c) What effect will using this figure, instead of the £1,750 trial balance figure, have on the profit for the year?

In order to account for a prepayment, it is necessary to:

- calculate the expense to be included in the income statement by taking the trial balance figure for the expense concerned and deducting the amount of the prepayment
- include the prepayment as a current asset on the statement of financial position.

Sam is now in a position to draw up an adjusted income statement and statement of financial position for Smart Sports, taking the known accruals and prepayment into account.

Demonstration Exercise 3.5

The trial balance for Smart Sports is given in Table 3.4:

Table 3.4

Smart Sports		
Trial balance as at 31 December 2011		
	Debit **£**	**Credit** **£**
Capital		10,000
Loan[1]		12,000
Sales		51,000
Purchases[2]	34,500	
Electricity[3]	1,920	
Insurance[4]	1,750	
Telephone	1,500	
Sundry expenses	1,650	
Drawings	7,200	
Accountant's fees	1,500	
Delivery costs	1,200	
Printing machine	5,500	
Computer	3,500	
Bank balance	11,080	
Trade receivables	4,100	
Trade payables		2,400
	75,400	75,400

1. Betty's loan to the business was interest-free for the first six months of the year, after which time interest was to be paid at the rate of 6% per annum. No interest had been paid during the year.
2. Purchases remaining unsold in inventory at the year-end amounted to £2,700.
3. Electricity used but not yet paid for as at the year-end amounted to £480.
4. Insurance had been prepaid by £351 at the year-end but not yet accounted for.

Using the partially completed financial statements to guide you, prepare the income statement for Smart Sports as at 31 December 2011 (Table 3.5) and the statement of financial position (Table 3.6) as at that date.

Table 3.5

Smart Sports		
Income statement for the year ended 31 December 2011 (after adjusting for accruals and prepayments)		
	£	£
Sales		----------
Less: Cost of sales		
Purchases	----------	
Less:	________	

Gross profit		----------
Less: Expenses		
Electricity	----------	
Insurance	----------	
Telephone	----------	
....	----------	
....	----------	
....	----------	
....	----------	
	________	
		________
Net profit		========

Table 3.6

Smart Sports		
Statement of financial position as at 31 December 2011 (after adjusting for accruals and prepayments)		
	£	£
ASSETS		
Non-current assets		
....		-----------
Computer		________
Current assets		
Inventory	-----------	
....	-----------	
Prepayment	-----------	
....	________	
		________
Total assets		========
CAPITAL AND LIABILITIES		
Capital at the beginning of the year		-----------
Add:		-----------
Less:		-----------
Capital at the end of the year		-----------
Non-current liabilities		
....		-----------
Current liabilities		
Trade payables	-----------	
....	________	-----------
Total capital and liabilities		========

Ponder Point

Why do you think a statement of financial position is referred to as a 'snapshot'?

The historic cost concept

The accounts that have been prepared up to now have been applying both the historic cost and the going concern concepts.

Terminology

The cost of sales is the cost of goods sold in a period, taking into account movements in inventories.

The historic cost concept requires transactions to be recorded at their original cost to the business, and as a result, the assets of a business are included at their historic cost on the statement of financial position.

The main advantage of the historic cost concept is that historic cost is a known amount that is indisputable.

Ponder Point

Is the historic cost of an asset likely to always be the most meaningful measure of an asset's value? Can you think of other ways that an asset could be valued?

Recent developments in accounting have led to a gradual move away from the use of historic cost and the inclusion instead of assets at 'fair value', which is a measure of their current market value.

The going concern concept

Terminology

The going concern concept means that, when producing accounts, there is an assumption that the business will continue to operate for the foreseeable future unless there is any evidence to suggest that it will not.

If a business is not a going concern, then a statement of financial position should include assets at the amount they could be sold for. These amounts may be very different from the amounts at which they had originally been shown. For example, if Smart Sports had to sell its inventory very quickly, Sam would probably have to accept a much lower price for the goods in order to dispose of them quickly.

Ponder Point

How long do you think the foreseeable future is, and can you think of any signs that might indicate that a business is not a 'going concern'?

Summary of Key Points

- A statement of financial position is a snapshot of the business's assets and liabilities at one point in time.
- The statement of financial position also shows the amount the owner has invested in the business, known as the owner's capital.
- Non-current assets are assets intended for long-term use in the business, such as plant, equipment, and motor vehicles. They are also known as fixed assets.
- Current assets and current liabilities are the short-term assets and liabilities of the business.
- An accrual is an amount owing at the end of the accounting period for an expense incurred but not yet paid for.
- A prepayment is an amount that has been paid by the end of the accounting period but the business has not yet had the benefit of that expense.

Smart Questions: a wider perspective

1. In addition to the statement of financial position, what other documents might a bank ask to see to determine whether to lend money to a business?
2. How might someone preparing accounts know whether the business has accruals and prepayments at the year-end?
3. Will the amount of an accrual always be an exact known amount, or could it be an estimate?
4. If a statement of financial position balances, does this confirm that it is correct?

Wider Reading

Perks, R., and Leiwy, D. (2010) ***Financial Accounting, Understanding and Practice,*** **3rd edition, McGraw Hill.** Chapter 1 gives an introduction to statements of financial position (balance sheets), including their content and particularly their limitations.

Practice Questions

3.1 Nick's Office Supplies

The trial balance in Table 3.7 was extracted from the records of Nick's Office Supplies as at 31 December 2011.

Table 3.7

	Debit £	Credit £
Capital		208,160
Loan[1]		10,000
Inventories at 1 January 2011	27,440	
Sales		477,600
Purchases[2]	322,400	
Wages	83,630	
Advertising	4,400	
Electricity[3]	5,050	
Insurance	16,080	
Premises	154,000	
Office equipment	27,900	
Bank balance	37,700	
Trade payables		61,720
Trade receivables	51,880	
Drawings	27,000	
	757,480	757,480

Additional information as at 31 December 2011:

1. The loan carries interest at 10%, and no interest has been paid during the year.
2. Inventories held were valued at £38,600.
3. Electricity owing amounted to £1,200.

REQUIRED:

a) Explain what is meant by a prepayment and how it is accounted for.

b) Explain what is meant by an accrual and how it is accounted for.

c) Prepare the income statement for Nick's Office Supplies for the year ended 31 December 2011.

d) Prepare the statement of financial position for the business as at that date.

3.2 Ming

Ming has been running a market stall in Beijing for some years. The stall sells hats and fans to holidaymakers. Ming works on the stall for three days a week and employs her younger sister to run the stall for the remaining three days a week that the market is open. Her trial balance as at 31 March 2013 is shown in Table 3.8.

Table 3.8

	Debit Yuan	Credit Yuan
Motor vehicle	75,000	
Trade receivables[1]	5,270	
Bank overdraft		540
Inventories as at 1 April 2012	59,830	
Sales		446,660
Purchases[2]	239,190	
Rent[3]	18,500	
Wages[4]	173,850	
Other expenses	23,230	
Capital account as at 1 April 2012		252,800
Drawings	105,130	
	700,000	700,000

1. Trade receivables arose from sales made on credit to a nearby hotel.
2. Closing inventories at 31 March 2013 were valued at 63,000 yuan.
3. Two months' stall rental had been paid in advance at the year-end. Rent is currently paid at the rate of 1,740 yuan per month.
4. Wages owing at 31 March 2013 amounted to 5,750 yuan.

REQUIRED:

a) Prepare Ming's income statement for the year ended 31 March 2013.

b) Comment on the profitability of the business and suggest how it might be improved.

c) Prepare the statement of financial position as at 31 March 2013.

Chapter Four
Accounting for Depreciation and Bad Debts
Smart Sports is called to account

Learning Objectives

At the end of this topic, you should be able to:

- understand why non-current assets need to be depreciated
- be able to use the straight-line and the reducing-balance methods of providing for depreciation
- explain why we need to provide for bad and doubtful debts
- prepare a final adjusted income statement and statement of financial position
- appreciate the limitations of a statement of financial position.

Introduction

Chapter 3 dealt with the preparation of a statement of financial position but ignored the need to adjust for depreciation and bad debts. In order to arrive at a meaningful profit figure and a final statement of financial position, it is necessary to make these adjustments.

Case Study
How to complete the final accounts

Sam Smart has been in business for a little over a year. He is in the process of preparing his income statement and statement of financial position for his business, Smart Sports, under the guidance of his friend Kim. He is keen to complete the financial statements and is aware that he needs to learn about depreciation, but Kim is on holiday for a few days. Sam gets chatting to an old friend, Dot, who claims to know something about accounting.

Dot explains to Sam that depreciation is something that affects motor vehicles and concerns the way they fall in value. At the end of the conversation, Sam decides to do a bit more research on the subject of depreciation as he is not convinced that Dot really understood it!

What is depreciation?

When a business purchases a non-current asset, it is shown as an asset on the statement of financial position as it will benefit the business over a number of years and enable it to generate profits. However, with the exception of land, non-current assets will not last forever.

To allow for the fact that non-current assets will benefit the business over a number of years, depreciation aims to spread the cost of those assets over the years in which the benefit will be felt. There are two main methods of spreading the cost:

- the straight-line method
- the reducing-balance method.

Ponder Point

Was Dot right to think that depreciation will apply only to motor vehicles?

Terminology

Estimated useful life is the expected length of time that a non-current asset will be used in the business.

Residual value is the estimated amount that a non-current asset will be worth at the end of its useful life.

The straight-line method

This is the simplest and most common method of providing for depreciation and aims to spread the cost of the asset evenly over its useful life.

Demonstration Exercise 4.1

Danni, the drinks seller, buys a fridge costing €630 that is expected to be used by the business for three years, at the end of which time it is estimated that it will be worth approximately €30, known as the residual value.

The total depreciation that must be provided over the asset's life is therefore €600:

$$\begin{aligned} \text{Total depreciation} &= \text{Cost} - \text{Residual value} \\ &= €630 - €30 \\ &= €600 \end{aligned}$$

To depreciate the fridge, this total amount needs to be charged to the income statement over the fridge's useful life. Each year, the value at which the fridge is recorded on the statement of financial position falls by the amount of the depreciation charged.

a) If the total depreciation that has to be charged is €600, and the fridge has a life of three years, what should the annual depreciation charge be, if the charge is to be spread evenly?

b) Complete Table 4.1 showing the statement of financial position values during the asset's life.

Table 4.1

Value when purchased	Value at end of 1st year	Value at end of 2nd year	Value at end of 3rd year
€630	€430	€............	€............

c) Explain how the depreciation on the fridge will affect the profits in each of the three years that the fridge is owned.

Demonstration Exercise 4.1—solution

a) Annual depreciation charge = €600/3 = €200 per annum.

b) The completed statement of financial position is given in Table 4.2.

Table 4.2

Statement of financial position—fridge values			
Value when purchased	Value at end of 1st year	Value at end of 2nd year	Value at end of 3rd year
€630	€430	€230	€30

c) The depreciation charge will reduce the profits by €200 each year.

Note that this fridge is an example of an asset being depreciated on the straight-line basis as each year's depreciation charge on the fridge will be the same. The value of the fridge shown on the statement of financial position is known as the net book value.

In the above exercise, the fridge may, or may not, have been owned for the whole financial year. It is common practice to use a full year's depreciation charge in the first year of ownership, regardless of the period of time that an asset has actually been owned.

Terminology

The straight-line method of providing for depreciation charges an equal annual amount as an expense so that the asset falls in value evenly throughout its useful life.

The depreciation charge is the amount charged to the income statement to spread the cost of non-current assets over the life of those assets. Non-current assets have a finite useful life, and they will be used in the business to help generate profits over that period.

Accumulated depreciation is the total depreciation that has been charged on an asset since it was purchased. This is deducted from the cost of an asset to arrive at its net book value.

The net book value (NBV) is found by taking the cost of an asset and deducting the accumulated depreciation that has been charged on that asset since it was purchased. This is the value of the asset shown on the statement of financial position.

Demonstration Exercise 4.2

Smart Sports purchased a printing machine for £5,500, and having done some research, Sam estimates that it should have a useful life of four years, at the end of which time it is likely to have no residual value.

If the straight-line depreciation method is going to be used:

a) What rate, given as percentage, should depreciation be charged at, if the machinery is to be written off over four years?

b) What will be the annual depreciation charge?

c) Knowing that the NBV of the machinery is the cost less the accumulated depreciation charged on it, calculate the NBV of the machinery at 31 December 2011 and at subsequent year ends, using Table 4.3.

Table 4.3

At the first accounting year-end, 31 December 2011			
	Cost £	**Accumulated depreciation** £	**Net book value** £
Printing machine	5,500		
At the second accounting year-end, 31 December 2012			
	Cost £	**Accumulated depreciation** £	**Net book value** £
Printing machine	5,500		
At the third accounting year-end, 31 December 2013			
	Cost £	**Accumulated depreciation** £	**Net book value** £
Printing machine	5,500		
At the fourth accounting year-end, 31 December 2014			
	Cost £	**Accumulated depreciation** £	**Net book value** £
Printing machine	5,500		

Ponder Point

Why is the net book value zero at the end of the fourth year?

The reducing-balance method

When the reducing-balance method is used, the depreciation charge is highest in the first year and reduces annually thereafter. This is achieved by applying the depreciation percentage to the NBV of the asset.

Demonstration Exercise 4.3

Smart Sports purchased a computer for £3,500. Kim advises Sam to depreciate it on the reducing-balance basis at the rate of 40% per annum.

a) Complete the working in Table 4.4 to find the depreciation charge for each of the first three years:

Table 4.4

	£
Cost of the computer	3,500
1st year's depreciation charge (40% × 3,500)	1,400
Net book value at 31 December 2011	2,100
2nd year's depreciation charge (40% × 2,100)	____
Net book value at 31 December 2012	
3rd year's depreciation charge (40% × 1,260)	____
Net book value at 31 December 2013	====

In summary, the annual depreciation charged to the income statement for the computer is shown in Table 4.5:

Table 4.5

	Depreciation charge for the year £
For the year to 31 December 2011	1,400
For the year to 31 December 2012	840
For the year to 31 December 2013	504

b) Show the statement of financial position entries for the computer, using Table 4.6.

Table 4.6

At the first year-end, 31 December 2011			
	Cost **£**	**Accumulated depreciation** **£**	**Net book value** **£**
Computer	3,500	1,400	2,100
At the second year-end, 31 December 2012			
	Cost **£**	**Accumulated depreciation** **£**	**Net book value** **£**
Computer			
At the third year-end, 31 December 2013			
	Cost **£**	**Accumulated depreciation** **£**	**Net book value** **£**
Computer			

Terminology

The reducing-balance method of providing for depreciation applies the depreciation rate to the NBV of the asset, so that the depreciation expense is greatest in the first year of ownership and falls every year thereafter.

Ponder Point

The reducing-balance method is a popular method of providing for depreciation in practice. Can you think of at least one reason that a business might choose this depreciation method?

Case Study
The Strikers Club is in trouble

Sam's business has been growing very rapidly, and he has made sales to sports clubs over a wide geographical area. He has just received some bad news from Dot regarding one of his customers, the Strikers Club. Sam has learned that all of its players have left and that the club has no money or any other assets left to pay off their outstanding liabilities. Unfortunately, Sam had made a number of sales to the Strikers Club, and they currently owe Smart Sports over £800.

Dot apologizes for having originally introduced Sam to the Strikers Club but explains that bad debts happen occasionally in business and are an unfortunate result of making sales on credit.

Bad and doubtful debts

Terminology

A bad debt arises when a customer who owes money to the business for goods or services received on credit becomes unable to pay the amount due. At that time it should no longer be included in the trade receivables figure as it does not represent an asset.

A debt should not be written off as a bad debt until it is definitely irrecoverable.

In order to account for a bad debt, it is necessary to:

- deduct the amount of the bad debt from the trade receivables figure
- show the total bad debts written off in the accounting period as an expense in the income statement.

Ponder Point

What steps can a business take in order to minimize its bad debts?

Bad debts tend to be written off as they arise during a financial year. Where this has happened, the trial balance will show a debit balance for bad debts. This amount should then be taken as an expense to the income statement.

As well as the bad debts that have been written off, businesses often know from experience that a proportion of their year-end trade receivables will eventually turn bad. To allow for this, a provision for doubtful debts should be set-up. Often this is calculated as a percentage of the trade receivables figure.

In order to account for the provision for doubtful debts, it is necessary to:

- deduct the total provision required from the trade receivables figure
- charge any increase in the provision as an expense in the income statement.

When there is a decrease in the required provision, then the amount of the decrease is added back in the income statement and increases the profit for the year.

Accounting for bad and doubtful debts is a clear example of the accounting concept of prudence in practice. This concept guides preparers of financial statements to take a cautious approach to preparing accounts and, in doing so, to ensure that any anticipated costs are taken into account.

Terminology

The provision for doubtful debts is an amount deducted from trade receivables to recognize that a proportion of those amounts will eventually not be received by the business.

The prudence concept requires that, when accounts are being prepared, income should never be anticipated but all possible costs should be taken into account. That means that a cautious, but realistic, approach should be taken to ensure that profits are not overestimated.

Demonstration Exercise 4.4

The trial balance for Smart Sports is given in Table 4.7, along with additional information in the table footnotes that will enable the final version of the income statement and statement of financial position to be prepared.

Table 4.7

Smart Sports		
Trial balance as at 31 December 2011		
	Debit £	**Credit** £
Capital		10,000
Loan[1]		12,000
Sales		51,000
Purchases[2]	34,500	
Electricity[3]	1,920	
Insurance[4]	1,750	
Telephone	1,500	
Sundry expenses	1,650	
Drawings	7,200	
Accountant's fees	1,500	
Delivery costs	1,200	
Printing machine[5]	5,500	
Computer[5]	3,500	
Bank balance	11,080	
Trade receivables[6]	4,100	
Trade payables		2,400
	75,400	75,400

1. The loan was interest-free for the first six months of the year, after which time interest was to be paid at the rate of 6% per annum. No interest was paid during the year.
2. Inventory held at the year-end was valued at £2,700.
3. Electricity used but not yet paid for as at the year-end amounted to £480.
4. Insurance had been prepaid by £351 at the year-end.
5. Depreciation is to be charged on non-current assets as follows:
   Printing machine: 25% per annum on the straight-line basis.
   Computer: 40% per annum on the reducing-balance basis.
6. A bad debt of £820 is also to be written off at the year-end.

Using the partially completed financial statements to guide you, prepare the income statement for Smart Sports as at 31 December 2011 (Table 4.8) and the statement of financial position (Table 4.9) as at that date.

Table 4.8

Smart Sports		
Income statement for the year ended 31 December 2011 (final version)		
	£	£
Sales		51,000
Less: Cost of sales	-----------	
....	-----------	
Less:	______	
		______
Gross profit		-----------
Less: Expenses		
Electricity	-----------	
Insurance	-----------	
....	-----------	
....	-----------	
....	-----------	
....	-----------	
....	-----------	
....	-----------	
Depreciation charge on printing machine	-----------	
Depreciation charge on computer	-----------	
Bad debt	______	
		______
Net profit		======

Table 4.9

Smart Sports			
Statement of financial position as at 31 December 2011 (final version)			
	Cost	**Accum. depn**	**Net book value**
ASSETS			
Non-current assets			
Printing machine	5,500		
Computer	3,500	____	____
	====	====	====
Current assets			
Inventory		--------	
....		--------	
....		--------	
....		____	
			____
Total assets			====
CAPITAL AND LIABILITIES			
Capital at the beginning of the year			--------
Add:			--------
Less:			____
Capital at the end of the year			--------
Non-current liabilities			
....			--------
Current liabilities			
....		--------	
....		____	
			____
Total capital and liabilities			====

Uses and limitations of the statement of financial position

The statement of financial position shows the assets a business owns and the liabilities it owes. This information can be useful to anyone wishing to find out more about a business.

Ponder Point

If you were advising Smart Sports' bank manager, would you recommend that an overdraft facility be provided for 2012? What other information would you require from Sam?

The statement of financial position, however, does have a number of limitations:

Limitation 1 – Historical cost

A significant limitation of the statement of financial position is that assets are generally recorded at historical cost, which is not always the most meaningful measure. The historical cost of a non-current asset may bear little resemblance to its actual value to a business, particularly if it was purchased some years ago.

Limitation 2 – Estimates and judgements

The preparer of the income statement and statement of financial position has to make a number of estimates and judgements:

- to decide whether individual expenditure is capital or revenue
- to determine which depreciation methods and rates to use
- to determine how much to provide for accruals and prepayments
- to decide which trade receivables are definitely bad and write them off
- to decide how much to provide for doubtful debts.

All of the above will require personal judgements to be made. It is therefore not possible to declare that there is only ever one possible profit figure and only one possible statement of financial position for a given set of business transactions. In fact, there are usually many possible variations of the financial statements that can justifiably be prepared, based on the same financial information.

Limitation 3 – Missing assets

The statement of financial position will include all known tangible assets but will not include any intangible assets, except in very specific, more unusual, circumstances.

Terminology

An intangible asset is an asset without any physical substance. Examples include goodwill and brand names.

Just because an asset does not have a physical presence, it is no less important than a tangible asset would be. Intangible assets can result in substantial financial benefits to the business in the future.

Ponder Point

Can you think of any intangible assets that Smart Sports might have now or hopes to have in the future?

Summary of Key Points

- Non-current assets are written off over their useful lives by charging depreciation to the income statement.
- There are two popular methods of providing for depreciation: the straight-line method and the reducing-balance method.
- The straight-line method of charging depreciation charges an equal annual percentage based on the cost of the asset.
- The reducing-balance method charges depreciation by applying a chosen percentage to the net book value of the asset. The depreciation charge is greatest in the first year of ownership and decreases every year thereafter.
- The statement of financial position shows non-current assets at their cost to the business less accumulated depreciation, known as the net book value.
- A bad debt arises when credit customers are unable to pay the amount they owe for goods or services they have received.

- A provision for doubtful debts is an allowance against existing debts turning bad. Based on past experience, it is usually calculated as a percentage of the trade receivables figure.

Smart Questions: a wider perspective

1. Does the statement of financial position include every significant asset from which the business benefits?
2. Would it be easy to value these assets in order to include them on the statement of financial position?
3. Will all businesses use the same depreciation methods and rates for similar assets?
4. Property is included as a non-current asset on the statement of financial position at cost less accumulated depreciation. Is this likely to be the most relevant value for all users of the accounts?
5. The provision for doubtful debts is based on a percentage of trade receivables at the year-end, a percentage which varies from business to business. Why is there no common percentage for all businesses?
6. Does the prudence concept mean that accountants always take a very pessimistic approach towards arriving at the profit for the year?

Wider Reading

Dunn, J. (2010) ***Financial Reporting and Analysis*, Wiley.** Chapter 8 provides an interesting overview of accounting for tangible non-current assets.

Practice Questions

4.1 Douggen

Douggen manufactures and installs specialist industrial pumps. The business commenced trading on 1 January 2012 and purchased the following assets:

Plant and machinery	£80,000
Motor vehicles	£24,000

Before preparing the financial statements, Douggen needs to decide how the business is going to depreciate these various assets.

REQUIRED:

a) Explain why the above assets should be depreciated.

b) If plant and equipment is to be depreciated on the straight-line basis, what should the depreciation charge be for 2012 and 2013, given that it is expected to have a useful life of four years and a scrap value of £8,000 at the end of that time?

c) Describe the business's depreciation policy for plant and equipment by completing the following statement:

'Plant and equipment is to be depreciated at ... % on the straight-line basis.'

d) Douggen is considering depreciating motor vehicles either:

- at the rate of 25% per annum on the straight-line basis
- at the rate of 35% per annum on the reducing-balance basis.

(i) Which of the two policies will lead to the smallest depreciation charge for:

(a) the year ended 31 December 2012

(b) the year ended 31 December 2013

(c) both years combined?

(ii) Which policy should Douggen choose if the business wants to maximize its profit for those two years?

e) Show the entry for non-current assets on the statement of financial position at 31 December 2012, assuming that Douggen depreciates the motor vehicles at 25% per annum on the straight-line basis.

4.2 Russells

The trial balance of Russells as at 31 December 2012 is shown in Table 4.10.

Table 4.10

	Debit €	**Credit €**
Sales		220,360
Freehold premises[1]	67,500	
Plant and equipment[2]	39,000	
Fixtures and fittings[2]	15,000	
Trade receivables[3]	11,750	
Bank balance	4,200	
Trade payables		15,100
Inventories at 1 January 2012	7,800	
Purchases[4]	92,000	
Motor expenses	4,450	
Electricity[5]	8,000	
Wages[6]	43,600	
Bad debts	110	
Other business expenses	3,050	
Drawings	24,000	
Capital as at 1 January 2012		85,000
	320,460	**320,460**

1. No depreciation is to be charged on freehold premises.
2. All depreciation is to be provided on the straight-line basis. Plant and equipment is to be depreciated at 30% per annum and fixtures and fittings at 20% per annum.
3. A provision for doubtful debts of 4% of trade receivables is to be established.
4. Inventories held at 31 December 2012 were valued at €8,200.
5. Electricity owing at the year-end amounted to €1,200.
6. Wages due to staff at 31 December 2012 amounted to €4,800.

REQUIRED:

Prepare the income statement for Russells for the year ended 31 December 2012 and a statement of financial position as at that date.

4.3 Poppy

Poppy started a business on 1 July 2011 as a personal fitness instructor and put in €8,000 capital to fund it. She prepared her first year's accounts to 30 June 2012.

During her first year, she purchased lightweight transportable equipment: a rowing machine for €2,500, a cycling machine for €3,000, and a treadmill for €2,500. She expects all the equipment to last for five years and have no residual value.

Clients pay her €250 per month for ten sessions. During the year, she took on 12 clients, 10 of whom joined at the start, while 2 joined on 1 January 2012. All clients pay her promptly at the beginning of each month, but one customer owes her a total of €1,250 at the year-end.

Poppy's average costs of running each session are €5. She purchased consumables, including sports wear, for a total of €1,500 during the year.

Poppy made drawings of €2,000 each month.

REQUIRED:

a) Compute Poppy's sales income for the year.

b) What will Poppy's bank balance be at 30 June 2012?

c) Prepare Poppy's income statement for the year ended 30 June 2012.

d) Prepare Poppy's statement of financial position as at 30 June 2012.

e) Although Poppy is delighted with how well the business has done, she is exhausted by the number of hours she is working. She would like to employ an assistant, at a cost of €600 per month. Advise Poppy on the viability of employing an assistant.

Chapter Five
Company Finance
Growing the business

Learning Objectives

At the end of this topic, you should be able to:

- discuss the nature of a limited company
- describe the main external sources of finance available to limited companies, and discuss their characteristics
- appreciate the role of a stock exchange
- outline the reporting requirements placed upon the directors of a company.

Introduction

Once businesses reaches a certain size, it is common for owners to form the business into a limited company for a variety of reasons. One key consideration is that a limited company often has greater options available to it for raising long-term funds, including the issue of shares or loans. Understanding the nature of share capital will enable us to appreciate the risks and rewards that shareholders accept.

Case Study
Should Sam form a company?

Smart Sports has grown considerably since the business was launched from Sam's garage. The number of customers and the demand for printed sports kits has grown sharply, with the volume of enquiries and orders showing a month-on-month increase. Sam realizes that, to deal with orders in the future, he will need to find larger premises and invest in bigger and more efficient printing equipment, as his existing printer is rather slow. He decides to phone Kim, his accountant, to discuss the options available to him.

During the conversation, Kim establishes that Sam has friends and family who would consider investing in Smart Sports. He advises Sam that he should consider converting his business into a limited company as this would enable him to offer potential investors a stake in the company in return for their investment. These funds could then be used to enable the business to move to new premises and expand.

Before deciding on this course of action, Sam needs to understand more about the nature of limited companies.

The nature of limited companies

Company formation

It is relatively straightforward to form a company. Various information and documents have to be filed with the relevant authorities, detailing the company name, the directors, the objectives of the business, and the company's internal rules and regulations.

Separate legal entity

A limited company has a separate legal identity, separate in law from the shareholders who own it and the directors who manage it. As a result, it can sue and be sued in its own name.

Limited liability

When a business becomes a limited company, the shareholders have limited liability, which means that they stand to lose only the amount they have invested in the company. Their personal assets are safe should the company become unable to pay its liabilities.

Ponder Point

Does a sole trader have limited liability?

Perpetual life

Another important feature of limited companies is that they have a perpetual life. Their existence is not dependent on the continuing life of the shareholders.

Terminology

Limited liability means that, should the company be wound up, shareholders stand to lose only the amount that they have invested in the business. (This assumes that their shares have been fully paid for.)

A private company is restricted from issuing its shares to the general public.

A public company can offer its shares for sale to the general public.

Directors are those employees elected by the shareholders to run the company. Every limited company must have at least one director.

Demonstration Exercise 5.1

a) What might be the main benefits to Sam of forming a company?

b) Would you expect Smart Sports to be formed as a private or public company, and how will this affect the company name?

c) If Sam cannot advertise his shares to the public, who might he approach with a view to investing as a shareholder?

d) Sam intends to become a director of the company. What does this mean? What do you think his role will involve?

e) Can Sam be a shareholder as well as a director?

Demonstration Exercise 5.1 – solution

a) The main benefit would be that the company could raise additional capital by offering investors a share in the business.

   Other benefits would include having limited liability and the enhanced status that a business trading as a company is perceived as having.

b) A private company, which in the UK will be identified by the use of 'Ltd' at the end of the company name.

c) Sam could consider approaching family members, friends, colleagues, customers, or others who know Sam and the business.

d) A director of the company is a senior employee of the company, responsible for running the business and taking key decisions. In a small company, the directors may be the only managers, but in a larger company, where there may be many layers of management, the directors will comprise the top tier.

e) Yes, Sam can be a shareholder as well as a director. However, a director does not have to be a shareholder in the company.

Share capital

Ordinary shares

When a company is formed, the required share capital is divided into evenly sized 'nominal' amounts or shares, and each shareholder acquires some of these shares. All companies have to issue ordinary shares, often known as equity shares.

Shareholders invest in a company with the hope that they will eventually be rewarded by the receipt of dividends from the company and by an increase in the value of their shares.

The ordinary shareholders' investment is known as the equity of a company.

Preference shares

A relatively small number of companies also issue preference shares in addition to ordinary shares. Preference shares have very specific characteristics, which usually include the following:

- They are entitled to receive a fixed rate of dividend if a dividend is paid. For example, a 5% £1 preferance share will entitle its holder to receive a 5 pence dividend each year.
- An ordinary dividend cannot be paid until any preference dividend has been paid.
- Preference shares are usually cumulative, such that if the dividends are not paid in one year, then the preference shareholders are entitled to receive arrears of dividend in subsequent years.
- If the company is wound up, the preference shareholders are entitled to be repaid before the ordinary shareholders.
- Preference shares do not usually carry voting rights.

Ponder Point

Preference shareholders are sometimes said to receive preferential treatment over ordinary shareholders. By referring to each of the above characteristics, do you agree that this is so?

Terminology

Ordinary shares entitle their owner to receive an ordinary dividend from the company. Ordinary shareholders are the owners of the company and are entitled to vote at general meetings, which gives them control over the business.

Preference shares entitle their owners to receive dividends at a fixed rate before the ordinary dividend can be paid. Preference shareholders are not generally entitled to vote at general meetings.

The nominal value of shares represents their face value and is nearly always the amount at which the shares are issued when the company is formed.

A dividend is a payment made to a company's shareholders to reward them for investing.

Demonstration Exercise 5.2

Sam has decided that he will form a company, Smart Sports Ltd, and aims to raise £50,000 from the issue of ordinary shares.

a) Would you recommend that the company issue 50,000 shares of £1 nominal value, 5,000 shares of £10 nominal value, or 500 shares of £100 nominal value? Explain your answer.

b) Shares are normally issued at nominal value when a company is formed. When might shares be issued at a price greater than nominal value?

c) Sam's mother, Betty, has never previously owned shares in a company. Explain the benefits that such an investment might bring and the possible drawbacks.

d) How might Betty find a buyer for her shares in a few years' time?

Case Study

Will Betty be able to sell her shares?

Betty is concerned about whether she will be able to sell her shares in the future and wants to find out whether it is likely to be possible. Sam asks Kim and explains to him that a number of his friends as well as his mother, Betty, are interested in becoming shareholders if a company is formed. With the exception of Betty, they are all experienced investors who understand the risks attached to any such investment, and Betty is taking independent financial advice. Sam explains that Betty's main concern is that she may want to sell her shares in a few years' time and is wondering whether that might be possible.

Kim decides to outline for Sam the role of stock markets for very large companies and the role of venture capital for smaller, less-established, businesses.

The stock exchange

The stock exchange is one of the best known marketplaces where shares are bought and sold. The price at which they are traded is dependent on supply and demand, which will depend on investors' views on the prospects for that business, the sector it is in, and the economy as a whole.

In order for a company's shares to be traded in this way, the company has to be listed.

Ponder Point

Can you name some stock exchanges?

Being listed also enables companies to raise new capital when needed.

The disadvantages for a company of having its shares listed are that it is an expensive and time-consuming process, and once listed, the company becomes subject to much higher levels of public interest. Investors, analysts, and journalists study its results and announcements, with the directors put under constant pressure to meet their expectations. The regulatory requirements are more extensive and deadlines for reporting on financial results are much tighter for listed companies. As a result, it is usually appropriate only for large businesses to obtain a stock exchange listing.

Ponder Point

What benefits might a company gain from having its shares listed on a stock exchange?

Venture capital

Venture capital is long-term capital for small and medium-sized businesses for whom a stock exchange listing would not be appropriate. Venture capitalists are prepared to invest in smaller, usually riskier, businesses and normally take an equity stake in the business, although some debt may be involved.

In addition to providing capital for the business, the venture capitalists will also usually expect to have a representative on the board of directors to advise the business and to represent the venture capitalist's interests.

Terminology

A stock exchange is a market where new capital can be raised and existing shares can be bought and sold.

Venture capital is long-term funding, usually equity capital, provided to small and medium-sized businesses to enable them to grow.

Demonstration Exercise 5.3

Sam is interested in making contact with venture capitalists to see whether Smart Sports is a business in which they might be prepared to invest in the future.

a) What might be the main benefits to Smart Sports of obtaining venture capital finance?
b) Can you list the sort of information that the venture capitalists would be interested in. (Hint: Do not just consider financial information.)
c) What might be the main drawbacks of obtaining venture capital finance?
d) What sort of investment in the company do venture capitalists require, and how would they expect to benefit from their investment?

Having explored the requirements of venture capitalists, Sam concludes that they would be unlikely to invest when the company is formed. However, in a couple of years' time, they may well provide a suitable form of funding for the business.

Loan capital and debentures

Many businesses raise finance from loans as well as share capital. A contract is drawn up between the company and the lender that specifies the amount of the loan, the interest rate, and any security provided on the loan.

Ponder Point

What do you understand by a company giving security on a loan? What sort of assets might be offered as security?

Debentures are one form of long-term loan that is usually divided into units such that there can be a number of debenture holders lending money to the company. Debentures can be listed on a stock exchange and traded like shares.

Terminology

Debentures are long-term loans raised by a company where security is usually provided for the loan.

One major advantage of debenture or loan interest is that it is an expense that is allowable for tax purposes, whereas dividends paid are not. However, while companies can choose whether or not to pay a dividend, interest on loans and debentures does have to be paid when due.

Retained profits

Companies can, as we have seen, raise long-term funding from both share issues and loan issues. A third and often more significant source of long-term funding for most companies is the profits that are retained by the business every year.

Demonstration Exercise 5.4

Sam has now decided to form his company, Smart Sports Ltd, and to issue 50,000 £1 ordinary shares at £1 per share. In addition, the company will take out a five-year loan for £18,000 from Green Bank. Sam will acquire 70% of the ordinary shares issued, his friends Dot and Dan will acquire 12% each, and his mother Betty will acquire the rest of the shares.

a) Who will be the owners of the new company, Smart Sports Ltd?

b) Will Sam be able to continue making drawings from the business once it is converted into a company?

c) If not, how do you suggest that Sam is rewarded for his efforts in the company?

d) How will Green Bank be rewarded for making the loan?

e) What would be the implications for Smart Sports Ltd if the loan raised a bigger amount and the company issued fewer ordinary shares than Sam is planning?

f) If in two years' time, Betty sells her shares for a profit, will Smart Sports Ltd benefit from this profit?

g) Companies that make a profit can either pay it out as a dividend to share-holders and/or retain the profit in the business. What is the benefit to the company of retaining profits?

Reporting requirements

Forming a company will place significant extra reporting requirements on the business that the directors are required to meet. Typically, the directors will be required to:

- produce annual financial statements that comply with company law and accounting standards; the statements are then made available to the shareholders and other users
- if the company is above a certain size, arrange to have the financial statements audited
- file the company's financial statements, or sometimes just a summarized version, with the relevant authorities; the statements are then usually made accessible to the public
- submit various annual returns that give information on the company's main activities, address, and directors' details; this information is then made publicly available.

Summary of Key Points

- Forming a limited company is a relatively straightforward process.
- A company has a separate legal identity.
- Shareholders in a company are protected by having their liability limited. This is different to the situation for a sole trader, who has unlimited liability for the business's debts.
- All companies issue ordinary shares, known as equity shares. Shareholders usually hope to be rewarded by the payment of a dividend that companies may decide to pay. In addition, shareholders hope to benefit from a capital gain as a result of the value of their shares increasing over time.
- Companies may issue preference shares, but they are issued far less frequently than ordinary shares. Preference shareholders are usually entitled to receive a fixed rate of dividend, which has to be paid before the ordinary dividend can be paid out.
- A stock exchange listing enables a company's shareholders to buy and sell their shares freely and enables the company to raise new capital. It is appropriate only for very large businesses.
- Venture capitalists are a possible source of long-term funding for small and medium-sized businesses that are likely to be relatively more risky.
- Companies can raise funds from issuing debentures or long-term loans, where security is usually provided.

Smart Questions: a wider perspective

1. Shareholders in companies are protected by limited liability, which is a long-standing principle. Why do you think shareholders are given the benefit of this protection?
2. Ordinary shares are issued by all companies, and preference shares are issued more rarely. Who might be interested in buying preference shares in a company?
3. Given that companies issuing loans and debentures will be obliged to meet interest payments when they fall due, why do companies not just issue share capital only and avoid this obligation?
4. If a company has retained profits over a number of years, does this mean that the company must have large cash balances as a result?

Wider Reading

Pike, R., and Neale, B. (2009) ***Corporate Finance and Investment, Decisions and Strategies*****, 6th edition, FT Prentice Hall.** Chapter 16 is a very comprehensive chapter and explains multiple ways in which companies can raise long-term finance.

www.bvca.co.uk/About-BVCA. The British Private Equity and Venture Capital Association (BVCA) website outlines the BVCA's objectives and how the industry works.

Practice Questions

5.1 Monk Ltd

Chris Monk is planning to form a company, Monk Ltd, and needs to raise a total of £1,000,000. He is considering various ways of raising this sum:

Option 1 Issue 70,000 £10 ordinary shares at nominal value, £10 per share, and issue a £300,000 6% debenture, repayable in five years' time.

Option 2 Issue 40,000 £10 ordinary shares at par, 400,000 5% preference shares at par, and £200,000 6% debentures.

Option 3 Issue 50,000 £10 shares at par and £500,000 7% debentures. (The lender has made it clear that a higher rate of return would be demanded if £500,000 or more is borrowed.)

Any debentures issued would be secured on the company's property.

REQUIRED:

a) For each of the above options, calculate the debenture interest and preference dividends that Monk Ltd would be liable to pay.

b) Monk Ltd expects to make a profit before interest and dividends of £40,000 in its first year of trading and £95,000 in its second year. Calculate the profits that would be available to ordinary shareholders in years 1 and 2 under each of these options.

c) Calculate the profit available per ordinary share in years 1 and 2 under each of the options in (b).

d) Use your findings above to advise Chris on factors he should consider before deciding how to raise the long-term finance needed.

5.2 Herring

Jorge is planning to set-up a restaurant business called Herring, serving Scandinavian-style fast food. He has plans to start by opening one restaurant and then within months to open at least two more. He has a great deal of experience in the catering sector but has never previously set-up his own business.

He is confident of raising the necessary funds as he has substantial savings, the bank has indicated it would be prepared to make a loan, and his friend Ulrika has made it known that she would be keen to put money into the venture. He is considering whether to establish the business, Herring, as a limited company or as a sole trader.

REQUIRED:

List the advantages and disadvantages to Jorge of setting up the business as: a) a sole trader; b) a limited company.

Chapter Six
Company Accounts
Smart Sports turns corporate

Learning Objectives

At the end of this topic, you should be able to:

- prepare an income statement and a statement of comprehensive income for a limited company
- prepare a statement of financial position for a limited company
- understand the purpose of a statement of changes in equity
- understand the importance of reliable corporate governance.

Introduction

Once a business is formed as a company, the way in which the financial statements are prepared is governed by company law and the requirements of accounting standards. The exact requirements will differ according to the size of the company.

Case Study
How are company accounts prepared?

On 1 January 2012, Sam formed the business into a company, Smart Sports Ltd, in order to raise the necessary funds to grow the business. The company issued 50,000 ordinary shares of £1 each, of which Sam acquired 35,000. The remainder were acquired by his mother, Betty, and two of his friends, Dot and Dan.

The business moved during 2012 from Sam's garage to a small rented industrial unit and has bought faster printing equipment and a delivery van. The company employs two people to do the printing and packing, which leaves Sam more time to generate new business.

The company has been trading for just over a year, and Sam is keen to complete the company's financial statements. He decides to arrange a meeting with Kim to seek advice on how to prepare the company's income statement and statement of financial position.

Kim explains that company accounts share many similarities with the financial statements that Sam prepared for his business when he was a sole trader. There are, however, some extra requirements that apply to company accounts.

The income statement

Operating profit

The income statement for a company is very similar to that for a sole trader, except that expenses are usually categorized under a few key functions (administration and distribution). Gross profit minus these expenses is known as the operating profit. The operating profit is an important measure of how well the company has done during a financial year. It is the profit the business has made from trading before any financing costs, such as interest or taxation, are taken into account.

Profit for the year

A company is liable to pay taxation on its profits, and this amount has to be deducted in arriving at the profit for the year.

The profit for the year represents the profit after all expenses, interest, and taxation have been deducted. It is the amount available to shareholders, and some could be paid out to them as dividends while the remainder, sometimes referred to as retained profits, would be kept by the company to allow it to grow and expand. These retained profits should benefit the shareholders in the longer-term.

Ponder Point

Do you consider that all profitable companies should pay a dividend to their shareholders?

The dividends paid during the year are not deducted in the income statement but are deducted in the statement of changes in equity for the year.

Terminology

Operating profit is the profit arrived at after all operating expenses have been charged, but before any interest has been charged.

The profit for the year is the profit that a company has made after taxation. This profit can be either used to pay dividends to shareholders or retained by the business.

Retained profit is the profit that remains once taxation and dividends have been deducted, and retained profits enable the company to fund future growth.

Shareholders' equity is the share capital and reserves of the company. The main reserve is usually the company's retained profits.

The statement of changes in equity

This statement shows how the shareholders' equity at the beginning of the year reconciles to the shareholders' equity at the end of the year.

An example taken from Danni's Drinks GmbH is given in Table 6.1.

Table 6.1

Danni's Drinks GmbH			
Statement of changes in equity for the year ended 31 December 2012			
	Ordinary share capital €	**Retained profits €**	**Total shareholders' equity €**
At 1 January 2012	25,000	66,100	91,100
Profit for the year	–	13,190	13,190
Dividends paid	–	(11,500)	(11,500)
At 31 December 2012	**25,000**	**67,790**	**92,790**

Ponder Point

In the above example, how much profit did Danni's Drinks GmbH make? Do you consider that the business has retained adequate profits for future growth (based on the limited information available)?

Interest and dividends

Interest and dividends are paid to providers of capital to a company. Interest has to be paid to lenders, and any interest payable, whether or not it has actually been paid, is deducted in the income statement.

Dividends are not deducted in the income statement but are shown in the statement of changes in equity. Only dividends that have actually been paid are deducted.

Demonstration Exercise 6.1

Balances extracted from the books of Smart Sports Ltd after it has been Trading for one year are given in Table 6.2.

Table 6.2

Smart Sports Ltd	
Balances extracted at 31 December 2012	
	£
Sales	153,000
Cost of sales	90,900
Administration expenses*	33,700
Distribution expenses*	12,400
Dividends paid	2,500
Interest paid	1,260
Ordinary shares of £1 each	50,000
7% loan (2017)	18,000
Retained profits at 1 January 2012	nil

* Expenses including depreciation have been categorized according to function.

Note: Taxation due on profits for the year amounted to £4,650.

Using the information given above for Smart Sports Ltd:

a) Complete the pro-forma income statement for the year ended 31 December 2012 (Table 6.3).

Table 6.3

Smart Sports Ltd	
Income statement for the year ended 31 December 2012	
	£
Sales	153,000
Less:	
Cost of sales	
Gross Profit	
Less:	
Administration expenses	
Distribution expenses	
Interest	
Profit before tax	
Taxation	
Profit for the year	

b) What is the operating profit for the year ended 31 December 2012?

c) Complete the pro-forma statement of changes in equity for the year ended 31 December 2012 (Table 6.4).

Table 6.4

Smart Sports Ltd			
Statement of changes in equity for the year ended 31 December 2012			
	Ordinary share capital £	**Retained profits £**	**Total shareholders' equity £**
At 1 January 2012	50,000	–	50,000
Profit for the year			
Dividends paid			
At 31 December 2012			

Demonstration Exercise 6.1 – solution

a) **Table 6.5**

Smart Sports Ltd	
Income statement for the year ended 31 December 2012	
	£
Sales	153,000
Less:	
Cost of sales	90,900
Gross profit	62,100
Less:	
Administration expenses	33,700
Distribution expenses	12,400
Interest	1,260
Profit before tax	**14,740**
Taxation	4,650
Profit for the year	**10,090**

b) Operating profit = £62,100 – (33,700 + 12,400) = £16,000.

It is the profit before interest is deducted.

c) **Table 6.6**

Smart Sports Ltd			
Statement of changes in equity for the year ended 31 December 2012			
	Ordinary share capital £	**Retained profits £**	**Total shareholders' equity £**
At 1 January 2012	50,000	–	50,000
Profit for the year		10,090	10,090
Dividends paid		(2,500)	(2,500)
At 31 December 2012	**50,000**	**7,590**	**57,590**

Information on dividends is often quoted as the dividend per share. In Smart Sports' first year of trading, a dividend of five pence per share was paid.

Total dividend paid = dividend per share × number of shares
= 5 pence × 50,000 shares = £2,500

The statement of financial position

The statement of financial position for a company is similar to that of a sole trader. The main area of difference is the capital section. Where a company has been formed, there are many owners of the business, and their investment in the business is known as the equity of the business.

The equity section of a statement of financial position details separately the share capital and any reserves the company may have.

Share capital and share premium

Each share issued has a nominal, or par, value, and when the first shares are issued, they are normally issued to shareholders at this amount. Once the company has been trading for some time, companies will usually issue shares at an issue price that exceeds their nominal value. Any difference between the issue price and the nominal value of the shares is taken to the share premium account.

Demonstration Exercise 6.2

Danni's Drinks GmbH issues 10,000 €1 ordinary shares at €1.40 per share.

Required:

a) How much cash will be raised from this share issue?

b) By how much will the ordinary share capital increase as a result of this share issue?

c) What is the total share premium arising from this share issue?

Demonstration Exercise 6.2 – solution

a) The share issue will raise cash of €14,000 (10,000 shares at €1.40 each).

b) The ordinary share capital account will increase by €10,000, which represents the nominal value of the shares issued.

c) The total share premium arising from the shares issued is €4,000 (10,000 shares at 40 cents premium per share).

Terminology

The equity of a company comprises the ordinary and preference share capital and all other reserves, including the share premium and retained profits.

The share premium is a reserve that records the premium amounts raised when a company makes a share issue. The premium is the difference between the issue price and the nominal value of the shares issued.

An example of the equity section of a statement of financial position is given in Table 6.7.

Table 6.7

Extract from Danni's Drinks GmbH statement of financial position as at 31 December 2012		
	€'000	**€'000**
Equity		
Share capital		
Ordinary shares of €1 each		35,000
5% preference shares of €2 each		5,000
		40,000
Reserves		
Share premium	4,000	
Retained profits	86,000	
		90,000
Total equity		**130,000**

Demonstration Exercise 6.3

The trial balance of Smart Sports Ltd as at 31 December 2012 is given in Table 6.8.

Table 6.8

Smart Sports Ltd		
Trial balance as at 31 December 2012		
	Debit £	**Credit** £
Ordinary shares of £1 each		50,000
7% loan (2017)		18,000
Sales		153,000
Cost of sales	90,900	
Operating costs, including depreciation	46,100	
Dividends paid	2,500	
Interest paid	1,260	
Printing machine	24,000	
Accumulated depreciation on the printing machine, as at 31 Dec 2012		6,000
Motor vehicle	28,000	
Accumulated depreciation on the motor vehicle, as at 31 Dec 2012		7,000
Computer equipment	6,700	
Accumulated depreciation on the computer, as at 31 Dec 2012		2,680
Bank balance	11,440	
Inventory as at 31 Dec 2012	20,200	
Trade receivables and prepayments	21,090	
Trade payables and accruals		15,510
	252,190	**252,190**

Note: Taxation due on profits for the year amounted to £4,650.

Remember that you have prepared the income statement and statement of changes in equity in Demonstration Exercise 6.1.

a) Does the company owe any interest on the loan at the year-end if the loan was taken out at the beginning of the year?

b) Unusually for a company trial balance, there is no figure shown for retained profits at the beginning of the year. Why is this?

c) Complete the statement of financial position for Smart Sports Ltd as at 31 December 2012 (Table 6.9).

Table 6.9

Smart Sports			
Statement of financial position as at 31 December 2012			
	Cost £	**Accum. dep'n £**	**NBV £**
ASSETS			
Non-current assets			
Printing machine	24,000	6,000	18,000
Motor vehicle	----------	----------	----------
Computer	______	______	______
	======	======	----------
Current assets			
Inventory		----------	
....		----------	
....		______	
			______
Total assets			======
EQUITY AND LIABILITIES			
Equity			
Ordinary shares of £1 each			50,000
Retained profits			______
Total equity			----------
Non-current liabilities			
....			----------
Current liabilities			
....		----------	
Taxation due		______	
			______
Total equity and liabilities			======

Case Study
Do assets have to be shown at cost?

While completing his first statement of financial position for the company, Sam took the opportunity to look at the accounts of some of his suppliers. He noticed something different about the way they valued some assets, and he decides to speak to Kim.

Sam understands that he has been applying the historic cost concept but has seen that some companies include properties on their statements of financial position at valuation rather than at cost. Kim explains that it is common practice for companies to do this but that any gain made on revaluation should not be included as part of the profit for the year.

Revaluing assets

Companies can choose to include their properties at fair value on their statement of financial position, whereby the net book value of the asset is replaced with a current valuation.

Ponder Point

Why do you think that companies might choose to include their properties at valuation?

The difference between the valuation and the net book value, if a positive difference, is known as the revaluation gain and is taken to a revaluation reserve. This reserve is shown as part of the company's reserves on the statement of financial position.

Revaluation gains are never included to increase profits in the income statement. Instead, they form part of the company's 'other comprehensive income' for the year.

If a revaluation loss arises, then the loss is taken as an expense to the income statement.

The treatment of revaluation gains and losses can be seen as a clear example of the prudence concept in practice. Revaluation gains are not included in arriving at the profit for the year, but revaluation losses are charged as an expense.

Ponder Point

Once properties have been revalued, companies are required to carry out subsequent revaluations on a regular basis. Why do you think this is required?

The statement of comprehensive income

This is a statement prepared as an addition to the income statement and starts with the profit or loss for the year and then adds items of 'other comprehensive income', including revaluation gains.

Companies can choose to prepare an income statement and a separate statement of comprehensive income, or a statement that combines the two. In this book, we will always prepare two separate statements:

1. The income statement that arrives at the profit or loss for the year.
2. The statement of comprehensive income, which starts from the profit or loss for the year and then lists items of 'other comprehensive income'.

Demonstration Exercise 6.4

One of the suppliers whose accounts Sam had been reading included the accounts of Zippy Shirts SA, a company based in France. Extracts from the company's financial statements as at 30 June 2012 and 30 June 2011 are given in Tables 6.10 and 6.11.

Table 6.10

Zippy Shirts SA	
Statement of comprehensive income for the year ended 30 June 2012	
	€'000
Profit for the year	574
Gain on property revaluation	650
Total comprehensive income for the year	**1,224**

Table 6.11

Zippy Shirts SA		
Extracts from the statement of financial position		
	At 30 June 2012 €'000	**At 30 June 2011 €'000**
Ordinary shares of 10 euros each	300	200
Share premium	1,100	600
Revaluation reserve	650	–
Retained profits	1,714	1,200
Equity	3,764	**2,000**

a) What is the nominal value of the company's shares?

b) The ordinary share issue was made in August 2011. How many ordinary shares did Zippy Shirts SA issue at that time?

c) How much did the share issue raise?

d) The company owns one property, which was on the statement of financial position at €1,850,000 before it was revalued. What valuation was placed on the property?

e) If a dividend of €2 per share was paid in February 2012, what is the total dividend that was paid?

f) Complete the statement of changes in equity for Zippy Shirts SA for the year ended 30 June 2012, using the pro-forma given in Table 6.12.

Table 6.12

Zippy shirts SA					
Statement of changes in equity for the year ended 30 June 2012					
	Ordinary share capital €'000	Share premium €'000	Revaluation reserve €'000	Retained profits €'000	Total equity €'000
At 1 July 2011	200	600	–	1,200	2,000
Share issue					
Total comprehensive income					
Dividends paid					
At 30 June 2012					

Corporate governance

Smart Sports Ltd is a small private company, and Sam is its sole director. In a larger public company, there would be more directors who may or may not be shareholders in the company. It is therefore important that the directors always act in the best interests of the company and all of its shareholders, and not simply seek to pursue what is best for them personally. This is what the corporate governance rules and regulations seek to ensure.

Ponder Point

Can you think of instances when a director's personal interests might conflict with the best interests of the company?

There are a number of basic principles that guide corporate governance practice, the main ones being:

Responsibility: Directors are expected to manage and lead the business and to do so within a framework of prudent controls.

Accountability: Shareholders should have the right to receive information from the company and should be able to remove directors from the company if they are unhappy about the direction the business is taking.

Transparency: Financial and other information released to shareholders should be clear and understandable. The way in which the business is run and controlled should be made clear in the financial statements.

Fairness: All shareholders should be treated fairly and equally.

Ponder Point

What do you understand by insider trading? Would it be acceptable under the principles of good corporate governance?

Summary of Key Points

- A full set of financial statements for a company will include:
  a) an income statement
  b) a statement of comprehensive income
  c) a statement of changes in equity
  d) a statement of financial position
  e) a statement of cash flows—this is covered in Chapter 7.

  Items (a) and (b) can be shown as one combined statement.
- The income statement for a company shows the operating profit generated as well as the profit for the year arrived at after all expenses, interest, and taxation have been deducted.
- The statement of comprehensive income starts from the profit or loss for the year and then adds on items of other comprehensive income, including revaluation gains.
- The statement of changes in equity shows how the shareholders' equity at the beginning of the year reconciles to the shareholders' equity at the end of the year.
- The statement of financial position for a company shows the shareholders' equity investment, which comprises the share capital and all the reserves of the company. The reserves include the share premium, revaluation reserve, and retained profits.
- A share premium account arises when shares are issued by a company at a price in excess of their nominal value.
- Any gain arising when a property is revalued should be shown as 'other comprehensive income' and taken to the revaluation reserve.

Smart Questions: a wider perspective

1. A sole trader's statement of financial position shows the amount of capital that the owner has invested in the business. What is the equivalent figure or figures for a company?
2. A sole trader can take drawings from a business. How would someone who is a director and shareholder of a business be rewarded?
3. What are the implications for a company if some of its shareholders sell their shares at a profit? Will the share premium account be affected?

Wider Reading

Elliott, B., and Elliott, J. (2009) *Financial Accounting and Reporting*, 13th edition, **FT Prentice Hall.** Chapter 8 provides details on the structure and content of financial statements prepared by companies complying with international accounting standards.

International Accounting Standard 1, *Presentation of Financial Statements.* **Summary available from www.iasplus.com/standard/ias01.htm.** This provides a useful summary of the key requirements of the international accounting standard on the presentation of company financial statements.

Melville, A. (2009) *International Financial Reporting, A Practical Guide*, 2nd edition, **FT Prentice Hall.** Chapter 3 provides a straightforward guide to the structure and content of financial statements prepared by companies complying with international accounting standards.

Practice Questions

6.1 Adiga Ltd

Adiga Ltd is a company that has issued ordinary £1 shares and 7% £1 preference shares. The company's trial balance as at 31 December 2012, after the income statement has been prepared, is shown in Table 6.13.

Table 6.13

	Debit £	Credit £
Ordinary share capital		1,100,000
7% preference shares		400,000
6% debenture (2018)		300,000
Share premium		260,000
Non-current assets, at net book value	1,500,000	
Trade receivables	329,000	
Bank balance	190,000	
Trade payables		205,000
Accruals		44,000
Prepayments	59,000	
Inventories at 31 December 2012	430,000	
Profit for the year		151,000
Preference dividends paid	28,000	
Ordinary dividend paid	44,000	
Retained profits at 1 January 2012		120,000
	2,580,000	2,580,000

Notes: No ordinary or preference shares were issued during the year.
Taxation can be ignored.
There were no share issues during the year.

REQUIRED:

a) Prepare the statement of changes in equity for the year ended 31 December 2012.

b) Prepare the statement of financial position as at that date.

c) Deepak is an ordinary shareholder in Adiga Ltd and is a little disappointed at the level of dividends for the year. Comment on the level of dividends (both ordinary and preference) paid out during 2012.

6.2 Sacha SA

The trial balance in Table 6.14 was prepared for Sacha SA, a French winemaker, after the income statement for the year ended 31 March 2013 had been drawn up.

Table 6.14

	Debit €'000	Credit €'000
Ordinary share capital		1,000
5% debenture (2020)		600
Share premium		150
Property, at net book value	1,640	
Plant and equipment, at net book value	353	
Inventories at 31 March 2013	734	
Trade receivables	516	
Trade payables and accruals		604
Bank balance	30	
Prepayments		
Profit for the year		199
Ordinary dividend paid	60	
Retained profits at 1 April 2012		780
	3,333	3,333

Notes: The property was revalued at the year-end by an independent qualified valuer at €2,000,000.
No ordinary shares were issued during the year.
Taxation can be ignored.

REQUIRED:

a) The directors are keen for the property to be shown at the revalued amount in the accounts. Explain what the effect on the financial statements will be as a result of processing the revaluation of the property.

b) Prepare the statement of comprehensive income for the year ended 31 March 2013, starting from the profit for the year.

c) Prepare the statement of changes in equity for the year ended 31 March 2013.

d) Prepare the statement of financial position as at 31 March 2013.

6.3 Meditor

Casey, one of your friends, has recently inherited a small shareholding in an Irish company, Meditor Ltd, which manufactures diagnostic medical equipment. Casey knows very little about the company but has acquired extracts from its two most recent statements of financial position.

Table 6.15

Meditor Ltd				
Statements of financial position as at 30 September				
	2013		2012	
	€'000	€'000	€'000	€'000
ASSETS				
Non-current assets				
Property		3,500		2,240
Plant and equipment	2,230		2,100	
Less: depreciation	1,915		1,580	
		315		520
		3,815		2,760
Current assets				
Inventory	521		420	
Trade receivables	440		381	
Cash	640		–	
		1,601		801
Total assets		**5,416**		**3,561**
EQUITY AND LIABILITIES				–
Equity				
Ordinary share capital	1,000		700	
Share premium	600		–	
Revaluation reserve	1,260		–	
Retained earnings	2,308		1,942	
		5,168		2,642
Non-current liabilities				
Loan		–		600
Current liabilities				
Bank overdraft	–		111	
Trade payables	248		208	
		248		319
Total equity and liabilities		**5,416**		**3,561**

Note: No depreciation is provided on property.

REQUIRED:

Based on the statements of financial position given in Table 6.13, answer the following questions for Casey. Explain your answers.

a) Casey has not been given a copy of the income statement. Did the company make a profit during the year ended 30 September 2013?

b) What is the company's most significant asset?

c) How has the long-term funding of the company changed during the year ended 30 September 2013?

d) Casey comments that it looks as if the company bought new properties during the last year. Did it?

e) The company owns significant amounts of plant and equipment. Have these assets been purchased recently?

f) What can you tell about how the company's cash position has changed during the year to 30 September 2013?

Chapter Seven
The Statement of Cash Flows

Where has all the cash gone?

Learning Objectives

At the end of this topic, you should be able to:

- discuss the crucial importance of cash to a business
- explain the difference between profit and cash
- prepare a simple statement of cash flows.

Introduction

Many profitable businesses fail because, although profitable, they do not have adequate cash available. Without sufficient cash resources, a business will be unable to pay its suppliers, employee wages, interest on loans, and shareholder dividends.

The statement of cash flows, which is the third main financial statement, highlights the cash that has flowed into and out of a business during a financial period. This enables users to see whether the business has been generating cash and whether it seems to have any cash flow problems.

Cash includes cash and bank balances plus very short-term deposits.

Ponder Point

Is the profit that a business makes a reliable indicator of its cash balances?

Case Study
Smart Sports runs into cash flow problems

Since forming his company two years ago, Sam has grown the business rapidly. He has moved from rented premises to a new industrial unit that the business has bought. He also bought two new delivery vans to meet expected future demand and achieve better delivery times.

Sam knows that the company is making a profit because he has seen the income statement. However, he cannot understand why, with all the money raised from the share issue and increased sales and profitability, the company is getting close to reaching its bank overdraft limit. He is worried that in a couple of months' time the business will not have enough cash available to pay suppliers and employee wages.

Once again, he arranges to meet Kim to try to find some answers. Kim is also keen to understand where the cash has gone, and explains to Sam that a statement of cash flows will highlight the sources of cash that have come into the company and how that cash has been spent. He suggests that, to understand statements of cash flow, they start by considering Danni's Drinks business as it is a simpler business than Smart Sports.

The statement of cash flows

The statement of cash flows is the statement that highlights how well a business has generated cash during a financial period. It also shows whether any extra long-term funding has been raised or repaid and whether any long-term assets have been bought or sold during the period.

The statement of cash flows is the third main financial statement that companies are required to prepare, and it is a popular one with users because it allows them to see exactly how the business has funded its operations.

Demonstration Exercise 7.1

When Danni first started trading, he sold 2,000 cans of drinks in January, the first month. The drinks cost him €2 each, and he sold them for €3 each. During that month, he bought 2,400 cans and also purchased two fridges for a total cost of €730. Danni paid €500 into his business bank account at the beginning of the month.

a) How much profit did Danni make in January? (Ignore depreciation.)

b) What would Danni's cash balance be at the end of January?

c) Why is there a difference between the profit made and the cash balance?

   If some of Danni's customers had been allowed credit and owed him €100 at the end of the month.

d) Will sales made on credit affect the profit for the month?

e) Taking the credit sales into account, what would Danni's cash balance be at the end of January?

f) List all the factors that will result in profit and cash not being the same.

Demonstration Exercise 7.1 – solution

a) Danni's profit in January was €2,000.

	€
Sales (2,000 × €3)	6,000
Cost of sales	
Purchases (2,400 × €2)	4,800
Less closing inventory (400 × €2)	800
	4,000
Profit	**2,000**

b) Danni's cash balance at the end of January would be €970.

   Money banked = capital €500 + sales income €6,000 = €6,500.
   Money paid out = purchases €4,800 + fridges €730 = €5,530.
   Net bank balance = €6,500 – €5,530 = €970.

c) There is a difference between the profit made and the cash balance because:

   - inventory had been purchased that had not been sold by the month end
   - fridges had been purchased
   - Danni had put capital into the business.

Inventory held and the purchase of the fridges will have reduced the bank balance but not reduced the profit. The capital invested by Danni will have increased the bank balance without increasing the profit.

d) Credit sales will have no effect on the profit for the month.

A sale is recorded in the accounts when the customer takes delivery of the goods. Whether a sale is made for cash or on credit will make no difference to the sales or profit for the period.

e) The bank balance would be €870.

Danni's net bank balance as calculated in part (b) was €970, which would be further reduced by the customers who owe the business €100 at the end of the month. The bank balance would be €870.

f) The factors are as follows:

- Inventory held at the month end.
- Fridges purchased.
- Capital put into the business.
- Trade receivables who owe the business at the month end.

The statement of cash flows for Danni's Drinks is given in Table 7.1. All of the factors noted above are shown on the statement as it highlights the differences between profit and cash by reconciling the two figures.

Table 7.1

Danni's Drinks	
Statement of cash flows for January	
	€
Cash flows from operating activities	
Profit for the month	2,000
Working capital movements	
Less: Increase in inventories	(800)
Less: Increase in trade receivables	(100)
Cash generated from operations	1,100
Cash flows from investing activities	
Less: Purchase of fridges	(730)
Cash flows from financing activities	
Add: Capital introduced	500
Increase in cash balance	870

Table 7.1 shows that, although €2,000 profit was made during the month, €800 of that amount is now tied up in inventories and €100 is owed by credit customers. As a result, only €1,100 cash has actually flowed into the business from operating activities. The other cash received during the year was €500 that Danni put into the business.

The fridges, purchased for €730 during the year, resulted in the business having an increase in its cash balance of €870, which is considerably less than the profit made.

Ponder Point

What effect does the amount of inventory held by the business have on its cash position? Can you explain why this is so?

Sources of cash flow

In preparing statements of cash flow, all cash flows are categorized under one of three possible headings.

Cash flows from operating activities: This is the cash generated from the main trading activities of the business. It is usually found by taking the profit for the year and making adjustments for non-cash expenses and working capital movements.

Cash flows from investing activities: Included under this heading will be any cash flows arising as a result of the purchase or disposal of non-current assets.

Cash flows from financing activities: Financing activities are ones that alter the long-term funding of the company. This will include share issues and loan issues.

Demonstration Exercise 7.2

Decide whether each of the following would be classified as an operating cash flow, an investing cash flow, or a financing cash flow:

a) Proceeds of a share issue.

b) Purchase of property.

c) Purchase of a motor van.

d) Cash tied up in inventory.

e) Proceeds of a loan issue.

Terminology

Cash flows from operating activities are cash flows that arise from the normal trading activities of the business.

Cash flows from investing activities include the amounts paid out to purchase non-current assets and the proceeds received from selling non-current assets.

Cash flows from financing activities are cash flows that alter the long-term financing of the company. These include the proceeds of share issues or the amount paid out to redeem a loan.

Working capital is the amount invested in the short-term assets of a business. It is represented by inventories, short-term receivables, and cash balances less short-term liabilities.

108 Non-current assets and the statement of cash flows

The way in which movements in non-current assets are shown on the statement of cash flows needs careful consideration.

Depreciation

When a fixed asset is purchased, the full cost of the asset is borne by the company's cash balance at that time. Depreciation, which is the means whereby the cost of an asset is gradually charged to the income statement over the life of the asset, does not represent an expense where cash is spent. Depreciation is therefore a non-cash expense.

In order to reconcile profit to cash in the statement of cash flows, it is necessary to add back any depreciation deducted in arriving at the profit figure, as it does not involve an outflow of cash.

Purchase of non-current assets

When a non-current asset is purchased, then the full cost of any such asset bought during the year should be shown as a cash outflow in the year it is purchased.

Movements in working capital

Increases and decreases in a business's working capital will not impact on the profit figure, but they will have a direct effect on the cash balance.

Inventories

The more inventories a business holds, the more cash will have been used up in purchasing it. Hence, any increase in inventories should be deducted as an outflow of funds in the statement of cash flows.

Trade receivables

When sales are made on credit, the business is deprived of the cash owed by those credit customers. The more that trade receivables increase, the more the business will be deprived of cash. In the statement of cash flows, it is therefore necessary to deduct any increase in trade receivables as an outflow of funds.

Trade payables

Trade payables provide funding to a business in the short-term. The more a business owes to suppliers, the less cash will actually be paid out of the business. Hence, any increase in trade payables should be added on as a cash inflow in the statement of cash flows.

Ponder Point

If a company decides to change from a supplier who allows 30 days' credit to a supplier who demands all purchases are made for cash, what will be the effect on its cash flows?

Demonstration Exercise 7.3

Smart Sports Ltd's income statement for the year ended 31 December 2013 showed a profit for the year of £30,902. During that year, the company purchased new premises at a cost of £80,000, along with other non-current assets.

The statement of changes in equity for 2013 along with the statements of financial position at 31 December 2012 and 2013 are given in Tables 7.2 and 7.3.

Table 7.2

Smart Sports Ltd				
Statement of changes in equity for the year ended 31 December 2013				
	Ordinary share capital £	**Share premium £**	**Retained profits £**	**Total equity £**
At 1 January 2013	50,000	–	7,590	57,590
Share issue	20,000	10,000	–	30,000
Profit for the year	–	–	30,902	30,902
At 31 December 2013	**70,000**	**10,000**	**38,492**	**118,492**

a) Did Smart Sports issue any new shares during 2013? If so, how much did the share issue raise?

b) Did Smart Sports take out any new loans during the year?

c) How much depreciation was charged in 2013?

d) How much was spent on purchases of property, plant, and equipment during the year?

e) Using the financial statements in Tables 7.2 and 7.3, prepare the statement of cash flows for Smart Sports Ltd for the year ended 31 December 2013.

Demonstration Exercise 7.3 – solution

a) During 2013, 20,000 shares were issued, which raised a total of £30,000. The amount raised by the share issue is found by adding the increase in the share capital account to the increase in share premium account.

b) During the year, £12,000 (£30,000 – £18,000) of new loans were taken out. (This assumes that no loans were repaid during the year.)

c) Depreciation of £20,208 (£35,888 – £15,680) was charged in 2013.

d) The amount spent on purchases of property, plant, and equipment during the year was £96,000 (£154,700 – £58,700).

Table 7.3

Smart Sports Ltd				
Statements of financial position as at 31 December				
	2013		**2012**	
	£	**£**	**£**	**£**
ASSETS				
Non-current assets				
Property, plant, and equipment				
At cost		154,700		58,700
Accumulated depreciation		35,888		15,680
Net book value		118,812		43,020
Current assets				
Inventory	39,000		20,200	
Trade receivables and prepayments	35,780		21,090	
Bank balance	–		11,440	
		74,780		52,730
Total assets		**193,592**		**95,750**
EQUITY AND LIABILITIES				
Equity				
Share capital		70,000		50,000
Share premium		10,000		–
Retained profits		38,492		7,590
Total equity		**118,492**		**57,590**
Non-current liabilities				
Loans		30,000		18,000
Current liabilities				
Trade payables and accruals	34,670		20,160	
Bank overdraft	10,430		–	
		45,100		20,160
Total equity and liabilities		**193,592**		**95,750**

Note: No non-current assets were sold during the year.

e)

Table 7.4

Smart Sports Ltd	
Statement of cash flows for the year ended 31 December 2013	
	£
Cash flows from operating activities	
Profit for the year	30,902
Add: Depreciation	20,208
	51,110
Working capital movements	
Less: Increase in inventories	(18,800)
Less: Increase in trade receivables and prepayments	(14,690)
Add: Increase in trade payables and accruals	14,510
Cash generated from operations	32,130
Cash flows from investing activities	
Purchase of property, plant, and equipment	(96,000)
Cash flows from financing activities	
Proceeds of share issue	30,000
Proceeds of loan issue	12,000
Net decrease in cash	(21,870)
Cash balances at 1 January 2013	11,440
Cash balances at 31 December 2013	**(10,430)**

Demonstration Exercise 7.4

By referring to the statement of cash flows in Table 7.4, answer the following questions:

a) Explain why the business has an overdraft at 31 December 2013 despite all its fundraising activities and the profit made during the year?

b) What steps could Sam take to ensure that the business's overdraft does not continue to grow?

As a result of Sam's better understanding of working capital management, he resolves to keep his inventory holding to a minimum and to avoid making any significant capital expenditure in 2014.

Tax, interest, and dividends

During a financial period, there are three other significant cash payments that a company will often make: payments of interest, payments of tax, and payments of dividends. The amounts recorded on the statement of cash flows will be the amounts actually paid out during the financial period.

- A full statement of cash flows starts with the operating profit for the year.
- Payments of interest and tax are shown as deductions from the cash generated from operations.
- Payments of dividends are shown with the cash flows from financing activities.

Case Study
Branching out to India

One of Sam's employees, Raja, has been working for Sam for the last 18 months, and he is keen to return to India. He has discussed with Sam the possibility of opening a couple of branches in India where the company will sell printed sports kits and printed T-shirts directly to the public. He and Sam have been exploring this opportunity and found that they could rent small suitable retail units on a short-term lease. Market research suggests such outlets would be popular, and Sam has full confidence in Raja to run the shops successfully. Sam decides to go ahead with the Indian shops as he sees this as a good opportunity for the business to expand and the capital investment involved will not be great.

Demonstration Exercise 7.5

In January 2014, Raja invested £30,000 in Smart Sports Ltd by buying 20,000 shares in the business. In the same month, he set-up shops in Mumbai and Delhi and started trading, having appointed managers at each branch. The company results, including the Indian branches, show a profit for that year of £61,455 on which no tax was payable. Extracts from the financial statements are given in Tables 7.5, 7.6, and 7.7.

Table 7.5

Smart Sports Ltd	
Extract from the income statement for the year ended 31 December 2014	
	£
Operating profit	62,555
Interest	1,100
Profit for the year	61,455

Table 7.6

Smart Sports Ltd				
Statements of financial position as at 31 December				
	2014		**2013**	
	£	£	£	£
ASSETS				
Non-current assets				
Property, plant, and equipment				
At cost		214,800		154,700
Accumulated depreciation		66,493		35,888
Net book value		148,307		118,812
Current assets				
Inventory	57,600		39,000	
Trade receivables and prepayments	45,080		35,780	
Bank balance	17,170		–	
		119,850		74,780
Total assets		**268,157**		**193,592**
EQUITY AND LIABILITIES				
Equity				
Share capital		90,000		70,000
Share premium		20,000		10,000
Retained profits		82,447		38,492
Total equity		**192,447**		**118,492**

Table 7.6 *(continued)*

	2014		2013	
	£	£	£	£
Non-current liabilities				
Loans		10,000		30,000
Current liabilities				
Trade payables and accruals	65,710		34,670	
Bank overdraft	–		10,430	
		65,710		45,100
Total equity and liabilities		**268,157**		**193,592**

Table 7.7

Smart Sports Ltd				
Statement of changes in equity for the year ended 31 December 2014				
	Ordinary share capital £	**Share premium £**	**Retained profits £**	**Total equity £**
At 1 January 2014	70,000	10,000	38,492	118,492
Share issue	20,000	10,000		30,000
Profit for the year			61,455	61,455
Dividend paid			(17,500)	(17,500)
At 31 December 2014	**90,000**	**20,000**	**82,447**	**192,447**

Notes: There were no disposals of non-current assets during the year.
Betty sold her 5,000 shares in Smart Sports Ltd to Dot, an existing shareholder, during 2014.

Required:

a) In preparing the statement of cash flows, explain how the issue of new shares to Raja should be accounted for.

b) Describe the effect of Betty selling her shares to Dot on the statement of cash flows.

c) Using the financial statements in Tables 7.5, 7.6, and 7.7, prepare the statement of cash flows for Smart Sports Ltd for the year ended 31 December 2014.

Ponder Point

How can you check that the figure for closing cash balances shown on the statement of cash flows is correct?

What to look for in a statement of cash flows

The statement of cash flows shows exactly how cash has been generated during a financial period and how it has been spent. The statement can therefore be used to confirm whether a business has managed its cash flows appropriately and whether it has adequate cash balances for the future.

In order to interpret a statement of cash flows, there are certain questions that can be helpful to consider:

1. Have the company's cash balances increased or decreased over the course of the accounting period?
2. Can the cash generated from operations easily cover any interest, tax, and dividends that have been paid? These are essential payments, and if a business cannot easily meet these commitments, that would be a cause for concern.
3. What happened to the long-term funding of the company over the course of the accounting period?
4. Did the company make any significant investments in non-current assets during the accounting period, and how were they funded? One significant principle of cash management is that any investment in long-term assets should be funded by long-term sources of funds. For example, the purchase of non-current assets should be funded by cash generated from operations, a loan issue, or a share issue.
5. How well has the company managed its working capital over the accounting period?
6. Is the final cash balance likely to be adequate to allow the business to operate on a day-to-day basis in the subsequent period?

Demonstration Exercise 7.6

Using the statement of cash flows you prepared in Demonstration Exercise 7.5, and the 'What to look for' questions listed in the previous section, interpret Smart Sports Ltd's statement of cash flows for the year ended 31 December 2014.

Managing cash

It is clearly important that any business wishing to succeed must ensure that it carefully controls not only its profitability but also its liquidity.

Terminology

Liquidity means the level of cash, bank, and other liquid assets available to the business. The liquidity of a business must be sufficient to allow the company to meet its liabilities as they fall due.

All areas of working capital need to be carefully monitored and controlled. Managing inventory will ensure that there is not too much cash tied up in it. Controls should be in place to ensure money comes in from trade receivables after a reasonable period of time, in line with the business's credit terms. Similarly, the business should take full advantage of any credit terms offered by suppliers. It is helpful if credit terms offered by suppliers are at least as long as the credit terms given to customers.

If a business fails to manage its cash, there could be a number of serious consequences. Too much management time will be diverted to deal with liquidity problems. There are likely to be increased interest charges, and the business is unlikely to be able to negotiate the best credit terms with suppliers or to take advantage of bulk-buying opportunities. It is also unlikely that funds will be available to enable new non-current assets to be purchased when needed. Most seriously of all, the business may be unable to pay its suppliers and its employees, and ultimately the business may fail.

Summary of Key Points

- Every business needs cash in order to function. It is cash that enables suppliers and employees to be paid and for the business to grow in the future.
- Cash and profit are not the same. To be successful, a business must manage both.
- The statement of cash flows is the third main financial statement; it shows how much cash was generated from operations, along with other sources of cash and how that cash was spent.

- In the statement of cash flows, the cash flows are identified under one of three possible headings: cash flows from operations, cash flows from investing activities, and cash flows from financing activities.
- Careful management of the working capital of a business is a key factor in ensuring that the business has adequate cash available to it.

Smart Questions: a wider perspective

1. How is it possible for a profitable business to experience cash flow problems?
2. Why is working capital management key to managing cash in a business?
3. If a business generates significant cash flows from operations, is it always advisable to raise extra long-term funding (by issuing shares and/or loans) if the business wants to expand?
4. If a business found that there was a surplus on revaluing a property, what effect would this have on its cash position?
5. Statements of cash flow are prepared after the end of an accounting period. What technique could a business use to plan future cash movements and balances?

Wider Reading

Elliott, B., and Elliott, J. (2009) ***Financial Accounting and Reporting*, 13th edition, FT Prentice Hall.** Chapter 26 provides a more detailed explanation of the preparation and presentation of more complex statements of cash flow.

International Accounting Standard 7, *Statements of Cash Flow*. Summary available from www.iasplus.com/standard/ias07.htm. This provides a useful summary of the key requirements of the international accounting standard on statements of cash flow.

Practice Questions

7.1 Rory's Newsmart

Rory's Newsmart owns and runs four stationery shops in Edinburgh, supplying retail and trade customers. Rory, who is the managing director of the company, has asked for your help. He is very concerned because he suspects that one of the shop managers has been stealing money from the business. He comments as follows:

'During the last year, the company has been thriving, with increased sales, and a new successful branch has been opened. Funds were raised from a share issue, and the company has never paid any dividends. Despite this, the business has been increasing its overdraft throughout the year, and it currently stands at £70,000. Will you look at my figures for me, please?'

You agree to help, and he supplies you with relevant extracts from the company's financial statements (Tables 7.8, 7.9, and 7.10).

REQUIRED:

a) Prepare a statement of cash flows for the year ended 31 March 2014. (Note that no non-current assets were disposed of during the year.)

b) Comment briefly on the statement that you have prepared, and in particular, advise Rory on whether or not his concerns are justified.

Table 7.8

Rory's Newsmart Ltd	
Extract from the income statement the year ended 31 March 2014	
	£
Operating profit	**69,000**
Tax (all paid during the year)	21,000
Profit for the year	**48,000**

Table 7.9

Rory's Newsmart Ltd				
Statement of changes in equity for the year ended 31 March 2014				
	Ordinary share capital £	**Share premium £**	**Retained profits £**	**Total equity £**
At 1 April 2013	250,000	150,000	120,000	520,000
Share issue	50,000	70,000		120,000
Profit for the year			48,000	48,000
At 31 March 2014	**300,000**	**220,000**	**168,000**	**688,000**

Table 7.10

Rory's Newsmart Ltd						
Statements of financial position as at 31 March						
	2014			2013		
	Cost £	**Dep'n** £	**NBV** £	**Cost** £	**Dep'n** £	**NBV** £
ASSETS						
Non-current assets						
Property	440,000	82,000	358,000	320,000	72,000	248,000
Equipment	164,000	26,000	138,000	60,000	20,000	40,000
	604,000	108,000	496,000	380,000	92,000	288,000
Current assets						
Inventories		229,000			137,600	
Trade receivables		107,400			46,800	
Bank balance		–			133,600	
			336,400			318,000
Total assets			**832,400**			**606,000**
EQUITY AND LIABILITIES						
Equity						
Ordinary £1 shares			300,000			250,000
Share premium			220,000			150,000
Retained profits			168,000			120,000
Total equity			**688,000**			**520,000**
Current liabilities						
Bank overdraft		70,000			–	
Trade payables and accruals		74,400			86,000	
			144,400			86,000
Total equity and liabilities			**832,400**			**606,000**

7.2 Biscuit Barrels

A few years ago Sarah started a business making cookies, cakes, and biscuits and supplying them to coffee shops and cafés. The business has always been profitable, and during 2011 it diversified into the production and sale of cookie- and bread-making kits. This seems to have been a successful venture as the business showed a significant increase in its profits. However, in 2011, a bank overdraft was needed for the first time.

Table 7.11

Biscuit Barrels	
Statement of cash flows for the year ended 31 December 2011	
	$
Cash flows from operating activities	
Profit for the year	126,500
Add: Depreciation	11,400
	137,900
Working capital movements	
Less: Increase in inventories	(21,120)
Less: Increase in trade receivables	(7,310)
Add: Increase in trade payables	4,040
Cash generated from operations	**113,510**
Cash flows from financing activities	
Repayment of loan	(50,000)
Dividend paid	(31,000)
Cash flows from investing activities	
Purchase of equipment	(72,000)
Proceeds from sale of equipment	18,770
Net decrease in cash	(20,720)
Cash balances at 1 January 2011	15,480
Cash balances at 31 December 2011	(5,240)

REQUIRED:

Using Table 7.11, explain to Sarah what has happened during 2011 to cause the company's bank account to become overdrawn, and make suggestions as to how it can improve its cash flow position in the future.

Chapter Eight
Interpreting Financial Statements
Exploring India

Learning Objectives

At the end of this topic, you should be able to:

- identify who uses financial statements and what their needs are
- calculate and interpret ratios that enable you to comment on a business's profitability, liquidity, and efficiency.

Introduction

Financial statements are a useful starting point to understanding how well a business is doing. To obtain a fuller picture and understand movements and trends, we need to use techniques to analyse further the financial statements, and look beyond the accounting numbers.

Case Study
How to analyse financial statements

Smart Sports Ltd has been trading for several years. Started by Sam Smart, it began by printing and selling team kits and has since expanded into India.

In 2014, Sam's friend Raja went into business with Sam to open up the retail market for Sam's sports clothing in India. Raja rented two shop units, one in an established arcade in Delhi, and the other in a new shopping arcade in Mumbai. Completely separate accounting records are kept for each shop.

In January 2015, Sam rings Raja to let him know that he is planning a trip to India to visit the shops. He lets him know that he has fixed some dates in February to visit Raja in India and that he is looking forward to visiting the shops and discussing how well they are doing. Raja explains that the Delhi shop is bigger than the Mumbai shop and that he cannot see how any useful comparison can be made. Sam believes there must be a way to compare how well the two shops are doing and decides to do some research into this before he arrives.

Sam researches how to go about interpreting accounting information and finds that ratio analysis is a widely accepted method used by accountants and non-accountants alike.

Terminology

Ratio analysis can be used to highlight underlying trends not always immediately obvious from the figures themselves.

Ratio analysis

Types of ratio

Ratios can be classified as follows:

Category of ratio	What it reveals
Profitability	How successfully the business is trading
Liquidity	How easy it is for the business to pay its way
Efficiency	How effectively the short-term assets and liabilities of the business are being managed.

Demonstration Exercise 8.1

Who might be particularly interested in each of the following types of ratio:

- Profitability
- Liquidity
- Efficiency?

Ponder Point

Do you think that looking at a single ratio on its own is useful?

An accounting ratio is most useful when it is used to compare to any of the following:

- previous years
- other similar companies
- trade averages
- budgeted figures.

The pyramid of ratios

We can look at ratios by drilling down through a pyramid, as shown in Figure 8.1.

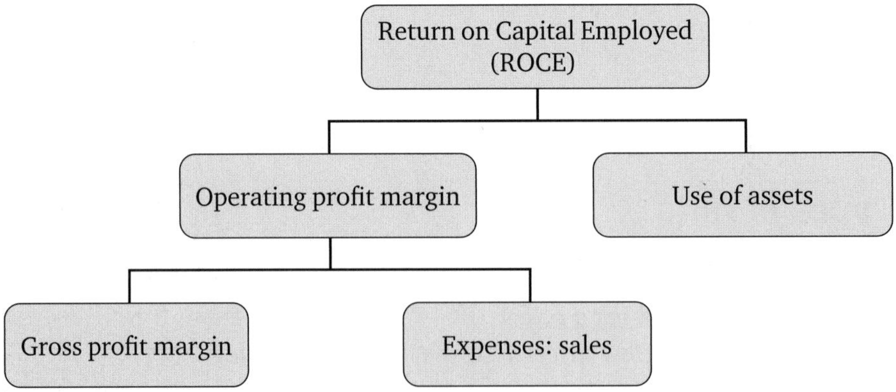

Figure 8.1

Profitability will be considered by looking at the return on capital employed ratio as the key ratio. Return on capital employed is itself a function of the profitability measure, operating profit margin, and the use of assets ratio.

Profitability ratios

Return on capital employed

Return on capital employed (also known as ROCE) is often seen as the key ratio as it indicates how effectively management is using the funds invested in the business to generate profits. There are many ways of computing this ratio, depending on whether long- and/or short-term capital is included and whether pre- or post-tax profits are used. A commonly used formula is:

$$\frac{\text{Operating profit}}{\text{Capital employed}} \times 100$$

$$= \frac{\text{Operating profit}}{\text{Shareholders' funds} + \text{long-term loans}} \times 100$$

where shareholders funds = share capital + reserves.

This ratio shows how effectively all the long-term funds at the disposal of the company have been used. It can be seen as a measure of management's ability to generate profits given the funds invested in it. It can be benchmarked against other investments or businesses.

Gross profit margin

$$\frac{\text{Gross profit}}{\text{Sales}} \times 100$$

This ratio reflects the margin that a business makes between the buying price and the selling price of goods. On its own, the gross profit margin for one business for one year is not particularly useful. But where it can be compared to previous years or to competitors, then the difference in the ratio can be more revealing.

Ponder Point

Can you think of reasons for a change in gross profit margin?

Operating profit margin

$$\frac{\text{Operating profit}}{\text{Sales}} \times 100$$

This ratio compares the operating profit margin to the turnover of the business. Changes in the gross profit margin will have an effect on this ratio. So too will expenses increasing at a rate significantly faster or slower than the rate of increase in sales.

Expenses: sales

$$\frac{\text{Expenses}}{\text{Sales}} \times 100$$

This ratio compares expenses incurred to sales made, to determine whether expenses are increasing at a faster or slower rate than the growth in sales made. To analyse this, it is necessary to investigate which type of expenses have changed and why they may have changed.

Use of assets

$$\frac{\text{Sales}}{\text{Capital employed}} = \frac{\text{Sales}}{\text{Net assets}}$$

This looks at how effective a company is at generating sales given the capital employed in the business.

Return on capital employed is a function of both operating profit margin and use of assets:

$$\text{Return on capital employed} = \text{Operating profit margin} \times \text{Use of assets}$$

Or

$$\frac{\text{Operating profit}}{\text{Capital employed}} = \frac{\text{Operating profit}}{\text{Sales}} \times \frac{\text{Sales}}{\text{Capital employed}}$$

In other words, any change in return on capital employed can be explained by either a change in the operating profit margin and/or a change in the efficiency with which the business uses its assets.

Demonstration Exercise 8.2

Shown in Tables 8.1 and 8.2 are the summarized income statements for the two Indian shops for the year ended 31 December 2014, plus the summarized total capital employed as at 31 December 2014.

Table 8.1

Summarized income statements for the two shops for the year ended 31 December 2014				
	Delhi		**Mumbai**	
	Rupees ’000	**Rupees ’000**	**Rupees ’000**	**Rupees ’000**
Sales		**6,500**		**2,700**
Cost of sales				
Opening inventories	100		100	
Purchases	3,840		1,900	
Closing inventories	140		140	
		3,800		1,860
Gross profit		**2,700**		**840**
Wages	900		420	
Depreciation	460		40	
Rent	300		160	
Other expenses	740		100	
		2,400		720
Operating profit		**300**		**120**

Table 8.2

Summarized total long-term capital employed as at 31 December 2014				
	Delhi		**Mumbai**	
		Rupees ’000		**Rupees ’000**
Total long-term capital employed (shareholders’ funds + long-term loans)		1,900		600

Required:

a) Calculate the return on capital employed, the gross profit margin, the operating profit margin, and the use of assets for the Mumbai branch. The ratios for the Delhi branch have been computed in Table 8.3.

b) Describe what Raja could report to Sam about the relative performance of each of the shops.

Table 8.3

	Delhi	Mumbai
Return on capital employed	$300 / 1{,}900 \times 100 = 16\%$	
Gross profit margin	$2{,}700 / 6{,}500 \times 100 = 42\%$	
Operating profit margin	$300 / 6{,}500 \times 100 = 4.6\%$	
Use of assets	$6{,}500 / 1{,}900 = 3.4$ times	

Liquidity ratios

Liquidity ratios look at the ability of a business to cover its short-term liabilities as they fall due. This is important as many companies that fail are profitable at the time they go bankrupt. It is lack of cash that forces them into liquidation.

Terminology

Liquidity is a measure of the ability of a business to pay its debts as they fall due.

Current ratio

$$\frac{\text{Current assets}}{\text{Current liabilities}} : 1$$

This ratio gives some indication of the short-term solvency of a business as it shows its ability to meet its debts as they fall due. Current assets will often exceed current liabilities. Current ratios will vary depending on the type of industry in which the business is operating, and this should be taken into account when interpreting these ratios. Generally, a business with a higher current ratio will be considered more liquid and hence less likely to suffer from cash flow problems.

Acid test ratio

$$\frac{\text{Current assets} - \text{inventories}}{\text{Current liabilities}} : 1$$

A limitation of the current ratio is the assumption that all current assets can easily be converted into cash. In the acid test ratio, inventories are excluded from current assets to recognize that they are not easily converted into cash. This ratio measures the very short-term liquidity of a business.

Ponder Point

Which, out of trade receivables and inventories, will take the longest to turn into cash?

There is no rule of thumb that can be applied to interpret the current ratios, as it depends on the nature of the business. If the company needs to hold large inventories and to offer long periods of credit to its customers, then a higher than average ratio will be expected.

If, on the other hand, it is a cash business that can turn over its inventories very quickly, then that type of business will have much lower than average current and acid test ratios.

Hence, when interpreting liquidity ratios, it is useful to:

- consider the nature of the business. Do they sell on cash terms or on credit? Are they a manufacturing, retailing, or service business?
- compare current and acid test ratios with previous years' ratios and with the ratios for similar companies.

Demonstration Exercise 8.3

The ratios in Table 8.4 have been computed for a manufacturing business and a supermarket.

Table 8.4

	Manufacturer of sugars, starches, etc. from carbohydrates	Supermarket chain
Current ratio	1.48:1	0.45:1
Acid test ratio	0.96:1	0.24:1

Discuss why it is possible for these two companies to operate successfully with such different liquidity ratios.

Demonstration Exercise 8.3 – solution

- Different types of business can operate successfully with very different current and acid test ratios.
- The manufacturing company will have large amounts tied up in inventories: raw materials, finished goods, and work in progress.
- You would expect the manufacturing company to be buying and selling on credit, not for cash. The company will therefore have significant amounts of trade receivables and trade payables.
- Hence, you would expect a manufacturing company's current and acid test ratios to be higher than average.
- The supermarket chain is a retailing business where the inventories turnover will be very fast, and with modern electronic point-of-sale equipment, levels of inventories can be tightly controlled. Relatively, the inventories figure will be very low, and as sales are made for cash, there will be no trade receivables.
- On the current liabilities side, suppliers may allow the supermarket chain credit terms of approximately 30 days, and hence trade payables will be a significant amount.
- You would therefore expect a supermarket to have very low current and acid test ratios. These ratios would have resulted from the nature of the business and would not necessarily indicate any liquidity problems.

The control of working capital

Working capital ratios (see Figure 8.2) give an indication of whether the inventories, trade receivables, and trade payables of the business are being effectively controlled. When calculating these ratios, use the year-end figures for inventory, trade receivables, and trade payables, for simplicity.

Terminology

Working capital is defined as the current assets less the current liabilities of a business.

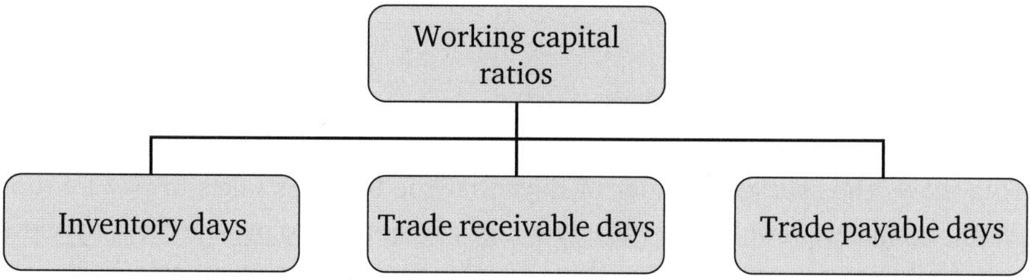

Figure 8.2

Inventory days

$$\frac{\text{Inventories}}{\text{Cost of sales}} \times 365 \text{ days}$$

This indicates the average number of days that goods are held in inventories. The resulting figure will depend on the type of business concerned. For example, we would expect the inventory turnover in a supermarket to be appreciably quicker than that in a furniture retailer.

Companies should strive to keep the inventory days as short as possible to minimize associated costs. However, inventory levels should always be sufficient to meet demand.

Ponder Point

What sort of costs are associated with holding inventory?

Trade receivable days

$$\frac{\text{Trade receivables}}{\text{Credit sales}} \times 365 \text{ days}$$

This shows the average number of days the business takes to collect its debts from customers and must be compared to the firm's credit terms. An increase in trade receivable days may be due to a change in the credit terms offered or to poorer credit control.

Generally, companies should be collecting debts due as quickly as possible to minimize the amount of funds tied up in trade receivables. This money could be more usefully employed elsewhere within the business.

Trade payable days

$$\frac{\text{Trade payables}}{\text{Credit purchases}} \times 365 \text{ days}$$

This shows the average number of days that the business takes to pay its suppliers. Businesses should take full advantage of credit terms provided by suppliers but should not risk antagonizing them by taking too long to pay them.

A change in the rate of payment of suppliers may well reflect an improvement or decline in the company's overall liquidity. For example, if the company was experiencing a shortage of cash, there will be a tendency for the trade payable days to increase.

Ponder Point

What would be the effect of having too little investment in working capital?

The working capital cycle

We can look at the working capital cycle as a whole in Figure 8.3.

The working capital cycle is computed by adding inventory days to trade receivable days and taking off the trade payable days.

From the working capital cycle in Figure 8.3, it can be seen that, to maximize the cash balance, it is necessary to:

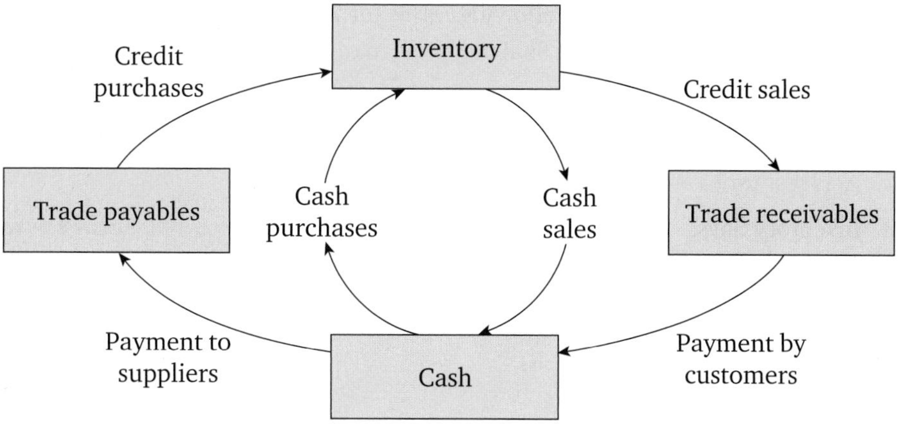

Figure 8.3

- collect trade receivables as quickly as possible without antagonizing customers
- pay trade payables as slowly as the credit terms allow without antagonizing suppliers
- keep inventories as low as possible while ensuring that they are sufficient to meet demand.

Ponder Point

Do you think that an increase in a working capital cycle of 21 days would indicate more efficient or less efficient management of assets?

Demonstration Exercise 8.4

Smart Sports Ltd has been approached by Running Fast Ltd, who run a small chain of sports stores in the London area, to supply them on a monthly basis with team kits.

The business has had a number of defaults on payments by small retailers, and Sam is keen to establish the viability of Running Fast Ltd, who wish to buy on 30 days' credit.

He has obtained copies of their most recent accounts, and summaries of the income statement and statement of financial position are given in Tables 8.5 and 8.6.

Compute and interpret the following ratios for 2015 and 2014, and prepare a list of points and questions that Sam may wish to raise during his discussions with Running Fast Ltd.

1. Current ratio.
2. Acid test ratio.
3. Inventory days.
4. Trade receivable days (10% of sales are on credit).
5. Trade payable days (all purchases are on credit).

Table 8.5

Running Fast Ltd				
Summarized income statements for the years ended 30 September				
	2015		2014	
	£'000	£'000	£'000	£'000
Sales		**388**		**360**
Cost of sales				
Opening inventories	40		20	
Purchases	310		300	
Closing inventories	47		40	
		303		280
Gross profit		**85**		**80**
Expenses (including interest)		72		70
Profit for the year		**13**		**10**

Table 8.6

Running Fast Ltd				
Summarized statements of financial positions as at 30 September				
	2015		2014	
	£'000	£'000	£'000	£'000
ASSETS				
Non-current assets		415		339
Current assets				
Inventories	47		40	
Trade receivables	8		5	
Bank balance	–		9	
		55		54
Total assets		470		393
CAPITAL AND LIABILITIES				
Ordinary share capital		220		220
Reserves		71		58
Non-current liabilities				
7% debentures		130		80
Current liabilities				
Trade payables	38		35	
Overdraft	11		—	
		49		35
Total capital and liabilities		470		393

Summary of Key Points

- Ratio analysis is a useful technique and can be used in interpreting accounting information.
- Ratios can be used to highlight underlying trends not always immediately obvious from the figures themselves.
- Ratios can be used to assess the profitability, liquidity, and efficiency of a business.
- An individual ratio is difficult to interpret unless it can be compared to a previous year's ratio and/or other meaningful ratios.
- Care is required in interpreting ratios, and it is essential to bear in mind the nature of the business being reviewed.

Smart Questions: a wider perspective

1. Would you expect the gross profit margin to be high or low for a luxury-products business?
2. Will a business that operates with a high gross profit margin necessarily achieve a high operating profit margin and a high return on capital employed?
3. If the current and acid test ratios fall sharply, does this necessarily mean that the business is experiencing liquidity problems?
4. What could happen if a company does not control its trade receivable days?
5. What is Just-In-Time inventory control?

Wider Reading

www.investopedia.com/university/ratios/. This web page offers an online financial ratio tutorial.

Practice Questions

8.1 TC Ltd

The following ratios were computed for TC Ltd based on the company's 2013 and 2012 accounts:

	2013	2012
Trade receivable days	39 days	43 days
Inventory days	44 days	38 days

REQUIRED:

Explain which of the following statements are true and which are false:

a) On average, TC Ltd's trade receivables are taking longer to pay in 2013 than in 2012.

b) On average, TC Ltd's inventories are being held for six days longer in 2013.

c) Give reasons why trade receivable days might decrease from one year to the next and why inventory days increase from one year to the next.

8.2 DogsRUs

Summarized in Table 8.7 is some data extracted from the accounts of three companies, all of which are in the wholesale dog food business:

Table 8.7

For the year ended 31 December 2012						
	DogsRUs		Fido		Happy Dog Foods	
	£'000	£'000	£'000	£'000	£'000	£'000
From income statement:						
Sales		8,200		6,200		9,500
Opening inventories	1,450		900		1,480	
Purchases	6,170		4,568		5,840	
	7,620		5,468		7,320	
Closing inventories	1,820		880		960	
		5,800		4,588		6,360
Gross profit		**2,400**		**1,612**		**3,140**
From statement of financial position						
Trade receivables		2,220		1,020		2,980
Trade payables		1,678		730		930

REQUIRED:

a) Calculate the following ratios for all three companies:

Gross profit margin
Trade payable days
Trade receivable days
Inventory days.

b) Comment on the ratios and suggest to management where improvements in performance may be possible.

c) Would your commentary be different if you knew that:

(i) Happy Dog Foods had an exceptionally large turnover in December 2012?
(ii) DogsRUs purchased a particularly large amount of inventory in December 2012 at an advantageous price?

Chapter Nine
Capital Structure and Investment Ratios
Sam gears up

Learning Objectives

At the end of this topic, you should be able to:

- calculate and interpret ratios that enable you to comment on a business's capital structure, investment returns, and performance
- discuss the limitations of ratio analysis.

Introduction

The analysis of capital structure and investment ratios are particularly relevant for existing and potential investors in a business.

Capital structure ratios consider where the long-term funds of the business have come from. They give an indication of the company's financial risk in relation to its ability to repay debt capital and debt interest.

Investment ratios look at how good the returns and performance of shares in a company are and help investors and potential investors to assess the likely potential of the company.

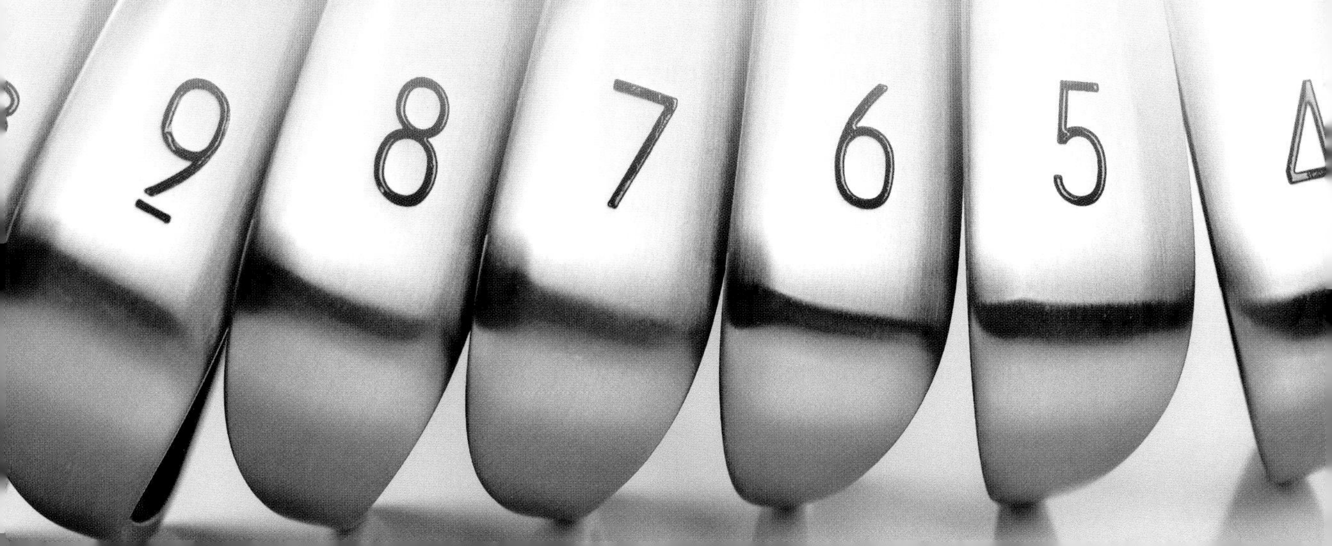

Case Study
Sam considers his capital structure

Sam Smart has been running Smart Sports, a sports equipment retailer, for several years. In 2016, Sam decides that he would like to further diversify his business and venture into the manufacturing of sports equipment. In order to do this, he will require extra funding. He decides to speak to his accountant, Kim as to the best way of funding the expansion; he arranges to meet Kim at the next Brookes Rangers football match, as they are both keen supporters.

Sam tells Kim that he is thinking of expanding his business into the manufacturing of sports equipment but that he will need extra funding to do this. He wants to know where he might be able to raise funding from, and Kim explains that there are a number of ways to get extra funding. He explains to Sam that, as the expansion is a long-term plan, he should use long-term external funding options. Sam could take out long-term loans, which may be in the form of a bank loan, or he could issue preference shares or more ordinary share capital. Sam asks what effect these three forms of financing will have on the performance of the business, and Kim goes on to explain that this can be explored by using ratio analysis to look at the alternative capital structures and their effect on Smart Sports Ltd.

Capital structure

Once a business borrows, it will have an obligation to pay interest on its debt and repay the loans when due.

Key ratios looking at capital structure are:

- gearing
- interest cover.

Gearing

Gearing measures the extent to which the company is financed by debt, or fixed-return capital, compared to equity capital, or shareholders' funds.

There are many ways of calculating gearing. This is a common one:

$$\frac{(\text{Long-term loans} + \text{preference shares})}{(\text{Ordinary share capital} + \text{reserves})} \times 100$$

A company may be financed entirely by equity, ordinary share capital, and reserves. More commonly, though, companies will raise some of their long-term funding by borrowing money on which interest must be paid, and occasionally issuing preference shares on which a fixed rate of dividend is payable.

The greater the proportion of financing that comes from debt and preference shares, the higher the gearing.

Terminology

Gearing measures the extent to which a business is financed by debt rather than equity capital.

Disadvantages of gearing

Gearing carries some risk, because the more highly geared a company, the greater the risk to the ordinary shareholders. The shareholders run the risk of:

- not receiving a dividend where there are insufficient profits available after the interest has been paid
- the debenture holders forcing the company into liquidation/bankruptcy if the company is unable to meet its interest obligations and capital repayments as they fall due.

Advantages of gearing

- When the company is trading successfully and generating increasing profits, the ordinary shareholders stand to reap disproportionate rewards in a highly geared company. That is, where a company can raise debt at x % but can generate a return greater than x % with the funds raised, then the ordinary shareholders will benefit from the 'gearing'.
- Companies with gearing are not solely reliant on retained profits and ordinary share issues to expand. Geared companies will have raised funds from loans and/or preference share issues.

Ponder Point

Why might a bank be interested in a company's level of gearing?

In summary, low gearing indicates a company that has low interest obligations and hence low financial risk. Shareholders will conclude that their dividends are more secure.

High gearing indicates a company that has high interest obligations but potentially better returns for company shareholders. Shareholders will conclude that their dividends are less secure.

There are no set limits as to what constitutes low or high levels of gearing, but as a rough guide:

Gearing $< 10\%$	Low level of gearing
Gearing $> 50\%$	High level of gearing
$10\% <$ Gearing $< 50\%$	Moderate level of gearing.

The level of gearing that a business is comfortable with will depend on the consistency of its profits and cash flow. A very volatile business will want to keep gearing low, whereas a company generating very steady, dependable profits will be able to operate reasonably securely with a higher level of gearing.

Interest cover

Interest cover tells you how many times the operating profit covers the interest expense. This is calculated as:

$$\frac{\text{Operating profit}}{\text{Interest expense}} \text{ times}$$

This ratio shows how easy it is for the company to cover its interest expense out of operating profit. A company with low interest cover will be at greater risk of not meeting interest payments than a company with a higher interest cover.

Terminology

Interest cover considers the number of times that operating profit covers the interest expense.

Demonstration Exercise 9.1

Kim has prepared the information in Table 9.1 so that Sam can consider whether to obtain external funding by issuing ordinary shares or by issuing debt. He has prepared alternative statements of financial positions for each option:

Table 9.1

	Sam Sports Ltd at 31 December 2016 finance raised by share issue £'000	Sam Sports Ltd at 31 December 2016 finance raised by gearing up £'000
ASSETS		
Non-current assets, at net book value	700	700
Current assets	400	400
Total assets	1,100	1,100
EQUITY AND LIABILITIES		
£1 ordinary shares	**250**	**50**
10% £1 preference shares	**130**	**200**
Share premium	**200**	
Retained profits	**500**	**500**
	1,080	**750**
Non-current liabilities		
5% loan	**20**	**20**
8% debentures	**–**	**330**
Total capital and liabilities	**1,100**	**1,100**

a) Calculate the gearing proportion for the alternative funding methods.

b) Calculate the profit available per ordinary share if the finance is raised by gearing and if profits before interest and dividends amount to £50,000. The workings have been done for the share issue option (see Table 9.2).

Table 9.2

	Sam Sports Ltd finance raised by share issue £	Sam Sports Ltd finance raised by gearing up £
Profit before interest and dividends	50,000	50,000
Less: Interest on loan	1,000	
(20,000 × 5%)		
Less: Interest on debentures		
Less: Preference dividend	13,000	
(130,000 × 10%)		______
Profits available to ordinary shareholders	36,000	______
Number of ordinary shares	250,000	______
Profit available per ordinary share	14.4p	______

c) If profits are likely to be less than £50,000, advise Sam as to whether he should fund the expansion by shares or by loans.

d) If profits for both scenarios are predicted to rise rapidly to £400,000 per annum in two years' time, calculate the profit available per ordinary share then (see Table 9.3). Note that there would be no new share or debenture issues in the intervening period.

Table 9.3

	Sam Sports Ltd finance raised by share issue £	Sam Sports Ltd finance raised by gearing up £
Profit before interest and dividends	400,000	400,000
Less: Interest on loan		
Less: Interest on debentures		
Less: Preference dividend	______	______
Profits available to ordinary shareholders	______	______
Number of ordinary shares	______	______
Profit available per ordinary share	______	______

e) Based on the calculations in Table 9.3, would you advise Sam to obtain external funding from shares or from loans?

Investment ratios

Investment ratios are particularly useful for existing and potential investors who are deciding whether to stay invested in a company or whether to buy or sell shares in that company.

Key investment ratios are:

- earnings per share
- price to earnings ratio
- dividend yield
- dividend cover.

Investment ratios draw upon figures not only from the financial statements but also from market information, in particular the company's share price. The share price is a measure of the future expected earnings of a business.

Earnings per share (EPS)

Earnings per share considers how much profit is being made for each share:

$$\frac{\text{Profit after tax and after preference dividends}}{\text{Number of ordinary shares}}$$

Earnings per share is expressed in pence. This is considered to be a fundamental measure of how well a share is performing. It is not meaningful to use earnings per share for comparisons between different companies. It is, however, useful for reviewing an individual company's profitability over time.

Terminology

Earnings per share (a fundamental ratio) shows how much profit is being made for each share.

Price to earnings ratio

The price to earnings (PE) ratio compares the market price of a share with the earnings per share:

$$\frac{\text{Market price per share}}{\text{Earnings per share}}$$

This ratio involves the share price and as such is a measure of the market's view of the expected future earnings of a business. A high PE indicates that investors are confident that the company's profits will increase in the future.

Ponder Point

Why might you pay more for shares in one business compared to another business?

Terminology

The price to earnings (PE) ratio compares the market price of a share with the earnings per share. It is therefore a reflection of the market's expectations for the company's shares.

Dividend yield

This ratio considers how much dividend an investor received compared to what it would cost to buy the shares at their current price. It gives a measure of the actual cash return that investors are receiving from the dividends on their shares.

$$\frac{\text{Dividend paid per share}}{\text{Market price per share}} \times 100$$

The dividend yield can be compared to the return expected to be received from other possible investments.

Terminology

Dividend yield compares the dividend received from a share with the market price of a share.

Ponder Point

Are dividends the only return that ordinary shareholders receive on their shares?

Dividend cover

This ratio looks at the extent to which a business is using available profits to meet dividend payments. This is usually referred to by the number of times that profit covers dividend:

$$\frac{\text{Profit for the year (after tax)}}{\text{Ordinary dividend paid}}\text{ times} = \frac{\text{Earnings per share}}{\text{Dividend per share}}\text{ times}$$

A high dividend cover indicates that the company can easily cover its dividend payments. A low dividend cover indicates that a company may find it difficult to afford the dividend payment and therefore is taking a greater risk with the payment. It also suggests that the company may find it difficult to maintain its current level of dividend payments into the future.

Terminology

Dividend cover considers the extent to which available profits can meet dividend payments.

Ponder Point

Why might an investor prefer to receive dividends rather than just benefit from an increase in share price?

Demonstration Exercise 9.2

Sam Smart has been very busy running his business Smart Sports for the last few years. Sam's cousin Dan, who lives in Australia, has been playing the lottery for the last five years and has recently struck lucky and won AU$20,000. Sam is in need of a holiday, and as both he and Dan have a passion for snowboarding, they have decided to spend $2,000 each on a holiday in the Victoria ski resorts near Melbourne. Dan intends to invest the remaining AU$18,000 in a company that makes snowboards. Being environmentally aware, he has reduced his list of possible investments to two Australian businesses well known for having good social and corporate responsibility. He is considering investing in Rick's Boards, based in Bunbury, Western Australia, or Peter's Snowsports from Melbourne. Dan knows Sam has learned much about accounting since he started his business and seeks Sam's advice on which company to invest in.

- Dan has obtained the financial statements to 30 September 2016 for both companies, extracts from which are given in Tables 9.5 and 9.6.
- Rick's Boards paid a dividend of AU$0.04 per share for the year to 30 September 2016, compared to Peter's Snowsports, who paid a dividend of AU$0.06 per share.
- The share prices of Rick's Boards and Peter's Snowsports were AU$1.80 and AU$2.30, respectively, as at 30 September 2016.
- The historical earnings per share for the two companies are shown in Table 9.4.

Table 9.4

	EPS for year ended 30 September			
	2013 cents	2014 cents	2015 cents	2016 cents
Rick's Boards	28	36	32	30
Peter's Snowsports	20	25	32	34

Dan is hoping that a long-term gain on his shares, plus any dividends he receives, will enable him to further indulge his passion for travelling.

Advise Dan as to which business would appear to be the best investment opportunity for him, by calculating and interpreting the following ratios for 2016:

1. Earnings per share.
2. Price to earnings ratio.
3. Dividend yield.
4. Dividend cover.
5. Interest cover.

Table 9.5

Summarized income statements for the year ended 30 September 2016		
	Rick's Boards AU$'000	**Peter's Snowsports AU$'000**
Sales	3,200	5,800
Cost of sales	2,100	2,500
Gross profit	**1,100**	**3,300**
Expenses (including interest)	830	970
Profit before taxation	**270**	**2,330**
Taxation	60	70
Profit for the year	**210**	**2,260**

Table 9.6

Statement of financial position extracts as at 30 September 2016		
	Rick's Boards AU$'000	**Peter's Snowsports AU$'000**
EQUITY AND LIABILITIES		
Equity		
AU$1 ordinary share capital	800	6,000
Share premium	150	3,000
Retained profits	1,350	6,600
Total equity	**2,300**	**15,600**
Non-current liabilities		
7% debentures	400	2,400
Total equity and non-current liabilities	**2,700**	**18,000**

Limitations of ratio analysis

Although ratios are a very useful tool, they suffer from a number of limitations:

- Ratios highlight underlying trends revealed by the financial statements. However, they do not provide explanations for changes found.
- Differences in accounting policies between companies may detract from the value of inter-firm comparisons.
- Financial statements and accounting ratios can be distorted as the result of a 'one-off' large transaction; for example, the disposal of a significant non-current asset.
- When interpreting ratios for seasonal businesses, some of the ratios can vary considerably over the year. Hence care must be taken when interpreting these ratios.
- Where a company undertakes a mix of activities, it is important to calculate separate ratios for each set of activities wherever possible.
- Consideration must be given to the nature of the business concerned when interpreting accounting ratios. For example, a supermarket is likely to have low liquidity ratios, because it has no trade receivables and a high rate of inventories turnover.

Summary of Key Points

- The gearing ratio can be used to consider to what extent a company is funded by debt and equity.
- Investment ratios (dividend yield, dividend cover, earnings per share, and price to earnings ratios) can be used to measure the return and performance of the company's shares.
- Although useful, ratios have limitations and need to be considered in relation to the nature of the business concerned and the broader economic environment.

Smart Questions: a wider perspective

1. What non-financial factors might you consider when deciding whether or not to invest in a business?
2. Why do investors pay more for a business than the statement of financial position value of the net assets?

3. Can investors rely on the accounting information given to them?
4. How can an investor explore the economic/market context in which the business operates?

Wider Reading

Marks, K., Robbins, L., Fernandez, G., and Funkhouser, J. (2008) *The Handbook of Financing Growth: Strategies, Capital Structure, and M&A Transactions*, **Wiley Finance.** A very useful book for students who want to understand more about how companies can finance growth.

Practice Questions

9.1 Dee Ltd

Dee Ltd manufactures sweets and chocolates. Extracts from Dee Ltd's statement of financial position as at 30 September 2013 is given in Table 9.7.

Table 9.7

Dee Ltd	
Statement of financial position as at 30 September 2013	
	£'000
ASSETS	
Non-current assets	277
Current assets	98
Current liabilities	(95)
Total assets	**375**
EQUITY AND LIABILITIES	
Ordinary £1 shares	90
Share premium	65
Retained profits	45
Total equity	200
Non-current liabilities	
Long-term loan	80
Current liabilities	95
Total equity and liabilities	**375**

REQUIRED:

a) Explain what you understand by the term 'gearing'.

b) Using the extracts from Dee Ltd's statement of financial position, determine Dee Ltd's gearing ratio.

c) What are the risks to a company of having a high level of gearing?

9.2 Joisa plc

Joisa plc is a business that specializes in the manufacturing of designer luggage. A luxury goods company Luxy Goods plc is considering buying Joisa plc so that they can expand their luxury goods business into luggage.

The financial information is available for the three years to June 2012 and is shown in Table 9.8.

Table 9.8

	30 Jun 2010	30 Jun 2011	30 Jun 2012
Profit after tax	£0.9m	£1.3m	£2.6m
Dividend paid	£0.5m	£0.7m	£0.9m
Number of ordinary shares in issue	6 million	6 million	6 million
Market price per share at the year-end	£1.1	£1.2	£1.85

REQUIRED:

a) Calculate the following for the three year period:

Earnings per share

Price to earnings ratio

Dividend yield

Dividend cover.

b) What would be your advice to Luxy Goods plc in relation to the potential purchase of Joisa plc?

Financial Accounting: Case Study
Foxgloves

Brother and sister Will and Alex have been working in the hotel industry for the last ten years. They decided to use the expertise they gained in this field to set-up a boutique hotel business, Foxgloves Ltd, by opening a small hotel in central London in June 2011. They funded their business partly from their own savings and partly from a bank loan. The hotel has been running for a year, and Alex has prepared the draft financial statements for the year ended 30 June 2012, subject to a number of adjustments.

The draft financial statements prior to adjustments, and the budgeted figures for the year ended 30 June 2012, are detailed in Tables FA.1, FA.2, and FA.3.

Table FA.1

Foxgloves Ltd		
Draft income statement for the year ended 30 June 2012		
	30 June 2012 **£**	**Budgeted figures** **£**
Sales	1, 400,000	1,600,000
Less:		
Cost of sales	560,000	650,000
Gross profit	**840,000**	**950,000**
Less:		
Operating costs	753,000	650,000
Interest	12,000	24,000
Profit before tax	**75,000**	**276,000**

Table FA.2

Foxgloves Ltd		
Draft statement of financial position as at 30 June 2012		
	£	£
ASSETS		
Non-current assets		
Buildings		850,000
Motor vehicle		20,000
Fixtures and fittings		106,000
		976,000
Current assets		
Inventory		–
Trade receivables		50,000
		1,026,000
Total assets		
EQUITY AND LIABILITIES		
Equity		
Ordinary shares of £1 each		400,000
Retained profits		75,000
Total equity		475,000
Non-current liabilities		
Loan (6%)		400,000
Current liabilities		
Bank overdraft	13,000	
Trade payables	138,000	
		151,000
Total equity and liabilities		**1,026,000**

Table FA.3

Foxgloves Ltd			
Draft statement of changes in equity for the year ended 30 June 2012			
	Ordinary share capital £'000	**Retained profits £'000**	**Total shareholders' equity £'000**
At 1 January 2012	400	–	400
Profit for the year		75	75
Dividends paid		–	–
At 30 June 2012	400	75	475

Budgeted liquidity and efficiency ratios for the year ended 30 June 2012 were as follows:

Current ratio	1.4:1
Acid test ratio	0.8:1
Inventories holding period	25 days
Trade receivable days	10 days
Trade payable days	42 days

Because the Olympics are currently taking place in London, the hotel is very busy, and you have been employed by Alex and Will to make the final adjustments to the accounts and to provide advice on accounting matters.

You also have the following information:

- The hotel industry generally struggled until April 2012, with many tourists choosing not to visit London before the Olympics. However, business picked up in May and June 2012, with improved weather bringing a surge of tourists.
- Globally, oil and food prices rose significantly over the period from June 2011 to June 2012 as a result of disruption to oil supplies from oil-producing nations.
- Labour in central London over the year to June 2012 was more affordable than it had been previously, as many workers from Europe sought work in London prior to the Olympics, driving wages down.
- Owing to global oversupply of wine, particularly New World wines, the cost of wine fell sharply. The wine cellar comprises around 25% of the total inventory value.

- Foxgloves Ltd also operates an online business selling the wine they stock for the hotel restaurant.
- Foxgloves Ltd has not yet paid a dividend.
- Capital repayments on the loan start in 2014.
- Operating costs include electricity, insurance, and salaries.

Adjustments required to be made are as follows:

1. Buildings are to be depreciated over 50 years using the straight-line method.
2. Depreciation on motor vehicles is to be charged at 30% using the reducing-balance method.
3. Fixtures and fittings are to be written off over four years using the straight-line method. They are not expected to have a residual value.
4. One of Foxgloves' customers, Gravel Ltd, has used the hotel regularly for its sales force in recent months, and the company currently accounts for 5% of Foxglove Ltd's trade receivables. Foxgloves has recently been informed that Gravel Ltd is being wound up and that its debt is very unlikely to be paid.
5. Inventory at the year-end was valued at £60,000.
6. Electricity of £7,000 was owing at the year-end.
7. Insurance of £24,000 was paid in January 2012 to provide cover for the year to 31 December 2012.
8. The interest rate on the loan is 6%, and six-monthly payments in arrears are made on 1 July and 1 January.

Required

a) Prepare the final income statement, statement of changes in equity, and statement of financial position for the year ended 30 June 2012.

b) Using the budgeted figures as comparators, calculate the following ratios:

- Return on long-term capital employed
- Operating profit margin
- Net profit margin
- Current ratio
- Acid test ratio

- Inventories holding period
- Trade receivable days
- Trade payables days.

c) Interpret the ratios you have computed for Foxgloves, under the headings of profitability, liquidity, and working capital management.

d) Alex and Will are considering paying a final dividend. Advise them on this matter.

e) Alex and Will are considering revaluing the building as they estimate it is now valued at £950,000. What effect would this revaluation have on the financial statements?

f) Alex and Will are thinking of expanding their business by buying another hotel in the West End of London. In order to do this they would need to raise extra finance. Calculate Foxgloves' current level of gearing, and advise Alex and Will on suitable ways in which they may be able to obtain the necessary finance.

Part Two

Management Accounting

Chapter Ten
Costs and Break-even Analysis

Smart Sports goes into production

Learning Objectives

At the end of this topic, you should be able to:

- explain the difference between management accounting and financial accounting
- distinguish between fixed and variable costs
- use break-even analysis as a decision-making tool
- be able to calculate and understand contribution, the break-even point and margin of safety
- discuss the limitations of break-even analysis.

Introduction

So far in this book we have been concerned mainly with financial accounting. This relates to the provision of financial statements (income statement, statement of financial position, and statement of cash flows) to shareholders and other users. Financial accounting is concerned with reporting on past events and recording most transactions at their historic cost. Management accounting is more concerned with planning for the future.

Management accounting

Management accounting is the term used to describe financial and non-financial information generated for business managers to help them in their day-to-day running of the business. It aids managers in the three key areas of: **decision-making** within the business, **planning** ahead, and **controlling** the business. One example of management accounting is the preparation of a cash budget.

Some key differences between financial and management accounting in companies are shown in Table 10.1.

Table 10.1

Financial accounting	Management accounting
Reports on past events	Often involves planning for the future
Highly regulated	Not regulated However, guidelines are set by professional bodies
Detailed annual financial statements	Frequent management accounting reports
Follows set format for statements	No pre-set and often detailed reports

Decision-making

Understanding in detail the future costs of a business helps a manager make informed decisions. Management accounting can provide such information by drilling down into the costs of the business and considering future as well as past costs. For example, Sam will need to understand the profitability levels of various products to find the sales mix that will give him the most profit, or to decide whether to expand his business or to buy-in or make a product.

Planning

Planning ensures that the business has direction and helps to ensure resources are used effectively. For example, Sam will want to plan his levels of production to ensure that he has sufficient materials in place for the production levels, or Sam could use his cash budgets to forecast whether he will require an overdraft facility.

Control

Management accounting techniques enable control to be exercised over the current and future strategy of the business. For example, by comparing budgeted figures to actual figures, management accounting can ensure the business is meeting its performance targets.

For the remainder of this book, we will be concerned with introducing some management accounting techniques.

Case Study
Sam considers manufacturing tennis racquets

Smart Sports has enjoyed international success selling printed team kits, starting with football clubs and moving into other sports, including tennis. Many of Sam's customers have enquired about other equipment, particularly tennis racquets. Until now, all Sam has had are financial accounts telling him how well he had done in the past and his current financial position. He is aware that management accounting techniques can be used in decision-making and has decided to discuss the issue with his accountant, Kim.

Sam explains to Kim that he has been looking at the possibility of manufacturing hand-strung tennis racquets as there has been a great deal of interest in these from clubs. Kim believes this will be an exciting new venture, but he warns Sam that he will need to consider carefully the feasibility of doing this; he tells him that management accounting techniques can help. Sam has already done a great deal of research into the costs involved, and Kim goes on to explain that Sam needs to start by splitting these costs into fixed and variable costs.

Fixed and variable costs

Terminology

Management accounting is the provision of information to internal managers for planning, decision-making, and cost control.

Variable costs vary directly with the number of units produced. For example, the cost of materials used in making a product would be a variable cost.

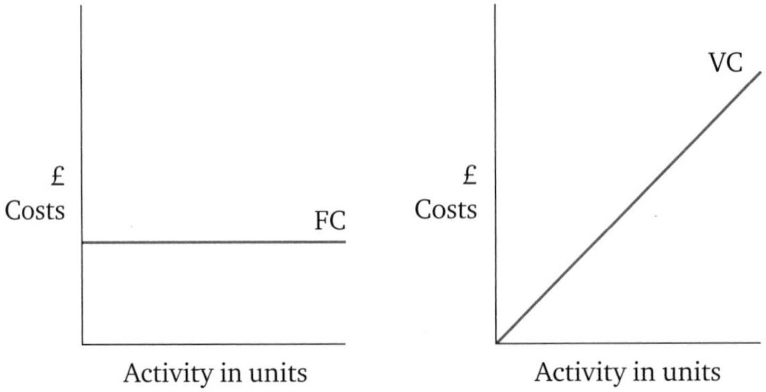

Figure 10.1 Fixed costs (FC) and variable costs (VC)

Fixed costs are those costs that remain the same whatever the level of output (over a limited range of output). For example, rent payable will be unchanged regardless of the number of units produced.

For decision-making purposes, it is often useful to classify costs as fixed or variable.
Fixed and variable costs can be illustrated graphically as in Figure 10.1.

Demonstration Exercise 10.1

Give three examples of variable costs and three examples of fixed costs that you might expect Sam to incur when manufacturing tennis racquets.

Demonstration Exercise 10.1 – solution

Examples of variable costs include:

- materials used in the manufacturing of the racquet, such as wood, carbon fibre, or aluminium
- strings of the racquet
- labour used to string the racquets
- fabric used to make the racquet grip.

Examples of fixed costs include:

- rent
- rates
- supervisors' salaries.

Ponder Point

Will fixed costs always remain fixed? When might they change to being variable?

Semi-variable costs

There are a number of costs that are not fixed and do not vary in direct proportion to activity.

Terminology

Semi-variable costs are costs that contain both a fixed and variable element. For example, telephone charges may include a fixed rental cost-plus a charge linked to telephone usage. These would show the type of cost behaviour demonstrated in Figure 10.2.

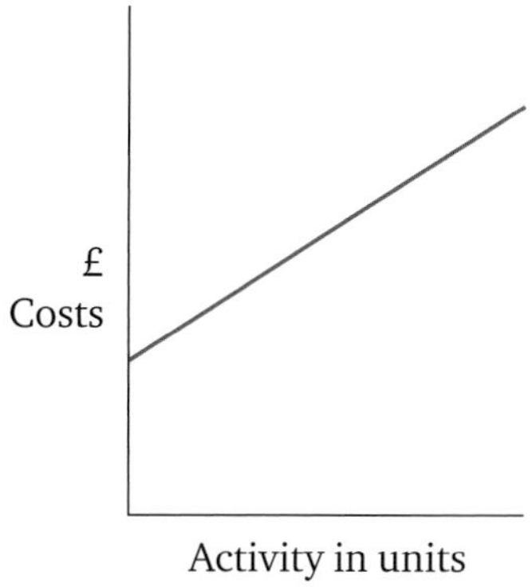

Figure 10.2 Semi-variable costs

Terminology

Step-fixed costs are costs that will remain fixed as output increases until the activity reaches a level where the costs have to increase sharply. One example is supervision costs, where an additional supervisor is required once a certain level of output is exceeded. These would show the type of cost behaviour demonstrated in Figure 10.3.

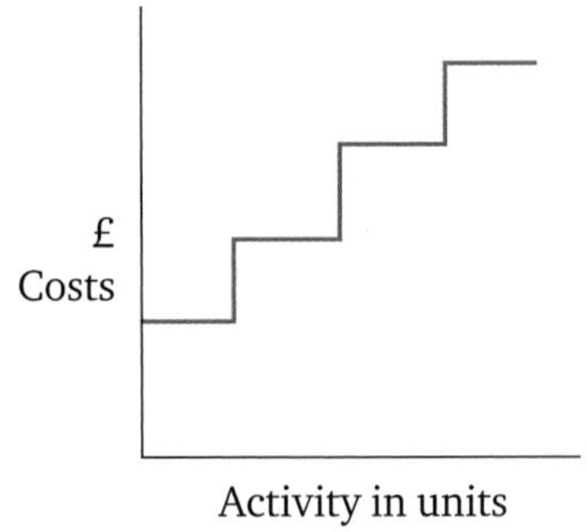

Figure 10.3 Step-fixed costs

Demonstration Exercise 10.2

In order to explore the feasibility of the venture, Sam is planning to undertake break-even analysis based on his estimates for the tennis racquet project.

Sam realizes that the first step in his analysis of the figures must be to identify those costs that are variable and those that are fixed.

Sam anticipates that the costs of producing tennis racquets would be as shown in Table 10.2.

Table 10.2

Hire of machine	£550 per month to hire
Material costs	£8.50 per racquet
Labour costs – Racquet framing – Racquet-stringing	£9 per hour The machine requires one person to operate it. Four racquets can be framed every hour. Staff who string racquets can hand-string two racquets in an hour.

Sam estimates that he will be able to produce 900 racquets in his first year.

a) From the following list of costs, decide which are fixed and which are variable:
- Hire of the machine.
- Material costs.
- Labour costs.

b) What is the variable cost per racquet?

c) What are the total fixed costs in a year?

Contribution

Once costs have been split into fixed and variable costs, this information can be used along with the sales price to understand the contribution of a unit, which is used for decision-making purposes.

Terminology

Contribution is defined as the difference between the selling price of a product and the variable costs incurred in producing that product.

So, for every extra unit produced and sold, there will be an increased total contribution. By adding together the contribution made by each product sold, the total contribution made for the business can be calculated. The total contribution is then available to cover fixed costs, and, hopefully, there will be an excess over fixed costs, which will represent the profit.

For decision-making purposes, all options providing a positive contribution are worthy of consideration.

Contribution per unit = Selling price per unit – Variable cost per unit

Demonstration Exercise 10.3

Sam has done some further research into the making and selling of tennis racquets and estimates that he can sell them for £25 each. For Sam's tennis racquet costing, calculate the contribution for each tennis racquet sold.

Break-even analysis

Terminology

The **break-even point** is the situation where neither a profit nor a loss is made.

It is useful for decision-making purposes for businesses to know the break-even point at which they are making neither a profit nor a loss. This will be the point at which fixed costs are covered. At the break-even point, total contribution will equal total fixed costs.

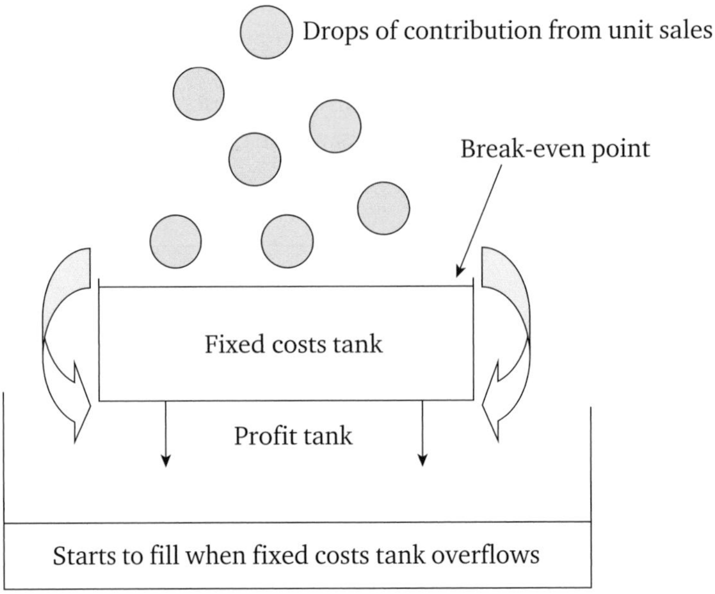

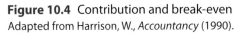

Figure 10.4 Contribution and break-even
Adapted from Harrison, W., *Accountancy* (1990).

The concept of break-even can be considered by thinking of two tanks as shown in Figure 10.4: a fixed costs tank that sits in a profit tank. The contribution from each sale made is represented as a drop of water dripping into the 'fixed costs tank'. The drops of contribution are needed to fill up the tank to cover the fixed costs. No drops of contribution 'water' can become profit until the fixed costs tank is full and the fixed costs have been covered. The point at which the tank is full but not overflowing is the break-even point. After that, every drop of contribution will now overflow into the profit tank, indicating that each of those further drops of contribution would be profit.

It is possible to represent the break-even concept in a 'break-even chart' as shown in Figure 10.5.

The break-even point is where the sales revenue line crosses the total costs line.

To the left of the break-even point, total costs exceed sales revenue, and the difference between the two at any given level of output will represent the loss made.

To the right of the break-even point, sales revenue exceeds total costs, and the difference between the two at any given level of output will represent the profit made.

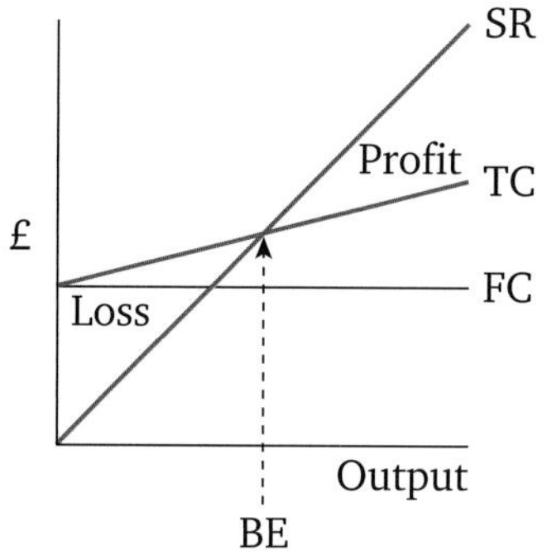

Key:
FC = Fixed costs
TC = Total costs = Fixed costs + Variable costs
SR = Sales revenue
BE = Break-even point

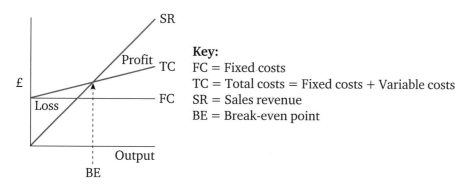

Figure 10.5 Break-even chart

The break-even chart is valid only over a range of output, known as the relevant range. After a certain level of output is reached, fixed costs will increase and unit variable costs and sales revenue may alter.

Computing the break-even point

At the break-even point:	**Profit = zero,**
Hence:	Sales – (fixed costs + variable costs) = zero
Or rearranged:	Sales – variable costs = fixed costs
That is, where:	Total contribution = fixed costs

To determine the break-even point (in units):

1. The fixed costs need to be determined first, as all these costs need to be covered.
2. The contribution per unit then needs to be calculated by taking the selling price per unit less the variable cost per unit.
3. The fixed costs must then be divided by the contribution per unit to give the point at which all fixed costs will be covered.

$$\text{Break-even (in units)} = \frac{\text{Fixed costs}}{\text{Contribution per unit}}$$

The number of units that would need to be produced and sold to make a certain profit level can be calculated by adding profit to the fixed costs.

$$\text{Units required to make profit of } \pounds x = \frac{(\text{Fixed costs} + \pounds x \text{ profit})}{\text{Contribution per unit}}$$

Demonstration Exercise 10.4

Sam's cousin Dan is over from Australia for the summer on a working visa and has decided to run football coaching days to help him fund his cycling tour of England.

He has negotiated with one of Sam's customers to hire their football pitch and other facilities for the day. He has agreed to pay them £100 for this. Sam also helped him find two qualified coaches, who will run the training sessions for a fee of £160 each. As an incentive to the players, he is going to give each of them a printed T-shirt that will cost him £6 to produce. He decides that he will charge the customers £25 for the day and expects to attract at least 40 players. He would like to know how many players he needs to make a profit.

Required:

a) What are the total fixed costs associated with this venture?

b) What would be the variable costs per player?

c) What would be the contribution per player?

d) What would be the break-even number of players?

e) If the coaching attracts 40 players, what profit will Dan make?

Demonstration Exercise 10.5

Sam's old friend Dot is considering setting up a business offering 'historical boating trips' along the River Thames. Dot thinks that she may be able to make a good living out of this. She has carried out market research and identified that there is a market for boating trips where everything is provided for customers, including someone to pilot the boat. Her anticipated costs are as follows:

- The business would operate for 20 weeks during the summer holiday season, from Wednesdays to Sundays inclusive (that is, 100 days each year).
- Ten second-hand boats would be rented for the summer season at a cost of £5,000. Dot would be responsible for maintaining them.
- Annual maintenance cost would be £100 per boat.
- Shared use of a ticket kiosk and the person to sell tickets would be £3,000 for the summer season.
- There would be two trips offered each day: one in the morning and one in the afternoon. Each would last for three hours.

- The food hampers would be purchased from Gourmet Picnics Ltd for £35 each as they are needed, and the historical guide will cost £12 per book. Each boat will be provided with one hamper and one historical guide.
- The boats will be piloted by boating staff who will be paid £7 an hour to be available and an extra £3 an hour if they are required to work. Assume that ten staff will be available for six hours during each working day.

Other costs include:

- Advertising: £1,250 per annum.
- Mooring costs: £2,600 per annum.
- Uniforms for boating staff: £600 per annum, assuming they need replacing each year.

Required:

a) What are the total fixed costs of this proposed business?

b) What are the variable costs of operating each trip?

c) If trips are charged at £150 for the three hour session, what will be the break-even number of boating trips? (The charge will be the same regardless of the number of people in the boat, up to a maximum of four).

d) If the business averages 10 trips in total per day (5 in the morning and 5 in the afternoon), what profit (or loss) should the business expect to make?

The margin of safety

The margin of safety is used to describe the difference between the break-even point and the anticipated level of output. In other words, the margin of safety measures the extent to which output can fall before a profitable operation turns loss-making.

$$\text{Margin of safety (in units)} = \underset{\text{(units)}}{\text{Expected sales}} - \underset{\text{(units)}}{\text{break-even point}}$$

It can also be expressed as a percentage:

$$\text{Margin of safety (as \%)} = \frac{\text{Margin of safety in units}}{\text{Expected sales in units}} \times 100\%.$$

Ponder Point

The margin of safety measures the riskiness of a project. Why?

Interpreting break-even analysis

Break-even analysis can be used in a number of ways. It can be used to determine the level of sales needed to cover all fixed costs. It can also provide guidance on the level of sales needed to achieve a required level of profit. This will enable the business to gauge whether its break-even point is too high, represented by a low margin of safety. The business can also consider what effect a change in contribution per unit (either changing the selling price, variable cost, or both) would have on the break-even point, by how much it would increase or decrease, and what would happen to the break-even point if you changed the fixed cost levels.

Demonstration Exercise 10.6

1. Compute and reflect upon the margin of safety for Dot's champagne boating business.
2. Would you consider it to be high risk for Dot?
3. What would be your advice to Dot in terms of whether she should undertake the business?

Ponder Point

What is the significance of the term 'relevant range' in break-even analysis?

Unit cost behaviour

Cost behaviour is such that the more you produce, the cheaper the cost of each unit produced becomes within a relevant range, as shown in Figure 10.6. This is because the fixed costs remain fixed and are spread out over a larger number of units, the greater the number of units produced.

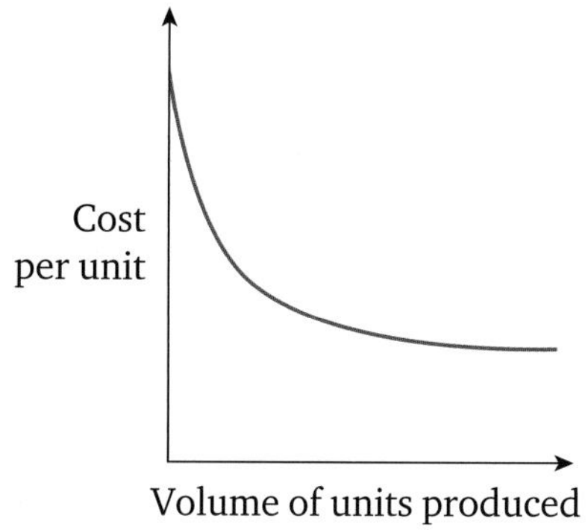

Figure 10.6 Unit cost behaviour

Demonstration Exercise 10.7

Using the information you obtained earlier:

a) How many racquets would Smart Sports need to sell to break-even?

b) What would the profit be if Smart Sports actually sold 1,100 racquets?

c) If you were Sam, would you go ahead? How risky is it?

Sam has also estimated how various levels of sales will affect his costs, in Table 10.3.

Table 10.3

Number of tennis racquets sold	Fixed costs £	Variable costs (£15.25 per unit) £	Total cost £
600	6,600	9,150	15,750
700	6,600	10,675	17,275
800	6,600	12,200	18,800
900	6,600	13,725	20,325
1,000	6,600	15,250	21,850

d) For each of the estimated levels of sales in Table 10.3, calculate the average cost per unit. What do you notice about the average cost per unit?

Assumptions underlying break-even analysis

There are many fundamental assumptions underlying break-even analysis:

- Costs can easily be divided into fixed and variable.
- Variable costs vary in direct proportion to activity within the relevant range.
- Fixed costs remain static over the relevant range.
- The unit selling price will remain constant throughout the relevant range.

These assumptions are not always realistic. For example, raw material unit costs may diminish with increased output as quantity discounts are received. There may be non-cost factors to consider, including the availability of finance and the implications for the workforce. In addition, a specific decision affecting one product may in turn affect other products; for example, if they are complementary products.

In conclusion, break-even analysis is a useful technique to adopt, but it does have severe limitations. It should therefore be used as a guide to decision-making, and other factors should be taken into account before a final decision is made.

Summary of Key Points

- Fixed costs remain the same whatever the level of output within the relevant range.
- Variable costs vary in direct proportion to the level of activity.
- Contribution per unit is the selling price less the variable costs per unit of production.
- The total contribution is used to cover the fixed costs. Once all fixed costs are covered, any further contribution generated will be profit.
- The break-even point is the level of activity at which neither a profit nor a loss is made.
- The margin of safety indicates the extent to which the forecast turnover exceeds the break-even point.

Smart Questions: a wider perspective

1. Can all costs be clearly categorized as fixed or variable costs?
2. Why is it cheaper per unit to produce more of a product?
3. Why is contribution different to profit?
4. How can you calculate break-even in a complex business with many different products?
5. What are the business consequences of classifying variable and fixed costs incorrectly?
6. It is assumed that a specific decision affecting one product will not affect other products. Do you think this will always hold true?

Wider Reading

Drury, C. (2008) *Management and Cost Accounting*, Cengage Learning. Part I introduces management accounting and looks at management accounting terms and concepts.

Practice Questions

10.1 Pippa

Pippa runs a photographic studio specializing in black and white portrait photography. Clients book a one hour studio session and are entitled to receive two large photographs of their choice from the sitting.

The following outgoings are associated with Pippa's business:

- Pippa rents the photographic studio for £12,000 per annum.
- Pippa employs two full-time photographers, each paid a salary of £22,000 per annum.
- She employs one photographic technician for one day a week. He is paid £120 per day, £6,240 per annum.
- Advertising costs are £550 per annum.
- Electricity costs are £1,100 per annum plus £4 per client hour. Each sitting takes two hours.
- Pippa acts as receptionist and general manager of the business and is paid £16,000 per annum.

- Fixtures, fittings, and equipment originally cost Pippa £12,800 and will depreciate by £2,560 per annum.
- Pippa expects to have 1,300 sittings per year; each sitting is charged at £80.

REQUIRED:

a) Identify Pippa's fixed costs and calculate the total fixed costs she will incur each year.

b) Comment on the level of fixed costs compared to variable costs and the implications of this for the business.

c) Calculate the break-even point and the margin of safety for Pippa.

10.2 Wanda

Wanda runs a home laundry service, Kwicky Washy Ltd, where customers' laundry is collected, washed, ironed, and delivered back to them for a set charge per bag. The service is offered to customers only within a limited radius of Oxford City Centre.

The following outgoings are associated with her business:

- Petrol costs average £2 per customer.
- The average customer sends two bags to the laundry service.
- The electricity costs for washing and drying are £1 per bag, and detergent costs 50 pence per bag.
- Wanda employs casual staff to handle, fold, and iron the laundry. They are paid £8 per hour, and each bag takes 1 hour, on average, of their time.

These staff are paid only for the hours they actually work.

- Wanda acts as delivery driver, book-keeper, and salesperson. She is paid a salary of £22,000 per annum.
- The delivery van depreciates at the rate of £4,000 per annum and the laundry machines (washers and dryers) at 20 pence per bag washed.
- Other van expenses include tax, insurance, and maintenance and amount to £2,000 per annum.

REQUIRED:

a) Identify which of the above costs are fixed and which are variable.

b) Calculate the variable cost per bag of laundry laundered.

c) Calculate the total fixed costs per annum.

d) Comment on the relative significance of fixed and variable costs in the above two businesses: Pippa's in question 10.1 and Wanda's Kwicky Washy in question 10.2.

Chapter Eleven
Absorption and Activity-based Costing
Sam's cost conundrum

Learning Objectives

At the end of this topic, you should be able to:

- understand why overheads need to be included when costing products
- calculate a simple 'blanket' overhead rate
- apply absorption costing methods to fully cost out a range of products
- understand the limitations of traditional costing methods
- calculate a simple activity-based cost.

Introduction

Understanding the costs within a company is key to many business decisions. A business needs to ensure tight overall control of its costs to maintain the profitability of its operations. Without detailed knowledge of its product costs, a business cannot set its prices appropriately or value its inventory. Businesses need to analyse how costs change according to circumstances, so that informed decisions can be made. We have seen how variable costs can be used to estimate the break-even point for a particular product. Management accounting can also be used to assess the 'full' cost of products, ensuring that a business includes *all* its costs in estimating the profitability of its products.

Case Study
Costing the new badminton racquet

Sam has now successfully launched his tennis racquet range, and it is selling well. He has used variable costing techniques to calculate how many tennis racquets he needs to sell to break-even. He has hired a machine to make the tennis racquet frames and employed two people to hand-string the racquet heads. He now wants to expand into badminton racquets as the equipment could be reset to manufacture a new shape of frame and the staff could be paid overtime to string the badminton racquet heads. He has appointed Anna as his production supervisor, but they are not sure how they should calculate the racquet costs.

When Sam was manufacturing just tennis racquets, the cost of the frame machine was charged to the frame-making department. However, they now have to find a way of spreading the costs fairly between both tennis racquets and badminton racquets. Variable costing techniques were appropriate when deciding whether badminton racquets should be launched, but a different method is needed for costing the racquets in the longer-term.

Direct and indirect costs

To understand how the different costs within a product change with volume, management accountants divide the costs into fixed and variable costs. This is used to calculate the contribution of a product, a useful tool in decision-making. This is often known as marginal or variable costing. However, the product costs can also be split into direct and indirect costs. Direct costs are those directly associated with a product, such as the string in the badminton racquets and the labour to hand-string them. Indirect costs are those that cannot easily be associated with a product, such as general factory costs, including rent, utilities, and depreciation. Indirect costs are also often known as overheads. These are used in the calculation of the 'full' cost of a product.

Ponder Point

How do variable costs differ from direct costs? How do indirect costs differ from fixed costs?

Absorption costing

The overhead costs incurred by the business need to be shared fairly between all the products. If a product is to be 'fully costed', its cost needs to include a proportion of all the indirect manufacturing costs incurred by the business or organization. For example, to make a single tennis racquet, the manufacturing process will have used a small part of the electricity paid for by the business. It will have taken up a tiny part of the supervisor's time so must carry a part of the supervisor's salary. A small proportion of each of these costs needs to be charged to every product made. Absorption costing tries to find the fairest way of achieving this but without creating a complex and costly accounting system.

Terminology

Direct costs are those costs directly associated with a product, such as material and labour costs.

Indirect costs are those costs that cannot be directly associated with a product, such as rent and depreciation. They are often called **overheads**.

Full costing takes into account both direct costs and indirect costs associated with the manufacture of a product.

Absorption costing is a management accounting technique where indirect manufacturing or overhead costs are spread fairly across the range of products made by the business.

Marginal costing is a method which only takes into account variable costs and ignores fixed costs. It can also be called variable costing.

Calculating a blanket rate

The simplest way of sharing overhead or indirect manufacturing costs between products is to create a blanket rate that can be charged out to each product. At the beginning of the financial year, the total budgeted overhead cost can be estimated and then divided by the budgeted number of products to be produced. This will create a rate or cost per product. This can then be charged to each product as it is produced.

If the total indirect cost is £500,000 and it is estimated that 100,000 products will be made, then each product can be charged with £500,000/100,000 = £5.

Demonstration Exercise 11.1

Sam estimates that his manufacturing overhead costs will be £85,100 in 2018. He forecasts that he will sell 15,000 team kits, 6,000 tennis racquets, and 2,000 badminton racquets. Calculate a blanket rate for Smart Sports.

Using the estimated direct costs for each product group, calculate the estimated product cost for each team kit, tennis racquet, and badminton racquet by completing Table 11.1.

Table 11.1

Product cost per unit calculated using a blanket rate			
	Team kits £	**Tennis racquets £**	**Badminton racquets £**
Direct materials	3.00	10.00	8.00
Direct labour	2.50	7.50	12.50
Overheads			
Total manufacturing cost per unit			

Ponder Point

What would happen if Smart Sports planned to make fewer team kits and racquets?

Over and under recovery

Usually, the calculation of the rate is based on estimated production volumes and costs at the beginning of the financial year. When the actual production volume and costs are known, they can be very different from the estimated amounts. For example, if the volumes have been higher than estimated, more overhead will have been 'recovered' or charged out, as the absorption rate is multiplied by a higher volume number. If the actual costs in total are higher than estimated but the volumes are in line with the estimate, then there will be an 'under' recovery, as insufficient costs have been 'recovered' or charged to the product.

This will have an impact on the profit or loss at the year-end. An accounting adjustment will need to be made in the accounts to compensate for the 'over' or 'under' recovery.

Terminology

The over recovery of overheads occurs after an absorption rate has been applied throughout the year and products have been charged with *more* than the actual overhead incurred by the year-end.

The under recovery of overheads occurs after an absorption rate has been applied throughout the year and products have been charged with *less* than the actual overhead incurred by the year-end.

For example, if Sam discovered that the business had actually made 24,600 units in total and had incurred £87,500 in actual costs, what would be its 'over' or 'under' recovery? What adjustment would it have to make in the year-end accounts?

Smart Sports will have 'recovered' or charged out its overhead costs at £3.70 per unit or £91,020 in total (£3.70 × 24,600 units). As it had incurred only £87,500 in actual costs, it will have overcharged its costs by £3,520. This is called an 'over' recovery. Smart Sports will have to increase the profit in the accounts by £3,520 (£91,020 – £87,500) as it has charged too much.

If Smart Sports had made only 20,000 units but still incurred £87,500 overhead costs, it would have 'recovered' or charged only £74,000 (£3.70 × 20,000 units). It would have 'under' recovered its costs by £13,500 (£87,500 – £74,000). It would then have had to reduce the profit at the year-end by this amount.

Demonstration Exercise 11.2

Sam estimates that the business will make 30,000 units in total and will incur £90,000 in actual costs. Calculate the blanket rate and then apply it in the following examples to calculate the 'over' or 'under' recovery of overheads. What adjustment would need to be made in the year-end accounts:

a) if the business actually made 30,000 units and incurred £100,000 in overhead costs?

b) if the business actually made 35,000 units and incurred £90,000 in overhead costs?

c) if the business actually made 35,000 units and incurred £100,000 in overhead costs?

Ponder Point

Why do these costs have to be based on estimated costs (predetermined costs) at the beginning of the year and not actual (historic) costs?

Calculating a departmental rate to fully cost the product

Allocate, apportion, and re-apportion indirect costs

To arrive at a more accurate method of charging out indirect manufacturing costs to products, a rate must be calculated for *each* manufacturing department in the business or organization. Rather than calculating one rate for the whole business, we need to calculate one for each manufacturing department, reflecting the characteristics of that department. For example, a blanket rate will ignore the differences between the frame-making and the racquet-stringing departments as the former is a machine-operation department and the latter is a labour-intensive one.

To calculate departmental rates, costs need to be collected by manufacturing departments in three stages, as shown in Figure 11.1.

Stage 1: Any costs that can be clearly identified with a specific department can be *allocated*. For example, the hire of the printing machine can be allocated directly to the team kit department.

Stage 2: Any costs that are general to all departments can be *apportioned* or shared. This can be done by taking each type of expense and finding an appropriate method of spreading the costs across departments. For example, the rent can be shared between the team kit, frame-making, and racquet-stringing departments according to how much space in the factory each uses.

Stage 3: If there are service departments that provide support to other departments, their costs need to *re-apportioned* over the manufacturing departments. For example, the maintenance costs could be shared between the team kit, frame-making, and racquet-stringing departments according to the number of employees in each department.

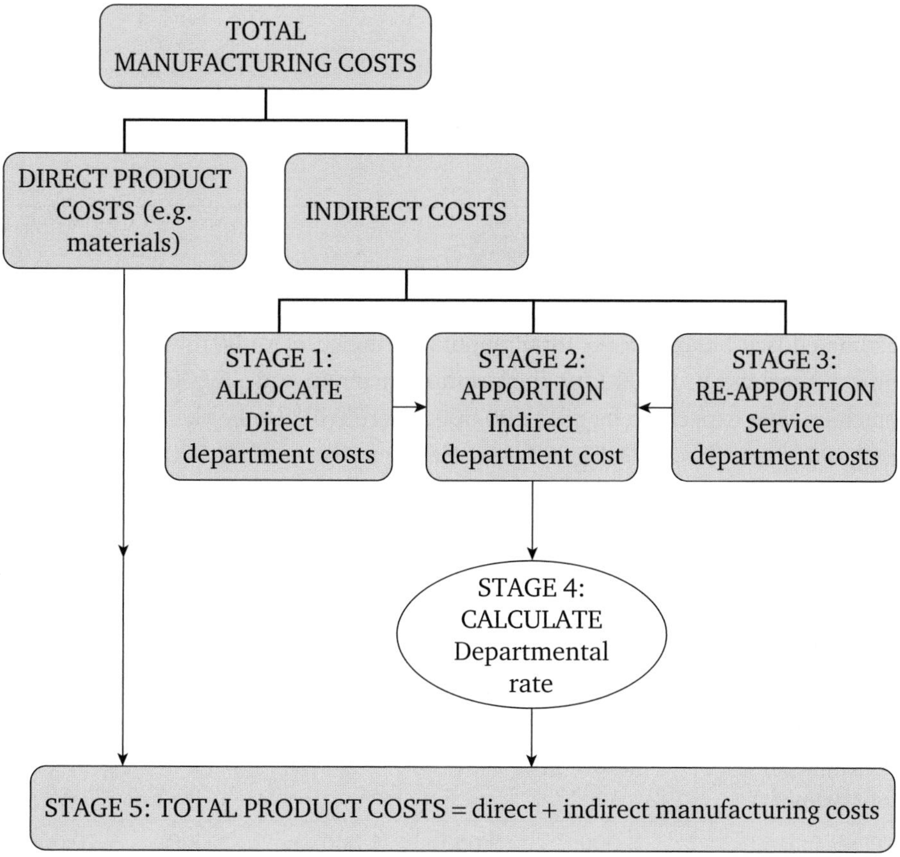

Figure 11.1 Calculating a departmental rate

Terminology

Allocated costs are those indirect costs that are directly associated with a manufacturing department, such as a production supervisor working for one particular department.

Apportioned costs are those indirect manufacturing costs that cannot be directly associated with a department and need to be shared between departments on a fair basis, such as rent.

Re-apportioned costs are the indirect costs of a service department (such as the canteen or maintenance departments) that are shared out between manufacturing departments on a fair basis.

Ponder Point

In what ways could you apportion: electricity, lighting, production director's salary, cleaning materials, and maintenance costs?

Demonstration Exercise 11.3

Anna has given Sam the following management accounting information. She has estimated that Smart Sports' total manufacturing costs for 2018 will include the hire of machinery: £4,000 for the printing machine and £6,600 for the frame machine. She expects to be paid £30,000. There will also be the factory rent of £40,000, depreciation of £3,000, and electricity costs of £1,500. She has also given Sam the data shown in table 11.2 for his manufacturing departments.

Table 11.2

Manufacturing department data					
	Team kit-printing	**Frame-making**	**Racquet-stringing**	**Maintenance**	**Total**
Supervisor (% time per department)	50%	25%	25%		100%
Floor space (square metres)	5,000	3,000	1,000	1,000	10,000
Net book value of equipment (£)	12,000	16,000	2,000	nil	30,000
Electricity used (kilowatt hours)	20,000	8,000	2,000	nil	30,000

Required:

a) Allocate and apportion these estimated costs to calculate a total estimated cost for the year for each of Smart Sports' manufacturing departments. Complete Table 11.3. The solution for team kit-printing has been given as an example.

Table 11.3

STAGES 1 & 2: Allocate and apportion indirect costs				
	Team kit-printing £	**Frame-making £**	**Racquet-stringing £**	**Maintenance £**
Hire of machinery	4,000			
Supervisor salary	30,000 × 50% = 15,000			
Rent	5,000/10,000 × 40,000 = 20,000			
Depreciation	12,000/30,000 × 3,000 = 1,200			
Electricity	20,000/30,000 × 1,500 = 1,000			
Total for each department	**41,200**			

b) Re-apportion the maintenance department's costs over the kit-printing and frame-making departments, assuming that the maintenance staff spend 3,000 hours in kit-printing and 2,000 hours in frame-making. Complete Table 11.4.

Table 11.4

STAGE 3: Re-apportion service department costs				
	Team kit-printing £	**Frame-making £**	**Racquet-stringing £**	**Maintenance £**
Total department				
Re-apportion maintenance				
Total manufacturing department costs				

Each manufacturing department now has a total budgeted overhead cost from which a departmental rate can be calculated.

Choosing and applying a departmental rate

Once costs have been collected by each manufacturing department, a rate needs to be calculated to reflect the characteristics of that department. In a similar way to the blanket rate, a rate can be calculated by taking the total departmental costs and dividing it by an appropriate measure, such as machine or labour hours, reflecting the work done (Stage 4 in figure 11.1). This rate can then be used to calculate the overheads that need to be charged to an individual product (Stage 5 in Figure 11.1)

Ponder Point

What would be the best method of arriving at a departmental rate for a highly mechanized department such as the frame-making department? And what would be best for a labour-intensive department, such as the racquet-stringing department?

Demonstration Exercise 11.4

Sam plans to make 15,000 team kits, 6,000 tennis racquets, and 2,000 badminton racquets. Anna has told Sam that it takes the labour hours presented in Table 11.5 to manufacture and string the tennis and badminton racquets.

Table 11.5

Machine and labour hours by department		
	Tennis racquet	**Badminton racquet**
Frame-machine hours	0.25	0.25
Racquet-stringing labour hours	0.5	1.0

Required:

a) Calculate the rate to be used for charging out team kits, using the total department cost and the number of team kits to be made. (Hint: this is just like the blanket rate, but for one department.)

b) Calculate the total estimated machine hours needed in the frame-making department and total estimated labour hours needed in the racquet-stringing department.

c) Calculate an appropriate departmental rate for the frame-making and racquet-stringing departments, using the total department cost and dividing it by the appropriate number of hours planned for each department (Stage 4 in Figure 11.1).

d) Use the departmental rate to cost a team kit, tennis racquet, and badminton racquet, and complete Table 11.6 (Stage 5 in Figure 11.1). Compare these to the costs calculated in Demonstration Exercise 11.1. Explain why they are different. The solution for tennis racquets has been given as an example.

Table 11.6

STAGE 5: Apply departmental rates to calculate product cost per unit			
Cost per unit	**Team kit £**	**Tennis racquet £**	**Badminton racquet £**
Direct materials		10.00	
Direct labour		7.50	
Overhead: team kit framing stringing		 3.71 1.18	
Total manufacturing cost per unit		**22.39**	

Ponder Point

Do you think that the manufacturing costs of these products are correct? On what does their accuracy depend?

Demonstration Exercise 11.5

Sam has been invited by a prospective supplier of shuttlecocks to visit his factory in Greece. Vas, the factory owner, has two manufacturing departments: first the cork-base department manufactures the bases by machine, and then the feather department manually applies feathers into the cork base. A canteen supports the two manufacturing departments. As Sam is surprised at the price of a box of 10 deluxe shuttlecocks, Vas gives him some information about the raw material and direct labour costs. He tells Sam that his overheads include rent of €45,000, insurance of €9,000, a supervisor of €40,000, and inspection costs of €8,000. He also charges depreciation of €45,000 to the cork-base department, €12,000 to the feather department, and €5,000 to the canteen. Use this information and Tables 11.7 and 11.8 to calculate the cost of a box of deluxe shuttlecocks:

a) Allocate, apportion, and re-allocate costs to the two manufacturing departments: cork-base manufacture and feather application.

b) Calculate an appropriate departmental rate for each department.

c) Using the direct cost information, calculate the cost of a box of deluxe shuttlecocks, assuming that 100 boxes can be made per hour in the cork-base department and 25 per hour in the feather department.

Table 11.7

Shuttlecock departmental information			
	Cork base	**Feather**	**Canteen**
Floor space (square metres)	35,000	45,000	10,000
Supervisor time (hours per week)	10	30	
Inspection time (%)	40	60	
Employees	15	30	5
Machine hours per annum	1,200		
Labour hours per annum	500	1,500	

Table 11.8

Direct costs per box of deluxe shuttlecocks	
	€
Direct materials: cork base	0.83
Direct materials: feathers	2.59
Direct labour: cork-base machine	0.45
Direct labour: feathering	1.53

Case Study
Customized tennis racquets

In response to customer feedback, Sam is considering launching a range of limited-edition tennis racquets. Customers would choose their own colour schemes and logos. However, he is concerned that the absorption costing techniques that Kim has shown him will not cost his new products accurately. First, absorption costing effectively averages costs over a range of products without looking at the effort needed to make individual products. A low-volume specialist range would not be charged with sufficient costs to reflect the extra effort involved. Second, this method of costing includes only manufacturing costs, and so any costs relating to processes occurring after the goods have been made (e.g. selling and delivery) are ignored.

Activity-based costing

Some management accountants have become concerned that traditional methods used to cost products no longer reflect changes in the business world. Absorption costing essentially depends on spreading costs across products based on some type of *volume* measure, such as units, machine hours, or labour hours. When overhead costs were a relatively small proportion of the total cost, this was a reasonable way to share out costs among different products. However, in the last few decades, overhead costs have significantly increased as a proportion of total costs, with direct labour costs falling and greater investment in automated machinery and technology.

In response to increasing global competition, products are changing very fast, with greater production complexity, increasing numbers of product varieties, and short product life cycles. The traditional volume-based overhead allocations are now seen as being too simplistic and not reflecting the costs of modern complex manufacturing processes. As rapid improvements have been made to information technology, both manufacturing systems and accounting systems can cope with more complex ways of costing products. One of these is activity-based costing (ABC).

Rather than looking at a production facility in terms of its manufacturing departments, activity-based costing looks at its activities. In Smart Sports, we have looked at the business as a group of manufacturing departments, such as team kit-printing, frame-making, and racquet-stringing. We can look at it another way: what activities do we need to do to make a tennis racquet? what drives those activities? How much does it cost to carry out these activities?

This should identify which products need more effort to produce them. It links the *cause* of costs to the activities needed to make the product, and so identifies the driver of the costs. For example, if Sam makes his customized tennis racquets, he will need to set-up his frame-making machine every time he manufactures a new type of racquet. As his production runs will be short, it will be very expensive, but traditional methods of costing will not show this. In this case, the activity is the set-ups, the cost pool is the annual cost of setting up the machines, and the cost driver is the number of set-ups in a year.

Terminology

Activity-based costing (ABC) is a costing method that analyses the processes or activities needed to make a product. By understanding the cause (or driver) of those activities, it links the cause and effect of costs on a product.

A cost pool is the total estimated cost of one activity, such as machine set-up.

A cost driver is the factor that causes the cost of the activity to change, such as the number of set-ups.

How to calculate an activity-based cost

There are six stages in activity-based costing:

1. Identify the activities involved in manufacturing the product.
2. Calculate the total cost of each activity: the 'cost pool'.
3. Identify what causes the activity: the 'cost driver'.
4. Calculate the cost per driver: the 'cost driver rate'.
5. Apply a cost driver rate to calculate product costs.
6. Add to direct costs to calculate full product cost.

Demonstration Exercise 11.6

Sam has talked through with his production supervisor, Anna, all the activities undertaken to make a tennis racquet. They have estimated costs by each activity and discussed what will drive these costs. The solution for writing a specification has been given as an example.

Required:

a) Calculate the cost per driver for each activity in Table 11.9.

Table 11.9

Activities, cost pools, and cost drivers for tennis racquets			
Activity	**Cost pool £ per annum**	**Cost driver**	**Cost per driver**
Writing a specification for each type of racquet	1,000	20 specifications	£50 per specification
Placing a purchase order for materials	3,000	500 purchase orders	
Frame machine set-up	2,000	30 set-ups	
Frame manufacture	18,624	1,687 machine hours	
Racquet-stringing	11,800	3,750 labour hours	
Delivery cost	5,000	270 deliveries	

Anna has given Sam and Kim information about making standard and customized tennis racquets, as shown in Table 11.10.

Table 11.10

Tennis racquet product data		
	Standard tennis racquet	**Customized tennis racquet**
Sales units	6,000	750
Number of specifications	5	15
Number of purchase orders for materials	350	150
Number of frame machine set-ups	15	15
Machine hours per racquet	0.25	0.25
Labour hours to string a racquet	0.5	1.0
Number of deliveries	120	150

b) Apply these rates to calculate the total manufacturing overhead for standard and customized tennis racquets in a year, using the information in Tables 11.9 and 11.10, laid out as Table 11.11.

Table 11.11

Total activity-based costs for standard and customized tennis racquets		
	Standard tennis racquet	**Customized tennis racquet**
Specification	£50 × 5 = £250	£50 × 15 = £750
Purchase orders		
Frame machine set-up		
Frame manufacture		
Racquet-stringing		
Total manufacturing costs		
Delivery costs		
Total manufacturing & delivery cost		

c) Using the product information in Table 11.12, estimate the cost of a standard and a customized racquet.

Table 11.12

Activity-based unit cost per tennis racquet		
	Standard tennis racquet £	**Customized tennis racquet £**
Direct materials	10.00	12.00
Direct labour	7.50	15.00
ABC manufacturing cost		
ABC delivery cost		
Total manufacturing and delivery cost		

d) Sam estimates that he could sell these racquets for £30. Would Sam market the customized racquets based on the standard manufacturing cost? Will he make a different decision now that he has activity-based costing information?

Ponder Point

How will activity-based costing change Sam's decision-making process? What could Sam do to make his customized tennis racquets financially viable?

Summary of Key Points

- Overhead costs need to be spread fairly across all products to find the full cost of a product.
- The simplest way of achieving this is to divide the total estimated manufacturing overhead cost by the estimated volume, called a 'blanket rate'.
- As actual volumes and actual costs are unlikely to be the same as those estimated at the beginning of the year, there will be an 'over' or 'under' recovery at the end of the year.
- Overhead cost allocation can be made more accurate by calculating a rate for each manufacturing department, called 'absorption costing'.
- Activity-based costing is a more recent technique of allocating costs to reflect the effort involved in making a variety of products.

Smart Questions: a wider perspective

1. What characteristics should a full costing system have?
2. Can overhead costs be allocated and apportioned fairly? On what does this depend?
3. Why does absorption costing not allocate or apportion non-manufacturing costs in the same amount of detail as manufacturing costs?
4. If there are two service departments (such as canteen and maintenance departments) that use the services of each other, how could their costs be apportioned across the manufacturing departments?
5. Will the total overhead cost each year calculated by activity-based costing be the same as that for absorption costing? If not, why not?
6. What are the advantages and disadvantages of investing in an activity-based costing system?

Wider Reading

Hughes, S., and Gjerde, K. (2003) 'Do different costing systems make a difference?', *Management Accounting Quarterly*, Fall 2003, Vol 5 No 1. This provides the results of a survey of how activity-based costing has made an impact on US manufacturing companies.

Major, M. (2007) 'Activity-based costing and management: a critical review'. In Hopper, T., et al., *Issues in Management Accounting*, 3rd edition, Pearson. This gives a comprehensive review of the latest thinking on activity-based costing.

Practice Questions

11.1 Elixir

A personal products company, Elixir, produces a range of soaps. The budget manufacturing overhead costs for the soap factory was £562,500 for the current year. A blanket rate was calculated on the basis of forecast sales of 450,000 bars of soap.

REQUIRED:

Calculate the under or over recovery for the following possible outcomes at the year-end. Explain what accounting adjustments would need to be made to the accounts in all cases:

a) Actual overheads of £583,750 and sales of 460,000 bars of soap.

b) Actual overheads of £525,450 and sales of 430,000 bars of soap.

c) Actual overheads of £533,550 and sales of 460,000 bars of soap.

d) Actual overheads of £595,250 and sales of 445,000 bars of soap.

11.2 Bambino

Bambino is an Italian company producing a range of dry baby food in packets and wet baby food in jars using different production processes. Carmelina, its management accountant, has estimated that the total manufacturing costs will include the supervisors' salaries of €50,000 for the packet department, €56,000 for the jar department, and €30,000 for the canteen. Other overhead costs include depreciation of €57,145, cleaning materials of €6,000, and factory administration of €9,240.

REQUIRED:

a) Using the factory information shown in Table 11.13, allocate, apportion, and re-apportion these estimated costs to calculate a total estimated cost for the year for each of Bambino's manufacturing departments.

b) Calculate a rate for each of the manufacturing departments, using a machine-hour rate.

Table 11.13

Baby food manufacturing department data			
	Packet department	**Jar department**	**Canteen**
Number of products produced per annum	560,000	480,000	
Number of cleaning times per annum	40	80	
Net book value of equipment	€458,200	€652,300	€32,400
Personnel per department	16	12	5
Machine hours per year	1,600	1,245	

11.3 Shamrock

Shamrock is a pizza manufacturer in Ireland and expects to make 1,345,000 Margherita and 882,000 pepperoni pizzas in the coming year. Paddy has been given information for the two manufacturing departments. Pizza bases are made in the bakery department, which has staff monitoring the production process and has estimated manufacturing overheads of €75,000. Once the pizza-base has been made, employees top the bases with tomato sauce, cheese, and a range of other ingredients by hand. The topping department has estimated costs of €87,000.

REQUIRED:

Using the machine and labour-hour information in Table 11.14:

a) Calculate a rate for the bakery department.

b) Calculate a rate for the topping department.

Table 11.14

Pizza-manufacturing data		
	Bakery	**Pizza topping**
Machine hours per 1,000 pizzas	0.75	0.25
Labour hours per 1,000 Margherita pizzas	0.1	5.0
Labour hours per 1,000 pepperoni pizzas	0.1	6.0

c) Apply these rates to calculate a cost of a Margherita and a pepperoni pizza (see Table 11.15).

Table 11.15

Pizza product cost data		
	Margherita per 1,000 pizzas €	**Pepperoni per 1,000 pizzas €**
Pizza-base cost	120.00	120.00
Topping-ingredient cost	345.00	479.00
Topping direct labour cost	45.00	57.00
Packaging cost	22.00	22.00

Chapter Twelve
Budgeting
Sam makes a Smart plan

Learning Objectives

At the end of this topic, you should be able to:

- understand why a business needs to prepare a budget
- explain the process of preparing a budget
- prepare a simple budget
- understand the problems of budgeting
- appreciate the purpose of simple variance analysis.

Introduction

In Chapter 10, we saw that there are three main purposes of management accounting: to aid planning, decision-making, and control. To achieve these at a business level, most businesses create a budget. This sets out the plans and targets for the coming year, usually broken down by month and by departments within the business. By comparing what actually happened to what it had planned to achieve, a business can gain greater control over its operations.

Case Study
Sam recruits his team

As Smart Sports is becoming a complex operation, Kim advises Sam that he needs to prepare a budget for the following year. Kim explains that the business needs to plan its future activities and be able to assess how well it has done. Sam has appointed a management team to help him make day-to-day decisions, including his production supervisor, Anna, his marketing manager, Juan, and his management accountant, Nina. Sam has to balance how far he can be involved in the day-to-day decision-making and what he can delegate. He needs to determine his overall objectives and plans and set targets and limits for his staff, as well as giving them the authority to make decisions with more independence. One management tool that can help him achieve this is budgeting.

The advantages of budgets

A budget is usually an annual financial plan agreed by management and is prepared by a business for a range of reasons. It is often considered to be the principal method of both planning and controlling the financial performance of a business. Without one, businesses will have little idea of where they have come from or where they are going to. Different businesses will have different needs and expectations from a budget.

Terminology

A budget is a financial plan, prepared and approved by management, usually for the year ahead.

There are many benefits to preparing a budget:

Planning: To enable a business to make sensible decisions, it must have an overall plan. A business working without a budget is like setting out on a journey without a road map. When faced with decisions such as pricing its products, buying raw materials and employing staff, Sam will need to understand how each decision will affect the overall profitability of the business.

Co-ordination and communication: Once a business reaches a certain size, one person alone cannot be responsible for all the decisions. Decision-making is delegated, often to marketing, production, human resources, and finance managers. However, managers must make decisions that are consistent with the overall business goals. A key part of this process is preparing and agreeing a budget together. For example, if Juan, Smart Sport's marketing manager, expects to sell a certain number of items, his production supervisor, Anna, needs to know how many so that she can purchase appropriate raw materials. Nina, the management accountant, can then use this and many other assumptions to estimate the profitability of the company.

Authorization: Once a budget has been agreed, managers will then have the authority, or permission, to incur certain costs to achieve the plan. For example, rather than having to go back to Sam each time Anna needs to make a purchase, she can set about achieving Smart Sports' budget with a degree of independence but knowing that it should be consistent with the business's overall goals. Managers should be responsible for the budgets over which they have control, known as 'responsibility' budgeting.

Ponder Point

What are the consequences if a manager has budget responsibility for areas over which he has no control?

Motivation: By setting objectives and targets within a budget, managers should be motivated to achieve them. In some cases, rewards or extra payments are given for achieving or exceeding plans.

Ponder Point

Should targets be easy or difficult to achieve?

Performance measurement and control: Once measurable objectives and targets are set, both at business and at individual levels, it is much easier to assess how well managers have performed. It is difficult to judge 'good' performance without some benchmark. A preferred method is to judge performance against what the company or an individual had planned to achieve. Other benchmarks may be useful, such as comparisons with the previous year's performance, but these might not take into account new factors, such as the expansion of the business, market conditions, or competitive activity. Once managers understand what has not gone to plan, appropriate corrective actions can be taken.

Ponder Point

What other comparisons might be useful in assessing the performance of a business?

The process of budgeting

Budget preparation often starts with the management of a business setting out its wider vision, mission, and long-term goals. Once this has been done, managers need to prepare a detailed plan of every operational and financial aspect of their business for the following year. First, the management team will need to consider what their limiting factor is. In most cases, the growth of the company will be limited by what it can sell. Occasionally, other factors can constrain growth, such as limits to the availability of a raw material, production capacity, or labour with specialized skills. Certain key assumptions will be agreed, such as market growth, the rate of inflation, expected pay rises, and the capital budget. The management team can then delegate the preparation of detailed budgets to various areas of the business. If sales growth is the limiting factor, the sales and marketing departments will need to first forecast what they expect to sell over the next year. This can then be used by the operational departments to prepare detailed production plans. These are often called 'functional' budgets and include materials, labour, and other departmental expense budgets.

Once each department has prepared individual (functional) budgets, the management accounting department can consolidate them to produce an overall business budget. Usually, this takes the form of a budgeted income statement and cash budget, but many businesses also produce a budgeted statement of financial position (or balance sheet). These statements are often called the 'master' budget (see Figure 12.1).

Terminology

The limiting factor is the constraint that will limit the business's growth in the following year. For example, the expected level of sales often determines how a business should start to plan its operations.

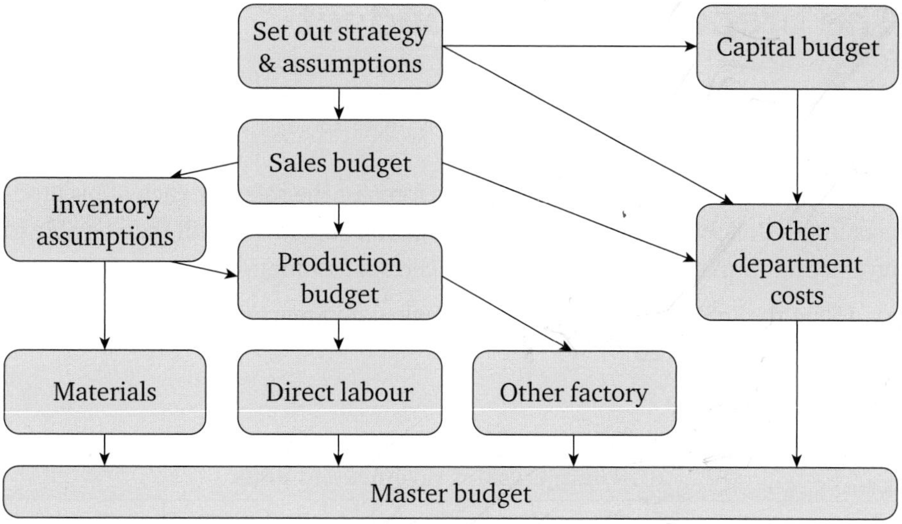

Figure 12.1 Budget process diagram

A master budget is the overall business financial plan, made up of a budgeted income statement, cash budget, and budgeted statement of financial position.

A functional budget is the individual departmental budget, for example of the sales, production, and finance departments.

This process is often 'iterative': a business may need several attempts to go through the process to obtain a final acceptable outcome. For example, when the management accountants add up the sales and expenses for the first time, there is often a much lower level of profit than expected. The management team must then go through the process again, trying to agree ways of achieving the desired profitability.

Ponder Point

Why might the process not achieve the desired result at the first attempt?

The preparation of a budget

Demonstration Exercise 12.1

Sam asks his marketing manager, Juan, to forecast the sales for each of his products for the following year. Anna, his production supervisor, will then be able to produce a raw materials budget based on certain assumptions.

a) Using the information in Table 12.1, calculate Smart Sports' total budgeted sales revenue for 2019.

Table 12.1

2019 budget: sales revenue and units				
	Team kits	**Tennis racquets**	**Badminton racquets**	**Total**
Sales units	16,000	10,000	5,000	
Sales price per unit	£15	£33	£35	
Total sales revenue				

b) Calculate how much of each type of raw material is needed and complete Table 12.3 using Anna's assumptions in Table 12.2. Assume that there is no change to finished goods inventory. The team kit solution has been given as an example.

Table 12.2

2019 budget: raw material usage assumptions			
	Team kits	**Tennis racquets**	**Badminton racquets**
Unprinted team kits	1 kit		
Aluminium per racquet (kilograms)		0.6	0.5
String per racquet (metres)		3.6	3.0
Accessory kits (including grip, plastic end, etc.)		1 accessory kit	1 accessory kit

Table 12.3

2019 budget: raw material usage				
	Numbers of unprinted team kits	**Aluminium (kilograms)**	**String (metres)**	**Accessory kits**
Team kits	16,000 × 1 = 16,000 kits			
Tennis racquets				
Badminton racquets				
Total	**16,000 kits**			

c) Using the costs for each raw material, calculate the unit raw material costs for each product and complete Table 12.4. The team kit solution has been given as an example.

Table 12.4

2019 budget: raw material cost per unit					
	Team kits @ £3.50 per kit	**Aluminium @ £12 per kg**	**String @ £0.50 per metre**	**Accessory kits @ £2 per kit**	**Total material cost per unit**
Cost per team kit	1 kit @ £3.50				£3.50
Cost per tennis racquet					
Cost per badminton racquet					

So far, the sales budget has been calculated in revenue and units. By using the raw material assumptions, the amount of raw materials needed can be calculated in total for each type of material. In the previous example, production units were the same as sales units because there was no change to levels of finished goods inventory held. However, this is unlikely to always be the case. In the next example, we will see the effect of a change of inventory levels on raw materials.

Once the required raw material quantities have been calculated, the raw materials that are already in stock can be deducted. However, if some inventory is needed at the end of the period, this will have to be added to calculate the total purchase requirements.

Units to be purchased = Units required – opening inventory units
+ closing inventory units

Demonstration Exercise 12.2

Anna estimates that raw material inventory levels will be 10% of production requirements at the beginning of the year and has made the following assumptions for closing raw material inventory levels: 1,700 kits, 800 kg of aluminium, 5,500 m of string, and 1,400 accessory kits at the end of 2019.

Calculate the purchase requirements for each raw material, taking into account the inventory level assumptions. Given Anna's cost assumptions above, how much will raw materials be expected to cost Smart Sports in 2019? Complete Table 12.5. The team kit solution has been given as an example.

Table 12.5

2019 budget: raw material purchases (units and cost)				
	Team kits	Aluminium	String	Accessory kits
Production requirement: units	16,000			
Opening raw material inventory: units	(1,600)			
Closing raw material inventory: units	1,700			
Purchase requirements: units	16,100			
Purchase cost	16,100 × £3.50 = £56,350			

Demonstration Exercise 12.3

Sam now needs to calculate the labour requirements to make the kits and racquets. He expects to pay all his direct labour staff at £10 per hour. A team kit requires 0.25 hours of direct labour to be printed. Both tennis racquets and badminton racquets require 0.25 direct labour hours each in the framing department, while in the stringing department, tennis racquets require only 0.5 direct labour hours, compared to 1.0 direct labour hours for badminton racquets.

Calculate:

- the direct labour cost per unit
- the total budgeted direct labour cost for each product for 2019
- the business's total direct labour budget for 2019.

Methods of budgeting

Every number so far in Smart Sports' budget has been calculated from first principles. Certain assumptions have been made, and every cost has been worked out from scratch. This is sometimes known as 'zero-based budgeting'. An alternative method is 'incremental budgeting', which takes the previous years' figures and adjusts them for expected changes such as inflation.

Demonstration Exercise 12.4

Sam and Anna discuss what assumptions are reasonable so that she can estimate the factory overhead costs for 2019 using incremental budgeting. Use the total factory overhead cost for 2018 (see Table 12.6) to calculate the Smart Sports' factory overhead rate for 2019 by applying a simple blanket rate (see Chapter 11).

Table 12.6

2019 budget: factory expenditure		
	2018 expenditure £	2019 assumptions
Hire of machinery	10,600	Same as 2018
Supervisor salary	30,000	Increase by 5%
Rent	40,000	Increase by 3%
Factory depreciation	3,000	Same as 2018
Electricity	1,500	Increase by 10%

Ponder Point

What are the advantages and disadvantages of incremental budgeting over zero-based budgeting?

Demonstration Exercise 12.5

Nina, Sam's management accountant, can now put together a budget income statement for 2019. She has agreed estimated expenses with Sam: sales and marketing of £98,000, distribution of £23,000, and administration of £67,250.

a) Calculate the unit cost for each product by adding together the raw material, direct labour, and overhead cost per unit.

b) Calculate the cost of sales from your previous calculations.

c) By putting together sales, cost of sales, and other expenses, how much profit can the business expect to make?

Terminology

An incremental budget is calculated by taking the previous year's actual figures and adjusting for changes such as price inflation.

A zero-based budget starts from first principles and calculates every number from scratch.

Demonstration Exercise 12.6

Sam is having discussions with a Croatian company that might supply him with folding chairs and tables for sports events. Sam has been quoted a price of 100 kuna per chair and 400 kuna per table. As Sam has queried the prices, he has been shown some assumptions on which the costings are based. Use the information in Table 12.7 to construct the following budgets for the company:

a) Total sales revenue and production budgets in units.

b) Raw material purchase budget in quantity and cost by each material type and in total, based on production units.

c) Direct labour budget based on production budget, in both cost and hours.

d) Use a departmental overhead rate to calculate the cost per chair and per table.

e) Use the cost of sales per unit, together with the budgeted sales units, to calculate a total cost of sales.

f) Prepare a budget income statement.

Table 12.7

Furniture budget: sales, inventory, and raw material assumptions		
	Chair	**Table**
Sales units	12,500	4,000
Opening inventory in units	1,200	230
Closing inventory in units	1,000	320
Raw material requirements:		
Plastic	3 kg	5 kg
Aluminium	1.5 kg	4 kg
Bolts	8 bolts	16 bolts
Units per direct labour hour	6 units	4 units

The factory overheads are charged to products on a direct labour hour rate, and further information is provided in Table 12.8.

Table 12.8

Furniture budget: raw material cost and factory assumptions	
	Kuna
Raw material cost:	
Plastic per kg	9
Aluminium per kg	3
Bolts per 100	50
Direct labour cost per hour	60
Factory overheads:	
Rent	65,800
Insurance	3,500
Administration	115,300
Salaries	42,600
Expenses:	
Marketing & sales	730,000
Head office charge	457,800

Problems of budgeting

While the purpose of budgeting is clear and the process might seem straightforward, businesses often find it difficult to agree and manage a budget. Above all, it can take a great deal of management time, especially if several iterations are needed to achieve the desired profit levels. Most companies find they need to update the budget throughout the year with detailed forecasts as circumstances change. Instead of good co-ordination and communication, there may be tensions between departments. Some may feel their targets are too hard compared to others. This leads to 'gaming' behaviour, such as building in slack. If managers know they are going to be rewarded for their performance against budget, it is in their interests to negotiate an easy target. Sales people might seek to negotiate a low sales target, while operational managers would be keen to obtain a high expenditure allowance. However, this undermines the budget as a useful planning tool. If the sales people underestimate their sales, the production department may not make enough to meet customer demands.

Budgets have been criticized for encouraging a 'top-down' approach, with the management team imposing their targets on the departmental managers. This can de-motivate managers, promote attitudes that avoid risk, and discourage people from taking the initiative. Budgets have been severely criticized for limiting entrepreneurial activity. Encouraging all managers to participate in budget preparation will present opportunities for those who have detailed knowledge of the business to offer new ideas. Managers will be more motivated to achieve targets if they have been involved in setting them. This is known as 'bottom-up' budgeting.

Terminology

A top-down budget is imposed by management from above, with little discussion about how targets are set.

A bottom-up budget is built up from detail provided by each manager responsible for a budget, with targets being agreed by all involved.

Ponder Point

What problems might occur if there is wide participation in the budgeting process?

Budgets to monitor performance and flexible budgeting

Once a budget has been agreed, a comparison of what actually happened against the plan each month will show how well or badly the company is performing. Differences between actual and budget are called variances and can be favourable or unfavourable. If sales are above budget or costs are less, the variance is said to be favourable. Both cases will result in a higher profit than planned. If sales are less than budgeted, or costs are greater than budgeted, there will be an unfavourable variance, leading to a lower profit than planned. Unfavourable variances can also be called adverse.

Terminology

A variance is the difference between budget and actual sales or expenditure.

A favourable variance occurs when sales value is more, or expenditure is less, than budgeted. This will result in a profit higher than budgeted.

An unfavourable variance occurs when sales value is less, or expenditure is greater, than budgeted. This will result in a profit lower than budgeted.

Once variances have been calculated, managers need to understand *why* they have occurred. Often, the management accountant will discuss performance with each operational manager so that a monthly report can be put together. This will include not only the key numbers showing performance against the budget but also a written explanation of why the variances occurred.

One key factor will be whether the business sold more or less than the planned number of products. This will affect other figures within the budget, such as sales revenue and variable costs. If sales volumes, the number of products sold, have been higher than planned, it is unreasonable to expect operational managers to make the products for the same total cost as in the original budget. They need to understand how much more they can reasonably spend to produce a higher number of products.

By 'flexing' the budget, a revised budget can be calculated to provide new targets based on revised sales revenue and expenditure figures. For example, if 3,000 tennis racquets were sold in the first three months of 2019, exceeding the budget of 2,500 racquets, we can calculate a realistic revised budget for the sales revenue and expenditure:

$$\frac{\text{Original budget sales revenue}}{\text{Original budget volume}} \times \text{actual volume} = \text{Revised sales revenue budget}$$

$$\frac{£82{,}500}{2{,}500} \times 3{,}000 \text{ racquets} = £99{,}000.$$

Similarly, the total variable costs of £46,250 can be divided by the budget volume of 2,500 racquets and then multiplied by the actual volume of 3,000 racquets to calculate a new target of £55,500 for variable costs (46,250/2,500 × 3,000). Had the production supervisor's performance been measured against the original budget, she could have been criticized for overspending. However, once the higher volume is taken into account, we can see that she actually saved the business £3,500 of variable costs (£55,500 – £52,000) (see Table 12.9).

Flexing the budget can also be used to calculate future costs by applying price and volume increases to actual sales and cost data. This can be used for calculating forecasts that provide continual updates to the budget during the year and for longer-term planning.

Table 12.9

Tennis racquets: three months Jan–Mar 2019 flexed budget					
	2019 budget	2019 actual	Variance	2019 flexed budget	2019 flexed variance
Tennis racquet units	2,500	3,000	500	3,000	
Sales in £	82,500	95,000	12,500	99,000	(4,000)
Variable costs £	46,250	52,000	(5,750)	**55,500**	3,500
Contribution £	36,250	43,000	6,750	43,500	(500)

Demonstration Exercise 12.7

Sam now wishes to assess how well the badminton racquets have performed in the first six months of 2019. Calculate a flexed budget in Table 12.10 based on the actual numbers of badminton racquets sold. Comment on the performance of the sales manager and the production manager.

Table 12.10

Badminton racquets: six months Jan–June 2019 flexed budget					
	2019 budget	2019 actual	Variance	2019 flexed budget	Flexed variance
Badminton racquet units	3,000	2,500			
Sales in £	105,000	90,000			
Variable costs £	66,000	60,000			
Contribution £	39,000	30,000			

Variance analysis

This principle of flexed budgeting is extended much further in management accounting to provide a detailed financial analysis of company performance. By setting standards (budgets) for every raw material and labour cost, in terms of both costs and quantities, flexed budgets can be produced at every level of the business. This allows for variances to be analysed by *volume* or *value*.

In the tennis racquet example in Table 12.9, we can see the effect of selling 500 more units than budgeted. By using the standard (or budgeted) contribution per unit, we can calculate that the business should have made an extra contribution of £7,250. This is the difference between the budgeted contribution of £36,250 and the flexed budget of £43,500. This is a sales *volume* variance as it was due to greater numbers of racquets being sold. We can also see the financial impact of selling the tennis racquets at a price below budget, as the actual sales of £95,000 are below that of the flexed sales of £99,000. This is a sales price or *value* variance.

We can apply this principle to both raw material and direct labour costs. For example, in Table 12.11 to make 12,000 tennis racquets, there would be a budget of £21,600 for string. This would be made up of 12,000 racquets using 3.6 m of string per racquet at a string cost of £0.5 per m. If the total actual costs were £20,520, made up of 12,000 racquets using 3.8 m per racquet of string at a cost of £0.45, we can calculate the material usage (*volume*) and material *price* variances.

Table 12.11

Tennis racquet string variance analysis			
Tennis racquet units: 12,000 actual units	**Price per metre of string per racquet**	**Metres of string per racquet**	**Total string costs £**
Budget	£0.50	3.6	21,600
Actual	£0.45	3.8	20,520
Variance	£0.05	(0.2)	1,080
Total price variance (price difference × actual usage per metre × actual units sold)	0.05 × 3.8 × 12,000 = 2,280 F		
Total usage variance (usage difference per unit @ budget price × actual units sold)		(0.2) × £0.50 × 12,000 = 1,200 U	Check: 2,280 – 1,200 = 1,080 F

Variances can be positive, i.e. favourable (F in Table 12.11), or negative, i.e. unfavourable, also known as adverse (U in Table 12.11). Variance analysis can become highly complicated and technical, so this attempts to illustrate the basic idea. Non-accountants need to understand the fundamental principle and then be able to interpret the information. A full understanding of how to calculate all variances in detail is outside the scope of this book.

Terminology

A price variance is the difference between budget and actual price multiplied by the actual sales volume. The same principle can be applied to material costs or labour rate variances.

A volume variance is the difference between the budgeted and actual volume, multiplied by the budget selling price. A similar principle applies to material usage and labour efficiency variances.

Demonstration Exercise 12.8

After six months of comparing the business's actual performance against budget, Sam is keen to understand why the labour costs are so high. Nina has given him a report on the variance analysis for the business's direct labour costs (Table 12.12). She has told him that the budgeted labour rate was £10 per hour but that it had actually cost £10.50 per hour. Consider the reasons that these variances could have occurred.

Table 12.12

Labour variances		
	Tennis racquets (12,000 sales units sold) £	**Badminton racquets (5,000 sales units sold) £**
Budget direct labour	90,000	62,500
Actual direct labour	88,200	78,750
Variance	1,800	(16,250)
Labour rate variance	(4,200)	(3,750)
Labour efficiency variance	6,000	(12,500)

Questioning assumptions

A budget is a financial plan based on estimates and forecasts of what a business expects to happen in the subsequent year. It can be highly subjective as many assumptions have to be made. In some cases, managers may not provide realistic estimates for a number of reasons. In other cases, managers might simply make misinformed judgements. It is therefore important that those involved in the preparation of budgets question the assumptions and judgements made by managers.

Summary of Key Points

- Budgets need to be prepared by businesses to plan and control their operations.
- Budgets can help a management team communicate and co-ordinate their plans, set limits on their activities, and measure their performance.

- Budgets are often made up of a business summary, known as a master budget, and individual departmental or functional budgets.
- There are many problems associated with budgeting, including how they impact on the behaviour of managers.
- Variance analysis allows performance to be analysed in more depth.

Smart Questions: a wider perspective

1. How can the accuracy of a budget be improved?
2. How can budgets motivate and de-motivate managers?
3. Which types of businesses might put more emphasis on planning rather than control in their use of budgets?
4. What conflicts can occur as a result of the different objectives of budgeting?

Wider Reading

Jackson, D., and Strovic, D. (2004) *Better Budgeting*, CIMA, available from www.cimaglobal.com. This article provides a review of recent debates on the role of budgeting.

Steven, G. (2007) 'Management accounting—performance evaluation', *Financial Management*, November 2007. Provides a comparison of different budgeting methods.

Practice Questions

12.1 Renata

Renata has set-up a jam-making business. As the fruit-picking season approaches, she needs to calculate her raw material requirements for the year ahead. Given her sales estimates in Table 12.13:

a) Calculate the production budget using the opening inventory assumptions in Table 12.13 and assuming that closing inventory should be 8% of sales units.

Table 12.13

Jam sales budget in units (jars)			
	Strawberry	**Raspberry**	**Kiwi**
Sales units	178,000	236,000	53,000
Opening inventory	16,300	25,000	4,200

b) Calculate how much raw material is needed by each type of raw material and in total using the assumptions in Table 12.14. Each jar of jam also requires one jar, one lid, and two labels.

Table 12.14

Jam raw material usage assumptions			
	Strawberry	**Raspberry**	**Kiwi**
Fruit	0.6 kg	0.5 kg	1.2 kg
Sugar	0.4 kg	0.5 kg	1.0 kg

c) Calculate the total raw material purchase budget if strawberries cost €1.32 per kg, raspberries cost €1.56 per kg, and kiwis cost €2.30 per kg. Sugar costs 20 cents per kg, jars cost 12 cents, lids cost 3 cents, and labels cost 2 cents each.

d) Calculate the cost per jar for each type of jam.

12.2 Turkish Teddies

A Turkish toy manufacturer makes luxury teddy bears and needs to calculate the labour requirements to make them. Each standard teddy takes 30 minutes to make, while 60 teddies can be packed every hour in the packing department. Some teddies are also dressed in T-shirts and require 15 more minutes in the teddy department. They expect to pay the direct labour staff in the teddy department 10 lira per hour and those in the packing department 8 lira per hour. Sales are expected to be 50,000 standard teddies and 15,000 dressed teddies.

REQUIRED:

a) Calculate the direct labour cost for the standard and dressed teddies.

b) Calculate the toy business's total direct labour budget.

12.3 Sole

The board of a shoe manufacturer, Sole, is reviewing the first draft of the budget for 2019, drawn up by the management accountant. The company operates in a very price competitive market with limited prospects for growth. General inflation is running at 2%. Head office costs are charged at a rate of 10% of sales.

REQUIRED:

Examine the budget in Table 12.15 and consider what questions you would advise the board to ask the management accountant.

Table 12.15

Sole: a comparison of 2018 actuals to 2019 budget		
	2018 actual	**2019 budget**
Number of pairs of shoes	85,400	89,670
	£	£
Average price per shoe	35.00	36.40
Revenue	2,989,000	3,263,988
Material cost	1,281,000	1,345,050
Direct labour cost	683,200	696,864
Factory rent	164,300	164,300
Factory utilities	65,800	69,090
Factory administration costs	87,290	78,561
Marketing costs	175,400	175,400
Selling costs	145,976	153,275
Head office charge	298,900	298,900

Chapter Thirteen
Pricing and Costs
Can Smart Sports compete?

Learning Objectives

At the end of this topic, you should be able to:

- understand how various methods of costing can impact on pricing
- calculate prices using cost-plus, sales-margin, and discount methods
- consider how various pricing strategies can be used, including how target and life-cycle costing can affect product pricing
- calculate internal transfer prices in a variety of ways.

Introduction

Management accountants use different methods of calculating costs in different situations. Marginal costing uses variable costs, absorption costing includes indirect costs, and activity-based costing considers what drives certain costs in a business. As understanding the costs of a business is key to most operating decisions, it is important to know which costing method should be used in each situation. This is particularly important when it comes to pricing products and services.

Case Study
Smart prices under pressure

Sam has a team meeting to review progress in 2019. Anna, his production supervisor, reports good manufacturing performance. However, Juan, the marketing manager, is more concerned about increased competition from rival manufacturers who are cutting their prices. As efficiency is improving, could there be an opportunity to reduce Smart Sports' selling prices? Sam also hoped to expand the range of racquets by launching a squash racquet. Would increased production volumes help to bring down costs by spreading fixed costs over more products? So far, the Smart Sports team have priced products in line with what they think customers are willing to pay. However, Sam is concerned that, as the business becomes more complex, he needs to understand a little more about how his costs and prices fit together.

Using cost information to price your product

Pricing a product depends on many factors, including the market in which the business is operating. Whichever method of pricing is chosen, knowing your product costs is vital so that you can assess the product's viability. Pricing your product in response to your competitors (market pricing) may be the most realistic method. However, many businesses use their costs to calculate their selling price. This can be done in two basic ways: cost-plus or margin pricing. Before looking at these two methods, an understanding of the distinction between gross profit margin and mark-up is essential. Consider Danni's drinks business, in which he buys drinks at €2 per can and sells them at €3 per can. He therefore makes a gross profit of €1 per can.

Danni's Drinks:

$$\text{Gross profit margin} = \frac{\text{Gross profit}}{\text{Sales}} = \frac{1}{3} = 33\%$$

$$\text{Mark-up} = \frac{\text{Gross profit}}{\text{Cost of sales}} = \frac{1}{2} = 50\%$$

Terminology

Cost-plus pricing is where the product is priced to achieve a standard mark-up.

Margin pricing is where the product is priced to achieve a standard margin based on the selling price.

Cost-plus pricing

When costs are used as the starting point for pricing, a business often applies a consistent percentage to its costs to reach a selling price. This method particularly suits retail businesses, where the managers will add an agreed percentage to the cost of purchases to cover their overheads and generate a profit.

For example, if your product cost is £9 and you wish to achieve a mark-up of 40%, you will need to multiply £9 by 1.40 (1 + 40/100). The selling price will be £12.60.

$$\begin{aligned}\text{Selling price} &= \text{product cost} \times (1 + \text{mark-up }\%)\\ &= £9 \qquad\qquad \times (1 + 40)/100\\ &= £12.60\end{aligned}$$

Sales-margin pricing

Some companies will set a price to deliver a certain profit margin. This is often the case in manufacturing companies where product margins are carefully monitored. The gross profit is the selling price less the cost of sales. The gross profit margin is the gross profit divided by the sales price, expressed as a percentage.

For example, if your selling price is £10 and your cost of sales is £6, the gross profit will be £4 (selling price less cost of sales), and your gross profit margin will be 4/10, or 40%.

$$\begin{aligned}\text{Gross profit margin }\% &= \frac{(\text{Selling price} - \text{cost of sales})}{\text{Selling price}} \times 100\\ &= \frac{(10-6)}{10} \times 100\\ &= 40\%\end{aligned}$$

This can be rearranged to calculate the selling price from cost of sales information and an agreed gross profit margin:

$$\text{Selling price} = \frac{\text{Cost of sales}}{(1 - \text{Gross profit margin \%})}$$

$$= \frac{6}{(1 - 40/100)}$$

$$= £10$$

Let's compare these two methods.

First, we start with the cost and need to calculate the selling price (see Table 13.1).

Table 13.1

	Cost-plus (with 20% mark-up)	Sales-margin (with 20% gross profit margin)
Selling price	120	125
Cost of sales	100 (multiply by 1.2 to give selling price)	100 (divide by 0.8 to give selling price)
Gross profit	20	25

Occasionally, it is useful to be able to calculate a required cost of sales from selling price information. These calculations can be reversed, as shown in Table 13.2, where this time we start with a selling price and need to calculate the cost of sales.

Table 13.2

	Cost-plus (with 20% mark-up)	Sales-margin (with 20% gross profit margin)
Selling price	120 (divide by 1.2 to give cost of sales)	125 (multiply by 0.8 to give cost of sales)
Cost of sales	100	100
Gross profit	20	25

Demonstration Exercise 13.1

Sam is considering cutting the price of his tennis racquets. If his cost of sales is £22, calculate a new price based on:

a) cost-plus pricing using a mark-up of 30% on cost of sales

b) margin pricing to give a 20% gross profit margin.

Demonstration Exercise 13.2

Sam is about to launch his new squash racquet. He knows that he must have a selling price of £45 to be competitive. Calculate what his cost of sales must be if:

a) he wants to make a gross profit margin of 40%

b) he uses mark-up of 70% on costs of sales.

Discounts and distribution margins

Customers often negotiate a discount on the selling price, usually expressed as a percentage. To calculate this, you need to deduct the percentage from 1 and then multiply the selling price by this. For example, if you are asked to give a 5% reduction, you can multiple the selling price by 95%.

Where a product is sold several times before reaching its final consumer, the margins made by all those involved are often expressed as percentages. For example, Sam could sell his squash racquets to a retail outlet that then sells them on to the final consumer. If Sam's price to the retailer is £35 and the retailer requires a 40% margin, the final selling price to the consumer will be £58. This applies the same calculation as sales-margin pricing above.

	£
Retailer's selling price to consumer	58
Sam's selling price to retailer	35
Retailer's gross profit	23
Retailer's gross profit margin	23/58 × 100 = 40%

To calculate the retailer's selling price from Smart Sports' selling price:

$$\text{Retailer selling price} = \frac{\text{Cost of sales (Smart Sports' selling price)}}{(1 - \text{Gross profit margin \%})}$$

$$= \frac{35}{(1 - 40/100)} = £58$$

Demonstration Exercise 13.3

Sam is negotiating with one of his customers over discounts. To help Sam in his decision-making, calculate the following discounts and margins:

a) The customer would like a 15% discount on Smart Sports' selling price of £20 for a team kit. If he agrees to this, how much will he be charged?

b) A tennis racquet has a retail price of £60. If the retailer makes a margin of 45%, what would be Smart Sports' selling price to the retailer?

c) Sam would like to ensure the business receives £51 for each badminton racquet sold. If it sells them through a retailer who requires a margin of 40%, what will be the final selling price of each racquet to the badminton player?

Choosing the appropriate costing method

In these examples, we have used cost of sales as the basis of calculation, but other cost methods can be used to set selling prices. However, the costing method must be chosen carefully and be appropriate for the particular situation. Marginal or variable costing can be used only in certain circumstances, whereas full costing methods such as absorption costing and activity-based costing should be used for long-term pricing.

Marginal costing: special prices

In the short-term and in certain circumstances, it may be advantageous for the business to price its products by using variable or marginal costs. It is usually an appropriate technique where there is spare capacity and an opportunity to make an additional contribution towards the costs of overheads by setting a price that is lower than full cost. However, the wider implications for the business must be carefully considered.

Demonstration Exercise 13.4

Sam's factory is busy most of the year, but in late autumn, there is not enough demand to keep the racquet frame machine operating. Lil, a tennis coach, has approached Sam with a one-off deal. She offers to buy 5,000 tennis racquets for £21. The usual price is £28, with variable costs of £19. Sam will have to pay £2,000 to deliver them to Lil. Should he accept the order?

Demonstration Exercise 13.4 – solution

In this case, Sam should accept the order as it will be filling up spare capacity in the factory. The fixed costs of running the frame machine will be incurred anyway, so any contribution the business can generate from selling additional racquets will increase its profits. It will make a contribution of £2 (£21 – £19) for every racquet sold, or £10,000 in total. Of course, it will then have to deduct the delivery cost of £2,000, but it will still make £8,000 contribution overall.

Demonstration Exercise 13.5

Sam is considering bidding for a contract to print 1,000 T-shirts for the UK national indoor hockey championships. These T-shirts would be needed in January, a time when business is slow, there would be capacity on the printing machine, and the permanent labour force is not fully employed. Material costs are estimated to be £8 per T-shirt. The business would have to employ some temporary labour, estimated to be £3,000 in total. This would be in addition to the permanent labour force, costing £2 per T-shirt. Delivery costs would be around £0.50 per T-shirt. What is the minimum price per T-shirt that Sam should charge?

Ponder Point

What other considerations should Sam take into account before agreeing to this 'special' price?

Full costing

Management accountants need to be very careful about when they apply marginal or variable costing techniques for pricing decisions. It can be very tempting to bid for extra business by reducing prices. However, in the long-term, this may be a misguided strategy. To appreciate this, consider the following example.

Demonstration Exercise 13.6

Sam sells a team kit for £15. He knows his direct costs are £11 and his indirect costs are £2.43. Jaz offers to make the product for £12. Should he accept Jaz's offer? What will happen to the cost of Sam's other products if he accepts it?

Demonstration Exercise 13.6 – solution

This looks like a good deal for Sam as he will make £3 (£15 – £12) for every team kit he buys from Jaz, compared to £1.57 (£15 – £11 – £2.43). But what will happen to the costs of his other products? This decision will have wider implications for the whole business. If Sam accepts this offer, the remaining products will have to bear a higher proportion of the overheads. For example, let's assume that Sam's total overhead cost is £92,340 and he is hoping to sell 20,000 team kits and 18,000 racquets. If he uses a blanket rate to share the overhead across all his products, he will charge each product with £2.43. However, if he buys the team kit shirts from Jaz, the £92,340 overhead costs will have to be shared between the racquets. The new blanket rate will be £5.13 (£92,340/18,000).

The cost spiral

Figure 13.1 illustrates why it is so important to use a cost that includes overheads such as absorption or activity-based costing to price your products. If Sam prices his products to cover just his direct or variable costs, he will not make sufficient contribution to cover his overheads. Table 13.3 compares various methods of costing.

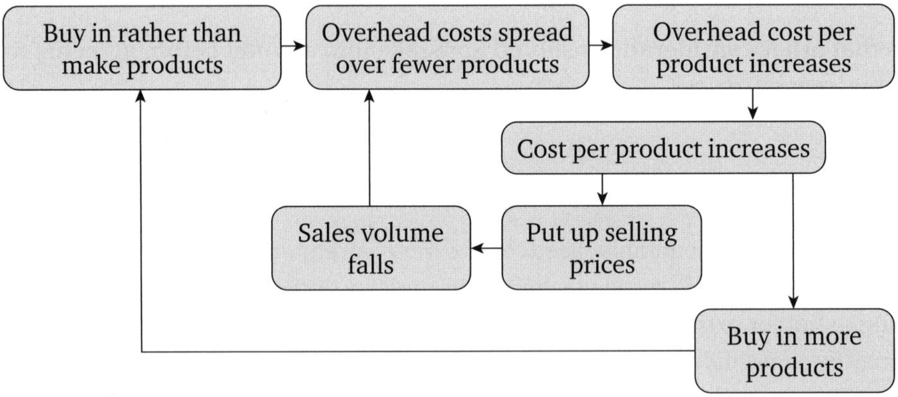

Figure 13.1 The cost spiral

Table 13.3

Alternative costing methods compared			
	Marginal costing	**Absorption costing**	**Activity-based costing**
What costs are allocated to products?	Variable costs only	Direct and manufacturing indirect/overhead costs	Direct and indirect overhead costs, including appropriate non-manufacturing costs
How are costs allocated or apportioned?	Variable costs are allocated directly as they are closely associated with the product	Indirect manufacturing costs are usually apportioned on a volume-based measure, such as machine- or labour-hour rate	By identifying activities, ABC allocates costs according to what drives those activities
Short- or longer-term decision	Short-term	Longer-term	Longer-term
When should it be used?	When making decisions that will not affect the fixed overhead costs, e.g. special prices	Where production overheads are shared between all the manufactured products; suits companies where the products are similar and production processes are predictable	Where production overheads are shared between all the products; suits complex businesses with a wide variety of products or services

Ponder Point

In the long-term, are all costs variable or fixed, and why?

Pricing and product strategy

Setting a price is only one part of the wider corporate and marketing strategy adopted by a business. Much depends on how the market operates and where the product is positioned in that market. If the product is very distinctive, customers are likely to buy, whatever the price. The demand for this type of product is described as 'inelastic' as customers are not price sensitive. Here, pricing strategy will be 'price skimming': setting high prices to take advantage of product innovations or branding. But where the market is competitive and customers *are* price sensitive, the demand for the product is considered to 'elastic'. Customers are prepared to buy more, if the price falls. Pricing strategy here will be 'penetration pricing': by setting lower prices than competitors, businesses hope to gain market share.

Terminology

Inelastic prices are those where customers are not sensitive to how high or low a selling price is set.

A price-skimming strategy is often used where prices are inelastic, setting prices high to take advantage of customers not being sensitive to prices.

Elastic prices are those where customers are sensitive to how high or low a selling price is set.

A penetrating price strategy is often used where prices are elastic, setting prices low to take advantage of customers being sensitive to prices.

Ponder Point

Would a can of drink have an inelastic or elastic price? What about the price of electricity? In what circumstances would a tennis racquet have an inelastic price?

Optimum pricing

To take advantage of price elasticity and inelasticity, judgements must be made about how many products could be sold at different pricing levels. If a business undercuts the prices of its competitors, it may be able to increase the number of products sold. On the other hand, if it increases its prices and makes a higher total margin, it may sell fewer products. By looking at the relationships between product volumes at different pricing points, the optimum price to maximize contribution can be calculated.

Demonstration Exercise 13.7

Use Sam's estimates in Table 13.4 to calculate the optimum price he should charge for his badminton racquets in order to maximize his profits. Base your calculations on direct costs of £24 per racquet, assuming that they are all variable.

Table 13.4

Badminton racquets optimum price			
Number of badminton racquets	Selling price per racquet	Contribution per racquet	Total contribution
5,000	£30		
4,000	£35		
3,000	£40		
2,000	£45		

Target costing

In reality, selling prices are often set by competitors. Depending on the market, selling prices can be the starting point (rather than the end result) of pricing calculations. Many large Japanese businesses have used 'target costing' to gain cost advantage in their manufacturing operations.

To achieve competitive advantage in this case, efforts should concentrate on controlling the costs of the product rather than focusing on pricing. This is called target costing (see Figure 13.2). A specification for a product is drawn up by the operational team (including the production, the research and development, and the marketing departments) and costed out by the management accountants. The level of required profit is set, usually by looking at the investment needed to launch the new product and the cost of financing this. A target cost can then be calculated and compared to the cost calculated by the team drawing up the

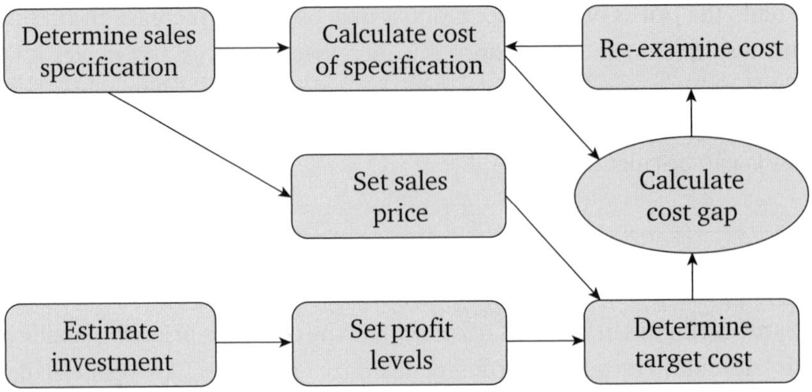

Figure 13.2 Target costing

product specification. Often there is a large gap between the costed specification and the acceptable cost of the product. The whole team then works to cut costs, but without compromising the product design.

Ponder Point

What problems might occur when using target costing?

Life-cycle costing

Life-cycle costing (see Figure 13.3) considers the costs incurred throughout the life of a product. There will be heavy investment initially in research and equipment, especially with technically advanced products. For example, Sam might consider funding research into new materials for manufacturing racquet frames. If the business could develop a stronger but lighter frame, it would be able to charge a price premium for the racquets. This is called the pre-manufacturing phase. After the product has been launched, the manufacturing phase begins, and costs will rise as sale volumes increase. As the product comes to the end of its life, sale volumes and manufacturing costs will decline, and the product may have to be supported with additional marketing and support-service costs. This is the post-manufacturing phase.

Let's compare this to how sales revenue is generated over time. Sales revenue will be generated only once the manufacturing phase has begun and will be low

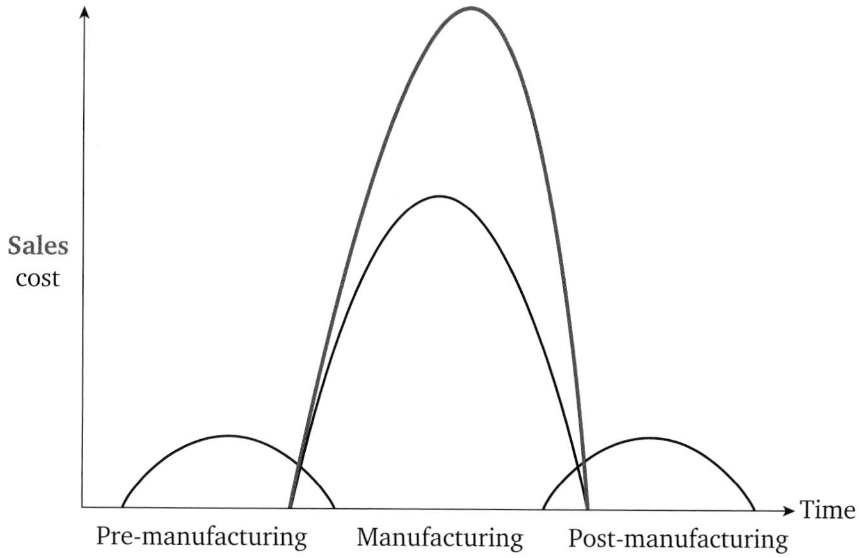

Figure 13.3 Life-cycle costing

at the beginning as the product gets established. Sales will increase steadily as volumes increase, but as the product reaches the end of its life, sale revenue will decline.

You can see that, by matching the revenue and cost profile at different stages of the product's life, the profitability can be very different. There will be heavy costs in the beginning, but profits will increase quickly in the manufacturing/sales growth stage. Careful management is needed at the end of a product's life to ensure that losses are kept to a minimum.

Pricing strategies may change throughout the life of the product. If a product is highly innovative at the beginning of its life, a price skimming strategy can be used. High prices and large profits can be made. But if many competitors develop similar products, penetration pricing may be needed, lowering prices to gain market share.

Ponder Point

In certain industries, 80% of costs are committed before the product is made. In which industries is this likely to occur, and what sort of costs might they be?

Terminology

Life-cycle costing considers the costs throughout the life of the product, including the pre-manufacturing, manufacturing, and post-manufacturing costs.

Target costing compares the selling price less the desired profit to the costed specification of the product before it is manufactured.

Transfer pricing

When a business transfers goods from one division to another, a price needs to be agreed for that internal sale. This is called a transfer price and can be set in various ways.

Sam is considering selling his team kit design to his Indian division but is unsure what price to charge them. He wants to ensure that his design team in the UK gets some benefit for their effort. However, he knows that he cannot charge too much, so that the team kits are competitively priced in India. Both businesses need to benefit, but he wants to make sure he maximizes the profit made by his whole group. He needs to agree a transfer price between his UK and Indian businesses. He can choose from two main methods of calculating a transfer price: cost-based or market-based price.

Cost-based transfer pricing

Products can be transferred to another division at cost: either variable or fully absorbed costs. Neither method is ideal. If products are transferred at variable cost, the selling division (in this case, the UK) gets no benefit. If a fully absorbed cost is used, including a share of the UK's fixed costs, this can lead to inefficiencies. There is no incentive for the UK to keep its costs competitive. Where transfer prices are set for products that are sold into regions with different tax regimes, it can be open to abuse. Profits can be increased in jurisdictions where tax is low, and costs increased where tax rates are high. As this method of transfer-pricing method can be subjective, it may be closely examined by the tax authorities.

Market-based transfer pricing

If a business is operating at full capacity, it will not be prepared to sell to another division at a price that will generate a lower contribution than it makes from its external customers. For example, if the UK division is selling squash racquets for £40 with variable costs of £22, it is making £18 contribution. It will want to make at least £18 contribution from any division. Any extra internal sale will mean a lost sale to an outside customer, so there will be an opportunity cost. In practice, the transfer price is often the market price of the product, which covers this opportunity cost. As there are external prices here that can be used as benchmarks, this method is considered more acceptable by tax authorities.

Terminology

A transfer price is the internal price set for the sale of goods from one division of a business to another. This can be a market-based price, set in line with the external market prices, or a cost-based price, calculated from the internal costs of the business.

Demonstration Exercise 13.8

The UK division of Smart Sports is supplying its sister division in India with a team kit design. The UK's variable costs are £1,250 for a design, which will be used on 500 team kits. However, the UK could charge £2,400 for design costs if they were selling them to external customers.

a) If the UK division has spare capacity, what transfer price should be used when supplying India?

b) If the UK division is working at full capacity, what transfer price should be used when supplying India?

c) If India found an alternative local supplier who would sell them a design at an equivalent cost of £3.75 per team kit, in what circumstances should they agree to buy from the UK?

Ponder Point

What are the benefits of letting each company negotiate its own transfer price? What are the disadvantages of doing this?

Summary of Key Points

- When setting prices, the method of calculating the cost of the product must be considered carefully.
- Companies may use cost-plus or sales-margin methods of calculating the selling price, depending on the nature of their business.
- Marginal costing should be used to set prices only in the short-term and in certain circumstances.
- A full costing method (such as absorption or activity-based costing) should be used for longer-term price setting.
- The wider marketing strategy must be considered when setting prices, including the relationship between price and volume of sales.
- Target costing can be used in competitive situations, driving down costs without compromising product quality.
- The profitability of products must be considered throughout the life of a product.
- Careful consideration needs to be given to setting transfer prices between different divisions so that the business maximizes its return but each division is appropriately rewarded.

Smart Questions: a wider perspective

1. When setting selling prices, what conflicting issues should be considered?
2. How should competitors be taken into account when determining pricing strategy?
3. Which costing methods should be used in assessing product profitability?
4. What wider considerations should be taken into account when setting transfer prices between divisions, particularly those in different countries?

Wider Reading

Scarlett, B. (2004) *Opportunity Knocks*, **CIMA Insider, April 2004, available from the CIMA (Chartered Institute of Management Accountants) website www.cimaglobal.com.** Provides a more detailed explanation of transfer pricing.

Practice Questions

13.1 Tatiana

Tatiana runs a Russian fashion accessory business and would like to know the selling price of her outfits. Based on the following cost of sales and cost-plus assumptions, calculate the selling price of:

a) a belt with a cost of sales of 800 rubles and mark-up of 25%

b) a handbag with a cost of sales of 1,500 rubles and mark-up of 40%

c) a scarf with a cost of sales of 1,200 rubles and mark-up of 30%.

Her supplier, Timur, needs to make certain sales margins on the following items. Calculate his selling price to Tatiana for:

d) a hat with a cost of sales of 630 rubles and a sales-margin of 30%

e) gloves with a cost of sales of 330 rubles and a sales-margin of 40%

f) a wrap with a cost of sales of 525 rubles and a sales-margin of 25%.

13.2 Nickolai

Nickolai sells outdoor clothing through his Russian retail outlet. He can sell the following goods at certain sales prices. Calculate his cost of sales if he is to achieve this for:

a) a raincoat with a selling price of 4,000 rubles and mark-up of 32%

b) a hat with a selling price of 1,200 rubles and mark-up of 25%.

Boris, one of his customers, is negotiating over his prices to Nickolai. Calculate the following:

c) Boris would like a discount of 15% on a pair of gloves with a selling price of 600 rubles.

d) If wellington boots have a retail price of 1,500 rubles, and Boris wishes to have a discount of 25%, what will Nickolai's price be to Boris?

13.3 St Pierre

St Pierre is a Canadian company that cans certain food products such as tuna. With a worldwide overcapacity in the food-canning market, pricing is very competitive. Although St Pierre sells its tuna under a brand name, it has been approached by a large European supermarket to supply tuna under their own label. Current costs per 1,000 cans are shown in Table 13.5.

Table 13.5

St Pierre tuna	
	C$
Tuna	180
Additional materials	20
Can	15
Label	5
Direct labour	105
Production overheads	85

St Pierre would have to invest C$200,000 in a new labelling machine to meet the specific requirements of the supermarket. Production overheads are absorbed on machine hours and are not variable. All other costs vary with volume. The supermarket has offered a contract for 500,000 cans at a price of C$0.70 per can for the next six months but would consider increasing it to one million cans if the price reduced to C$0.63 per can. Delivery would be in bulk and cost C$35,000 for 500,000 cans and C$50,000 for one million cans. Future sales are likely to be one million cans per annum, but these are not guaranteed until the first contract has been completed. Advise St Pierre on its decision.

Chapter Fourteen
Short-term Decision-making
Decision time

Learning Objectives

At the end of this topic, you should be able to:

- understand which costs are relevant in short-term decision-making
- assess whether an organization should make or buy products
- decide which products should be prioritized if there are limited resources
- assess whether upgrading a process would be financially beneficial
- determine whether a product should be discontinued or a location closed.

Introduction

In Chapter 13, we saw how different methods of costing should be used for different kinds of decision-making. It compared absorption and activity-based costing, which attempt to spread fixed costs fairly across all products, with marginal or variable costing. We have also seen in Chapter 10 how marginal costing can be used to evaluate the break-even point in a business. In this chapter, we will look at other applications of marginal costing in short-term decision-making. In particular, we will consider which costs are 'relevant' in making decisions.

Case Study
Evaluating business opportunities

Sam and his team take a day away from the office to consider expansion plans for Smart Sports. Juan, the marketing manager, has a vision of building a stronger brand through advertising campaigns. Anna, the production supervisor, has investigated hiring other machines to extend the Smart range of sports equipment. Nina has been negotiating a team kit contract with the British Olympic football team. Meanwhile, Sam wants to make sure they take sensible business decisions that do not undermine Smart Sports' success to date. They might even need to think about closing down some less successful parts of the business. Sam needs to analyse each project very carefully, assessing which types of cost need to be taken into account.

What are relevant revenue and costs?

When faced with a key decision, managers need to assess *which* costs they should consider. Some costs will be relevant to the decision, but others will not. We have seen how some decisions take into account variable costs only, such as setting a price for a special order. As the fixed costs were not going to change, whether or not the order was accepted, they did not need to be considered. They were not relevant to the decision.

Decision-making is about looking to the *future* and assessing the impact that a decision will have on the *cash* position of the business as a whole. Decision-making is about change. Relevant revenue and costs are those that are incurred as a direct result of a specific decision. They will be the extra or *incremental* costs and revenues that would not have been received or spent if the decision had not been made.

On the other hand, some costs will not change and so do not need to be taken into account. Any costs that have already been incurred are not relevant to the decision and are called *sunk* costs. Similarly, those costs that have been *committed* are considered non-relevant. Whatever decision is made, the commitment will have to be paid for. *Non-cash* items, such as depreciation, head office charges, or allocated costs, will not change the cash position of the business and must also be considered non-relevant.

Terminology

A relevant cost is one that results from a specific management decision and will affect the future cash position of the business by incurring incremental costs.

A relevant revenue is one that results from a specific management decision and will affect the future cash position of the business by the receipt of incremental revenue.

Non-relevant revenue or costs are those that remain unchanged following a specific management decision.

A sunk cost is one that has already been spent and is not a relevant cost as it will not change as a result of a management decision.

A committed cost is one that has to be paid for, whether or not management make a specific decision. It is a non-relevant cost.

Often decisions involve choosing between alternative courses of action. If a decision means that you cannot pursue another course of action, there is an opportunity cost to making that decision. For example, accepting a special order may mean that the business cannot take on another order. The contribution from the latter order should be considered to be an opportunity cost, as there would be a loss of the benefit that would otherwise be gained from accepting the latter order.

Terminology

An opportunity cost is the amount of benefit lost when a certain course of action is taken. This is a relevant cost for decision-making purposes.

Demonstration Exercise 14.1

Juan is very keen to run a major marketing campaign to support the Smart brand name. Until now, Smart Sports has used trade newspapers and the internet to advertise its kits and racquets, but Juan is now proposing to run a radio campaign. He has already spent £50,000 on production costs and is committed to radio slots in two regions at a cost of £10,000. He is considering whether to pay for three further regional slots. It has been forecast that the campaign will increase racquet sales, making a total contribution of £100,000. By running a radio campaign, the business will not be able to run a series of newspaper advertisements from which it had hoped to generate an additional £25,000 contribution. Nina helps Juan to assess whether it is financially beneficial to pay for the further three regional slots at £5,000 each. What will Nina advise?

Demonstration Exercise 14.1 – solution

Table 14.1

Marketing campaign: assessing relevant costs			
Relevant revenue	Contribution from increased sales	Relevant	£100,000
Relevant costs	£15,000 for three regional slots	Relevant	£(15,000)
Sunk cost	£50,000 production costs	Non-relevant	£nil
Committed cost	£10,000 regional slot cost	Non-relevant	£nil
Opportunity cost	Loss of contribution from newspaper campaign	Relevant	£(25,000)

Nina advises Juan that he should continue with the campaign, as relevant revenues of £100,000 exceed relevant costs of £40,000 (£15,000 + £25,000) (see Table 14.1).

Ponder Point

If Juan had not spent the money on production or committed to the radio slots, what would be Nina's advice?

Demonstration Exercise 14.2

Nina has been asked to assess the financial viability of a contract to supply the British football team with 20 sets of kit for the Olympic games, which would generate £75,000 of sales revenue. She has already had preliminary discussions with the Olympic committee and had to provide football kit samples at a cost of £2,400. Nina would buy-in each basic kit for £1,575 but print and add logos for the

Olympic team, using materials costing £50 per kit. Her production supervisor, Anna, would have to take on temporary labour, costing £15,700 to meet the extra demand. She would dedicate one existing supervisor, who is currently under-utilized, to oversee the project and whose salary for the period is £17,500. To cope with the specific logo designs, they would need to hire special equipment at a cost of £3,400. They could use their existing printing machine for much of the work at a depreciation charge of £2,700. Anna has also warned that they would have to turn down a tennis kit contract with an expected contribution of £15,200 should they accept the Olympic one. There would be an allocated charge to cover office costs of £3,200 on the Olympic contract.

Using Table 14.2, assess which revenues and costs are relevant to the decision. Then compare the relevant costs to the relevant revenues to assess its financial feasibility. Should Smart Sports go ahead with the Olympic contract?

Table 14.2

Olympic contract: assessing relevant costs			
	Detail	**Relevant/ non-relevant**	**Total relevant revenue/(costs) £**
Revenue	Contract value of supplying football team kits		
	Tennis kit contract		
Cost	Samples provided to secure contract		
	Hire of logo machine		
	Cost of basic kits		
	Cost of logo materials		
	Depreciation on printing machine		
	Temporary labour		
	Supervisor		
	Allocated office costs		
Net benefit/(cost)			

Make or buy decisions

Businesses may face choices over whether they make all the products they sell themselves or whether to buy-in some of them directly from suppliers. They may have expertise in certain areas of manufacturing but need other products, outside their experience, to complete a range for their customers. They may choose to buy-in components for their final product rather than manufacturing the components themselves. In these cases, the relevant costs of manufacturing must be compared to those of buying the product from a third-party supplier. As the revenue generated will be the same in both cases, this can be ignored. Similarly, the overhead allocation cost will be non-relevant as the fixed overheads of the business will not change in the short-term as a result of manufacturing or buying in the products.

Demonstration Exercise 14.3

Anna proposes to expand the range of sports equipment offered by Smart Sports. She would like to add hockey sticks, table-tennis bats, and cricket bats to the racquet collection. She is unsure whether it would be better to buy them in from another supplier or hire machines to make them themselves. She expects that the annual equipment hire will cost £5,000 to make hockey sticks, £9,000 to make table-tennis bats, and £8,000 to make cricket bats. Estimates for raw material and labour costs are set out in Table 14.3. Anna has quotations from other suppliers, should they choose to buy them in.

Table 14.3

Sports equipment: make or buy decision			
	Hockey sticks	Table-tennis bats	Cricket bats
Sales demand per annum (units)	5,000	18,000	2,000
Sales price per unit	£45	£8	£70
Bought-in price per unit	£38	£5	£52
Raw materials per unit	£22	£2	£32
Variable labour costs per unit	£10	£0.50	£18
Overhead allocation per unit	£4	£4	£4

Demonstration Exercise 14.3 – solution

To assess the financial viability of each product, the relevant costs of manufacturing need to be compared to the relevant costs of buying each product from a supplier. The cost of hiring equipment will be an incremental cost, so will have to be divided by the estimated sales demand. What sports equipment should Smart Sports buy-in, and what should they make themselves?

Table 14.4

Sports equipment: make or buy decision			
Per unit	**Hockey sticks**	**Table-tennis bats**	**Cricket bats**
Raw materials	£22	£2	£32
Variable labour costs	£10	£0.50	£18
Equipment hire	£1 (£5,000 ÷ 5,000)	£0.50	£4
Unit cost to make	**£33**	**£3**	**£54**
Unit cost to buy	**£38**	**£5**	**£52**

As Table 14.4 shows, Smart Sports should make hockey sticks and table-tennis bats but buy-in cricket bats. The overhead should not be included in these calculations, as it is an allocated cost.

Ponder Point

If the sales forecasts for the new equipment had been underestimated, what impact would this have on this make/buy analysis?

Demonstration Exercise 14.4

Smart Sports has relied on its own staff to manage all aspects of its business. However, it has grown sufficiently large to consider how best to manage certain support functions. Sam is considering whether he should employ an IT specialist to implement and maintain a new integrated software package or whether he should simply buy-in the expertise from consultants when he requires it. He estimates that the costs of employing a specialist would include a salary of £60,000 and a contribution to the pension fund of £5,000. To carry out the work, the specialist would require training on three courses per year at £500 each, use of the telephone of £200, and travel expenses of £500. The specialist would also be able to cover work currently carried out under contract, for which they pay £11,500 per annum. Nina estimates that it costs £1,500 on average for every member of staff to use the space in the office (covering rent, heating, and canteen) but that they would not need to increase the work space if the specialist joined them.

Nina has also investigated contract consultancy costs and estimated that they would need to hire an IT consultant for 34 weeks at £50 per hour with a working week of 35 hours, in addition to the existing contract.

a) Should Smart Sports employ a specialist or buy-in consultancy advice when they need it?

b) What other considerations should be taken into account before making the final decision over which products to make and which to buy-in?

Limiting factors

If a business is growing fast, it may be faced with not being able to meet all its sales demand. A number of constraints may limit how much it can produce. It could be the capacity of a machine, the supply of a certain raw material, or the availability of skilled labour. These are examples of 'limiting factors', and in any of these circumstances it is important that managers make the appropriate decisions about which product or service is restricted, so that the maximum contribution is made. It is not sufficient just to assess the contribution per unit of each product. Different products may use different quantities of the limiting factor. For example, a product may make the highest contribution but also take up most time on the production line. To carry out a comprehensive analysis, the following steps need to be taken:

1. Calculate the contribution per unit.
2. Calculate the usage of limiting factor per unit, such as quantity of raw material, labour hours, or machine time.
3. Divide the contribution by the limiting factor. This will show the contribution per limiting factor for each product.
4. Prioritize the products according to their contribution per limiting factor.
5. Calculate how much each product uses of the limiting factor, starting with the highest priority product.

Demonstration Exercise 14.5

The launch of the squash racquet has been so successful that the frame machines are being used to their full capacity of 1,400 hours for three months. Nina calculates which racquets should take priority until they can install another frame machine (see Table 14.5).

Table 14.5

Frame machine: limiting factor			
	Tennis racquet	**Badminton racquet**	**Squash racquet**
Potential racquet sales for next three mouths	3,000 racquets	2,100 racquets	1,500 racquets
Selling price per racquet	£35.00	£40.00	£42.00
Material costs per unit	£13.00	£11.00	£10.50
Variable labour costs per unit	£9.50	£15.00	£12.00
Contribution per racquet	£12.50	£14.00	£19.50
Machine time per racquet	0.25 hours	0.25 hours	0.4 hours
Contribution per machine hour	£50.00	£56.00	£48.75

Once the contribution per limiting factor has been calculated, the racquets can be put into order of priority—badminton, tennis, and then squash. Even though the squash racquet makes a larger contribution per unit, it takes up more time on the machine, so its contribution per machine hour is less than the other racquets. We can now calculate how many racquets should be made to maximize contribution.

Demonstration Exercise 14.5—solution

Table 14.6 shows that we can make sufficient tennis and badminton racquets to meet the sales demand but that we can make only 312 squash racquets (125 hours/0.4 hours per squash racquet) before reaching the full capacity of the frame machine.

Table 14.6

Frame machine: limiting factor			
	Tennis racquet	**Badminton racquet**	**Squash racquet**
Priority	2	1	3
Machine time per racquet	0.25 hours	0.25 hours	0.4 hours
Potential racquet sales for next three months	3,000 racquets	2,100 racquets	1,500 racquets
Machine time required	750 hours	525 hours	600 hours
Optimum use of machine hours for next three months	750 hours	525 hours	125 hours (1,400 – 750 – 525)
Optimum number of racquets	3,000	2,100	310

Demonstration Exercise 14.6

Anna has been told that racquet string will be in short supply owing to distribution problems. As they have now installed a new machine increasing frame capacity, there is no limitation on the number of racquet frames they can produce. Using Table 14.7, advise Anna on which racquets should now take priority, given a limited supply of string. They are expected to have 6,200 metres of string until further supplies can be delivered.

Table 14.7

String: limiting factor			
	Tennis racquet	**Badminton racquet**	**Squash racquet**
Sales demand for next month	1,250 racquets	600 racquets	500 racquets
Contribution per unit	£12.50	£14.00	£19.50
String required per racquet	3.6 metres	3.0 metres	2.8 metres
Contribution per unit			
Production priority			
String usage			
Optimum number of racquets			

Upgrading equipment

Businesses may face choices about how far to upgrade their processes to make cost savings. They need to balance increasing fixed costs against savings in variable costs. This can be assessed in the short-term by using a variation of the break-even equation. To calculate how many units need to be sold, the additional fixed costs can be divided by the variable-cost savings per unit. In Chapter 10, we used the following equation to calculate the break-even point:

$$\text{Break-even (in units)} = \frac{\text{Fixed costs}}{\text{Contribution per unit}}$$

This can be extended to assess the number of units which would need to be processed to justify the increased fixed costs as a result of upgrading the business's processes.

$$\text{Number of units} = \frac{\text{Additional fixed costs}}{\text{Savings in variable costs per unit}}$$

Demonstration Exercise 14.7

Anna has been looking at how her products are labelled before despatch. Currently, this is a labour-intensive process, with every product being labelled manually. While a fully automated packing and labelling machine would be too costly, she is considering buying small hand-held labelling machines to speed up the process. By purchasing one labelling machine for £200, she estimates that she would save one labour hour for every 1,800 products. Based on her current budget, labour costs are £11.50 per hour, and total estimated sales units for the year are 40,000.

Demonstration Exercise 14.7 – solution

By dividing the savings in labour cost per hour by the number of products labelled per hour, Anna can calculate the cost saving per unit (£11.50/1,800). She will therefore save £0.0064 for every product labelled. By dividing the cost of the labelling machine by this figure, Anna can see that she needs to label 31,250 products to break-even (£200/£0.0064 = 31,250 units). By comparing this with her budgeted sales units of 40,000, she finds that it would be worthwhile to purchase a labelling machine.

Demonstration Exercise 14.8

Lee, one of Smart Sports' clothing suppliers, is considering upgrading his cutting equipment. Currently, he has a manually intensive cutting process, but this could be more efficient with new cutting tools. Patterns are laid onto the material, and then ten layers of material are cut by hand before the garments are made on sewing machines. Each tool would cost £750 and would save ten minutes for every set of ten garments. He employs staff at a rate of £8.50 per hour. How many garments will he need to cut in his first year in order to break-even?

Closure of sites or discontinuing products

Marginal costing techniques can also be used to assess whether products should be discontinued, factories closed, or other operations shut down. In each case, only the relevant revenues and costs should be considered. These must be future cash costs that change as a result of the decision taken. If a product or operation is discontinued, allocated costs are unlikely to be saved but will be shared out between the remaining operations. Therefore, they should be considered as non-relevant costs and not be taken into account.

Many businesses analyse the profitability of their products, retail outlets, or operations, in a profitability statement. This usually includes some kind of allocation of fixed costs. To assess whether a product, retail outlet, or operation should be closed down, this should be reformatted into a contribution analysis, showing what each operation contributes to the overhead of the business as a whole.

Demonstration Exercise 14.9

Sam reviews the performance of his Indian operation with Raja. Their Indian retail business has been very successful overall, but some of the shops have been less successful than others. They consider the profitability of each shop to decide whether they should close those that are not performing so well. Raja runs his operation from a head office in Delhi, costs of which are charged out to stores in proportion to their sales revenue. Based on the information in Table 14.8, which shops should Raja and Sam consider closing and why?

Table 14.8

Indian branches: profitability analysis			
	Mumbai million rupees	**Delhi million rupees**	**Calcutta million rupees**
Sales revenue	31.5	52.2	21.0
Cost of goods sold	12.6	21.0	8.4
Rent of shop	4.4	6.5	5.2
Shop staff	3.5	3.8	3.3
Other shop expenses	4.2	5.1	3.0
Head office allocation	4.5	7.5	2.3
Shop profit/(loss)	2.3	8.3	(1.2)

Demonstration Exercise 14.9 – solution

To assess the viability of each shop, only those costs that will be saved as a result of closure are relevant. Although Calcutta looks as if it makes a loss, once the allocated costs are removed, it still makes a contribution. This takes into account sales revenue less cost of goods sold and other shop expenses but excludes head office costs (see Table 14.9). If Calcutta is closed, the head office costs will not be saved but will have to be shared between Mumbai and Delhi. No shop should be closed.

Table 14.9

Indian branches: contribution analysis			
	Mumbai million rupees	**Delhi million rupees**	**Calcutta million rupees**
Sales revenue	31.5	52.2	21.0
Cost of goods sold	12.6	21.0	8.4
Total shop expenses that would be saved on closure	12.1 (4.4 + 3.5 + 4.2)	15.4	11.5
Contribution per shop	6.8	15.8	1.1

Terminology

A profitability analysis looks at the profitability of a sector of the business, such as its products or operations. This usually includes an allocation of shared costs.

A contribution analysis looks at what each sector of the business contributes to the overheads. This excludes any allocated fixed costs.

Demonstration Exercise 14.10

Danni is reviewing the profitability of his range of drinks. He is considering discontinuing his energy drink products as they look unprofitable. Manufacturing costs are allocated on a volume-basis, and advertising costs and other expenses on the basis of sales. By closing the energy drink production line, he estimates that he would save €5,230 of utility costs and €13,450 of supervisory costs. His advertising costs largely promote the Danni's Drinks brand, but he would save €3,250 by not running advertisements in sports magazines. Using Table 14.10, what would you advise Danni to do?

Table 14.10

Danni's Drinks: cost data				
	Original €	Energy €	Sugar-free €	Total €
Sales	252,500	56,320	130,260	439,080
Cost of goods sold	101,000	34,918	58,617	194,535
Manufacturing	103,765	13,887	40,148	157,800
Advertising	31,226	6,965	16,109	54,300
Other expenses	26,022	5,804	13,424	45,250

Ponder Point

What other factors should Danni consider before discontinuing the energy range of products? How might he improve its contribution in other ways?

Summary of Key Points

- Marginal costing techniques can be used to assess short-term decisions.
- Relevant costs should include only future, cash, and incremental expenses.
- Opportunity costs, which equal the benefit lost through taking an alternative decision, are a relevant cost and should also be taken into consideration.
- Sunk and committed costs are non-relevant costs, as they will be incurred irrespective of the decision.
- Where supply of a key resource is limited, production should not be prioritized by the contribution made by each unit. Instead, the contribution per limiting factor must be calculated.

Smart Questions: a wider perspective

1. How can management improve the quality of decision-making?
2. For how long will fixed costs remain as fixed costs? Will they then be considered relevant or non-relevant?
3. Can qualitative factors in short-term decision-making ever be measured financially?

Wider Reading

Steven, G. (2005) 'Management accounting—decision management', *Financial Management*, July/August 2005, CIMA London. From the professional body for management accountants in the UK, this article discusses the limitations of marginal costing.

Practice Questions

14.1 Brookes

Brookes Ltd is a market research company providing data to consumer goods companies about the markets in which they operate. In order to tender for a contract, they have undertaken some initial research for a personal-product manufacturer, costing £10,000. As the bidding process has been competitive, their fee has been set at £75,000. They have employed a market researcher on a temporary basis, with a salary of £5,000 per month. This can be terminated if the contract is turned down, but if they continue, it is expected that the researcher will stay for six more months.

To undertake this project, they will need to purchase specialist software for £15,000 and will incur processing costs of £8,000, including IT, stationery, printing, and postage. They will be able to use existing staff to carry out interviews but will lose the contribution from another project of £14,000. The project will be charged with a cost to cover general overheads, calculated at 10% of fee income.

REQUIRED:

Assess whether they should they go ahead with the research project, by identifying the relevant revenue and costs and determining the net benefit or loss.

14.2 Carlos

Carlos, an Italian ice cream manufacturer, is considering extending his product range to include frozen yogurt, boxes of frozen chocolates, and sorbets. He could either buy in products made to his specification or consider manufacturing them himself. If he manufactures them, he would have to buy additional equipment for each product range. All manufactured products will be charged with 10% of sales revenue to cover the overheads of the business.

REQUIRED:

Use the data in Table 14.11 to assess which products he should buy-in or make himself:

Table 14.11

New frozen products: make or buy analysis			
	Yogurt	**Boxes of chocolates**	**Sorbet**
Sales demand per annum	1.0m units	1.25m units	2.0m units
Sales price per 100 units	€150	€225	€80
Equipment cost	€250,000	€350,000	€125,000
Bought-in price per 100 units	€95	€150	€60
Raw materials per 100 units	€30	€50	€20
Variable labour costs per 100 units	€20	€50	€10
Distribution cost per 100 units	€15	€30	€11.75
Allocation of overhead—10% of sales	€15	€22.5	€8

14.3 Fleur

Fleur runs a bookshop and is reviewing the profitability of her product sales. She allocates the rent and staff costs on a sales revenue basis, but promotional expenses are directly incurred by each product group. If she were to discontinue any of her product lines, she would be able to save some rent of £50,000 by sub-leasing the space out to a coffee shop. She would also save the cost of two part-time members of staff, at a cost of £25,000 per year.

Table 14.12

Book product group: revenue and cost data			
£	Adult	Children	Educational
Sales revenue	746,000	568,000	342,000
Cost of goods sold	373,000	430,800	102,600
Rent of shop	148,659	113,187	68,154
Shop staff	33,786	25,724	15,490
Promotional expenses	22,500	42,500	10,200

REQUIRED:

Using the information in Table 14.12, calculate the profitability by product group and then compare it to a contribution analysis to assess which product group should be discontinued.

Chapter Fifteen
Investment Appraisal Techniques

Smart4sport.com

Learning Objectives

At the end of this topic, you should be able to:

- discuss the nature and significance of appraising long-term investments
- use a range of investment appraisal techniques to assess and compare projects
- understand the advantages and limitations of each method.

Introduction

Longer-term decision-making is often particularly important to businesses because they tend to involve large capital outlays that will benefit the business over a number of years. To evaluate a particular project, it is necessary to forecast future costs and revenues, often for many years ahead. Making the right decision is important as, once the decision to proceed with a particular project has been made, it is usually impossible to reverse it.

Case Study
Building the online business

Since the company was formed a number of years ago, Smart Sports Ltd has had a website, initially developed for the business by Dot. It shows a range of the company's products and allows customers to order online. The order is then processed by one of the company's stores.

As the volume of internet orders have been steadily increasing, the number of queries and emails that have to be processed has grown hugely. Sam has been exploring the best way to grow this area of the business and has engaged a firm of management consultants to carry out a feasibility study. They have advised Smart Sports to establish a purpose-built automated warehouse to deal with internet orders, alongside a professionally developed website. This proposal will involve the business in a large capital outlay, and Sam is keen to assess the project carefully before deciding to go ahead with it.

Investment appraisal techniques

There are four well-established techniques for assessing possible long-term investment proposals:

- accounting rate of return
- payback period
- net present value
- internal rate of return.

Whichever of the techniques is employed, only the relevant costs should be taken into account. Sunk costs and committed costs are not relevant to the decision and should be excluded from the cash flows and profit calculations (see Chapter 14).

Accounting rate of return

The **accounting rate of return** (ARR) measures the average annual profit for a project expressed as a return on the average funds invested in the project:

$$ARR = \frac{\text{Average annual operating profit}}{\text{Average amount invested in the project}} \times 100\%$$

Demonstration Exercise 15.1

Table 15.1 shows figures taken from the management consultants' report prepared for Smart Sports Ltd into the launch of the new internet site and warehouse, identifying the forecast costs and profits associated with the project.

Table 15.1

The Smart Online Project		
Timing		**£'000**
Already paid	Cost of website development	25
At start	Cost of building and equipping the warehouse	2,000
After one year	Operating profit from online sales, before depreciation	350
After two years	Operating profit from online sales, before depreciation	675
After three years	Operating profit from online sales, before depreciation	1,200
After four years	Operating profit from online sales, before depreciation	850
After five years	Operating profit from online sales, before depreciation	550
After five years	Sale of warehouse	400

In order to simplify any appraisals, it will be assumed that all profits arise on the last day of a given year. The operating profits given in Table 15.1 exclude any depreciation that would be charged on the warehouse and website software.

Using the figures for the Smart Online project shown in Table 15.1, we can calculate the ARR for the project.

Demonstration Exercise 15.1 – solution

To find the average annual operating profit, the depreciation charge must be computed. If depreciation is charged on the straight-line basis, the charge will be £320,000 (£320k) per annum.

$$\text{Depreciation per annum} = \frac{\text{Cost less residual value}}{\text{Estimated useful life}} = \frac{£2{,}000k - £400k}{5 \text{ years}}$$

$$= £320k$$

The average annual profit will then be as shown in Table 15.2.

Table 15.2

Year 1	Operating profit after depreciation (£350k – £320k)	£30k
Year 2	Operating profit after depreciation (£675k – £320k)	£355k
Year 3	Operating profit after depreciation (£1,200k – £320k)	£880k
Year 4	Operating profit after depreciation (£850k – £320k)	£530k
Year 5	Operating profit after depreciation (£550k – £320k)	£230k
	Average for the five years (30k + 355k + 880k + 530k + 230k)/5	**£405k**

$$\text{Average amount invested in the project} = \frac{\text{Cost of project} + \text{residual value}}{2}$$

$$= \frac{(£2{,}000k + £400k)}{2}$$

$$= £1{,}200k$$

$$\textbf{ARR} = \frac{\mathbf{405}}{\mathbf{1{,}200}} \times \mathbf{100\% = 34\%}$$

Note that the amount of £25k that has already been spent on developing the website is not included in this analysis, as it represents a sunk cost.

The decision rule for ARR is that a project should be accepted if it can achieve the target ARR for the business. Where there is more than one project and not all possible projects can be undertaken, then the project or projects giving the greatest ARR should be chosen.

Ponder Point

Do you think that Sam should consider proceeding with the Smart Online project, based on the ARR calculated above? With what should Sam compare the ARR to decide whether it is acceptable?

Case Study
The bottles project

Sam and Danni, from Danni's Drinks, have been long-standing friends and are considering a joint venture to produce and sell lightweight, shatterproof water bottles that can be personalized for teams and individuals by the use of a heat moulding machine. The machine can mould logos and names permanently onto a thick reusable plastic bottle. It is anticipated that demand will be high from sports teams and individuals and for use by children, who frequently damage or lose bottles. The heat moulding machines are very easy to use, but as it is a new technology, they are expensive.

Demonstration Exercise 15.2

Initially, the bottle moulding machines will be installed in three new mobile outlets.

The cost of the moulding machines will be £1.5 million in total, and they will have a life of four years, at the end of which time they will have a scrap value of £100,000. Forecast outlays and profits from the project are shown in Table 15.3.

Table 15.3

The bottles project		
Time		**£'000**
In previous year	Cost of the time spent and the expenses incurred by Danni and Sam while researching this venture	40
At start	Cost of moulding machines	1,500
At start	Grant from The Ten Green Trust, who would support this project because of its positive environmental impact (non-refundable grant)*	200
After one year	Operating profit from bottle sales, before depreciation	360
After two years	Operating profit from bottle sales, before depreciation	550
After three years	Operating profit from bottle sales, before depreciation	710
After four years	Operating profit from bottle sales, before depreciation	340
After four years	Scrap value of machines	100

* The grant can be deducted from the cost of the moulding machines.

Danni and Sam currently achieve an average return on capital employed in their existing businesses of 21%.

Calculate the ARR for the bottles project, and advise Danni and Sam on whether they should consider proceeding further with this project.

Limitations of ARR

There are three major limitations of ARR.

1. ARR takes no account of the timing of the profit flows. Two very different projects, one where the most significant profits arise in year one, and the other where the most significant profits arise in year four, could give the same ARR. Logically, most managers would prefer the project that gives the greatest profits in the first year.
2. ARR ignores the time value of money. Where there is any sort of inflation, then £500 received now will always be worth more than £500 received next year and much more than £500 received in a few years' time. The ARR merely adds together all of the profits made to arrive at an average, ignoring the real value of each year's profits.
3. ARR could lead to the wrong project being chosen if only the ARR is considered and not the actual amount of the expected profits. It would be possible for a project to give the greatest ARR but, because of the project's size, for it to yield lower actual profits than an alternative project.

Payback period

The payback period is the length of time that the cash inflows from a project will take to cover the initial investment.

Ponder Point

In order to arrive at an approximate figure for the cash flows arising in a business, the figure for profit before depreciation is often used. Can you explain why it is necessary to exclude depreciation?

Demonstration Exercise 15.3

If we refer again to the cash flows that will arise from the Smart Online project, we can determine the payback period for that project.

Demonstration Exercise 15.3 – solution

The initial outlay for this project is £2,000k. In each subsequent year, the project will generate positive cash flows, and we can find the cumulative cash flows, as shown in Table 15.4.

Table 15.4

The Smart Online project			
	Cash inflow/ (outflow) £'000	**Cumulative cash flow £'000**	**Working £'000**
At start	(2,000)	(2,000)	
After one year	350	(1,650)	(2,000) + 350
After two years	675	(975)	(1,650) + 675
After three years	1,200	225	(975) + 1,200
After four years	850	1,075	225 + 850
After five years	950	2,025	1,075 + 950

After three years, the cumulative cash flows are positive for the first time (at £225k), showing that the payback period has been reached.

If we assume that the cash flows arise evenly over the course of each year, we can find the payback period to the nearest month as follows:

$$\text{Payback period} = 2 \text{ years} + \frac{975}{1{,}200} \times 12 \text{ months}$$

$$= 2 \text{ years and } 10 \text{ months}$$

The decision rule for using the payback period is that a project should be accepted if the payback period for the project is within the limits set by the business. Where there is more than one possible project under consideration and not all possible projects can be undertaken, then the project or projects giving the shortest payback period should be chosen.

Demonstration Exercise 15.4

Forecast cash outflows and inflows from the bottles project are shown in Table 15.5.

Table 15.5

The bottles project		
Time		**£'000**
At start	Cost of moulding machines, less grant	1,300
After one year	Cash inflow from bottle sales	360
After two years	Cash inflow from bottle sales	550
After three years	Cash inflow from bottle sales	710
After four years	Cash inflow from bottle sales	340
After four years	Scrap value of machines	100

Danni and Sam have agreed a target payback period of three years.

Calculate the payback period for the bottles project, and advise Danni and Sam on whether they should consider proceeding further with this project.

Ponder Point

Can you think of any advantages of using the payback period as an investment appraisal technique?

Limitations of the payback period

There are significant limitations to using the payback period as an investment appraisal technique:

1. The payback period takes no account of the cash flows that are expected to occur after the payback point has been reached.
2. The payback period ignores the actual timing of the cash flows. For example, the two projects in Table 15.6 would have the same payback period of three years. Clearly, any logical person would choose project 1, where the majority of the expected cash inflows are expected to occur in year 1.

3. Just as with the ARR, the payback period does not recognize the time value of money (that is, that cash received now is worth more than cash received in the future).

Table 15.6

Time	Project 1 Cash inflows/ (outflows)	Project 2 Cash inflows/ (outflows)
Year 0	£(20,000)	£(20,000)
Year 1	£15,000	£2,000
Year 2	£3,000	£3,000
Year 3	£2,000	£15,000

Terminology

Accounting rate of return (ARR) is an investment appraisal technique to calculate the average profit from a project given as a percentage of the average investment in the project.

The payback period is the length of time that the cash inflows from a project will take to cover the initial cash outlays.

Net present value

The net present value (NPV) technique of evaluating investments does not have the same limitations as ARR and the payback period, as the NPV method *does* take into account all of the cash flows and allows for the time value of money. It is the most meaningful method of assessing capital projects.

The NPV method recognizes that £500 received in a year's time is of less value to the business than £500 received immediately. There are various reasons for this:

- Income of £500 received immediately can be invested and earn interest over the subsequent year.
- The £500 income received immediately carries less risk than income that is expected to be received in a year's time. There is always the risk that this income may not be received in full if the project does not turn out as expected.

- Where there is inflation, the purchasing power of £500 now will be greater than the purchasing power of £500 in a year's time.

In order to take account of these factors, the NPV method discounts all the cash flows connected with a project, to their present value at the start of the project. The discount rate that a business uses should take into consideration all of the factors listed above.

Discounting to present value

A business that expects to receive £500 in one year's time will know that the true value of this cash flow will be less than if the £500 were received immediately. If the business would expect to be generating a return of 10% from sums invested, then £500 in one year's time will be worth £454.54 now, and this amount is known as the present value:

$$\text{Present value of £500 received in one year's time} = £500 \times \frac{1}{(1+0.10)}$$

$$= £454.54$$

Conversely, it can be shown that, if £454.54 is received now and achieves a return of 10% over the next year, then in one year's time it will have grown to a value of £500.

Future value in one year's time of £454.54 received now
$= £454.54 \times (1 + 0.10) = £500$

Any logical business should therefore be equally happy to receive £454.54 now or £500 in one year's time. If this business expects to receive £1,000 in two years' time:

$$\text{Present value of £1,000 received in two years' time} = £1{,}000 \times 1/(1+0.10)^2$$
$$= £826.45$$

In this case, the business should be equally happy to receive the present value of £826.45 now or £1,000 in two years' time. If the £826.45 is received now and earns a return of 10% over the next two years:

$$\text{Future value after one year of £826.45 received now} = £826.45 \times (1+0.10)$$
$$= £909.09$$

Future value after a second year = £909.09 × (1 + 0.10)
= £1,000

OR

Future value after two years of £826.45 received now
= £826.45 × $(1 + 0.10)^2$ = £1,000.

The NPV technique converts cash flows arising from a project into their present values, so that the amounts are then comparable. By adding together the present values of all of the cash flows associated with a project, the NPV can be found.

The NPV of the Smart Online project can be calculated as shown in Table 15.7.

Table 15.7

The Smart Online project				
		Cash flows	**Present value calculation**	**Present value**
Time		**£'000**		**£'000**
At start	Initial costs	(2,000)	No adjustment necessary	(2,000)
After one year	Net cash flow	350	350 / (1 + 0.1)	318
After two years	Net cash flow	675	675 / $(1 + 0.1)^2$	558
After three years	Net cash flow	1,200	1,200 / $(1 + 0.1)^3$	901
After four years	Net cash flow	850	850 / $(1 + 0.1)^4$	581
After five years	Net cash flow	550	550 / $(1 + 0.1)^5$	342
After five years	Sale of warehouse	400	400 / $(1 + 0.1)^5$	248
Net present value				**948**

Instead of using the workings shown above, a quicker way of arriving at the present values is to make use of discount factor tables, one of which is given at the end of this chapter (Table 15.14). Another useful tool is the NPV function that is available in computer spreadsheet applications.

Table 15.8 shows the NPV calculation for the Smart Online project using discount tables.

Table 15.8

The Smart Online project				
		Cash flows	**Discount factor**	**Present value**
Time		**£'000**		**£'000**
At start	Initial costs	(2,000)	1	(2,000)
After one year	Net cash flow	350	0.91	318
After two years	Net cash flow	675	0.83	560
After three years	Net cash flow	1,200	0.75	900
After four years	Net cash flow	850	0.68	578
After five years	Net cash flow	550	0.62	341
After five years	Sale of warehouse	400	0.62	248
Net present value				945

The small difference between the two NPVs is a rounding difference.

The decision rule for using the NPV technique is that a project should be accepted if it can achieve a positive NPV when the present value of all of the cash flows associated with the project are taken into account. Where there is more than one possible project and not all can be undertaken, then the project or projects giving the greatest NPV should be chosen.

Ponder Point

Refer to the limitations of the ARR technique and decide whether the NPV technique suffers from any of the same limitations.

Internal rate of return

Internal rate of return (IRR) is another technique that takes account of all of a project's cash flows and the time value of money. The IRR of a project is the discount rate that is needed in order for the NPV of all the cash flows to be zero.

If we consider again the Smart Online project, we found that, when a discount rate of 10% is applied to the cash flows, it results in an NPV of £948k. However if a higher discount rate is applied, the NPV of the project falls.

Table 15.9

Discount rate %	NPV £'000
10%	948
15%	562
20%	247
25%	(14)
30%	(232)

From Table 15.9, it is clear that, as the discount rate increases, the NPV falls, such that the NPV is very close to zero when the discount rate is 25%. In other words, the IRR for the Smart Online project is 25%.

The IRR is usually found by applying a variety of discount rates to ascertain which one gives an NPV closest to zero. Sometimes it may be necessary to interpolate between two whole-number discount rates to find the IRR to slightly greater accuracy. The IRR function in computer spreadsheet applications can be used as a quick way of calculating the IRR of a project.

The decision rule for using IRR as an investment appraisal technique is that a project should be accepted if the IRR of a project is greater than the rate of return required by the business for that project. Where there is more than one possible project and not all can be undertaken, then the project or projects yielding the greatest IRR should be chosen. However, if the IRR technique gives a different project choice to the NPV decision, then the project selection arising from the NPV technique should be used.

Ponder Point

It would be possible for two projects that are expected to yield identical IRRs to be very different in size. Is the relative size of a project likely to be of significance to the investment decision?

Demonstration Exercise 15.5

The joint venture that Sam and Danni are considering has the forecast cash outflows and inflows as shown in Table 15.10.

Table 15.10

The bottles project		
Time		**£'000**
At start	Cost of moulding machines, less grant	1,300
After one year	Cash inflow from bottle sales	360
After two years	Cash inflow from bottle sales	550
After three years	Cash inflow from bottle sales	710
After four years	Cash inflow from bottle sales	340
After four years	Scrap value of machines	100

Danni and Sam have agreed that a discount rate of 15% would be required from this project.

Required:

a) Calculate the NPV for the bottles project.

b) Estimate the project's IRR using trial and error.

c) Advise Danni and Sam on whether they should consider proceeding further with this project. Would your advice be different if they required a return of 20%?

Terminology

Present value (PV) is the value today of an amount that will be received in the future. To find the present value of a future cash flow, it has to be discounted using an appropriate discount rate.

Net present value (NPV) is an investment appraisal technique that calculates the present values of all the cash flows associated with a project and, by totalling them, calculates the net present value that a project would be expected to yield.

Internal rate of return (IRR) is the discount rate that, when applied to a project's cash flows, will yield a net present value of zero.

Comparing the techniques

In practice, most businesses will employ a range of investment appraisal techniques to evaluate long-term capital projects, as they all have something to contribute to the decision-making process. ARR is a measure that can easily be compared to the business's return on capital employed. The payback period is very simple to compute, and businesses will be acutely aware that the shorter the payback period, the sooner they will be able to invest in other projects. NPV and IRR are the most meaningful techniques because they consider all of the relevant cash flows and take account of the time value of money.

All of the techniques suffer from the major limitation that capital investment decisions rely on estimates of future cash flows that might involve forecasts for many years into the future.

Demonstration Exercise 15.6

Smart Sports is also planning to launch a range of drinks products. The products have been developed by Hydration Labs Ltd and are designed to be sold as powders that dissolve easily in water. They are based on natural fruit extracts with added vitamin and mineral supplements. Smart Sports have been offered the opportunity to buy the rights to package and sell the drinks under the Smart brand name for a four year period, for the sum of £250,000.

Some market research has been undertaken, and the likely cash flows associated with the project have been forecast as shown in Table 15.11.

Table 15.11

Sports drinks		
Time		**£'000**
Already paid	Market research and forecasting costs	10
At start	Cost of licence to market drinks	250
At start	Costs of designing the packaging plus cost of advertising campaign*	15
After one year	Cash inflow from drink sales	40
After two years	Cash inflow from drink sales	70
After three years	Cash inflow from drink sales	140
After four years	Cash inflow from drink sales	120

* The work on designing the packaging and the advertising campaign will largely be done by the two members of the marketing department at Smart Sports Ltd, both of whom have time available to complete the design. Of the costs, £4,000 will be spent on radio advertisements for the new drinks.

Smart Sports Ltd would usually require a return of between 10% and 15% on projects undertaken, depending on the risk of each project.

Assess this business project for Smart Sports Ltd by calculating its payback period, its net present value, and its internal rate of return. Advise Sam on whether the business should consider going ahead with this project.

Summary of Key Points

- There are four established methods of appraising capital investment projects: accounting rate of return (ARR), payback period, net present value (NPV), and internal rate of return (IRR).
- All of the techniques rely upon the use of forecast cash flows and profits, often for many years into the future.
- Whichever technique is employed, only the relevant cash flows should be included. Sunk costs and committed costs are not relevant to the decision and should be excluded from the cash flows and profits used in the appraisals.
- Accounting rate of return assesses projects by calculating the expected average return that the profits will yield.
- The payback period is the length of time that the cash inflows from a project will take to cover the initial investment.
- The net present value and internal rate of return techniques involve discounting cash flows to take account of the time value of money.
- The net present value technique is the most reliable method of assessing capital investment projects.

Smart Questions: a wider perspective

1. Discuss the sort of non-financial factors that a business should take into consideration when it is appraising a new capital investment project.
2. Given the limitations of the payback period as a method of assessing potential projects, why do you think it is still a commonly used technique in practice?
3. A business appraises its capital investment projects using the NPV method and is currently considering two competing projects. Why should the business not necessarily use the same discount rate in assessing both projects?
4. How could the NPV technique be used to assess the acquisition of a company?

Wider Reading

McLaney, E. (2006) *Business Finance Theory and Practice*, 7th edition, FT Prentice Hall. Chapter 4 gives a comprehensive explanation of discounting and investment appraisal techniques.

Practice Questions

15.1 Juliet

Juliet opened a coffee shop in Paris two years ago. The business has grown steadily, and the shop is frequently so full that some potential customers have to be turned away. She is considering three possible ways of expanding the business:

Option 1: Building an extension to the existing coffee shop.

Option 2: Establishing a canopied terrace area.

Option 3: Opening a second coffee shop in a road a few blocks away from the original shop.

She has researched the various options and has come up with the estimates shown in Table 15.12 for the next five years. Whichever option is chosen, Juliet plans to sell the entire business in five years' time.

Table 15.12

Time		Extension €'000	Terrace €'000	New shop €'000
At start	Cash outflow	(168)	(96)	(247)
Year 1	Cash inflow	51	30	60
Year 2	Cash inflow	56	40	65
Year 3	Cash inflow	61	44	72
Year 4	Cash inflow	63	46	78
Year 5	Cash inflow	68	50	80
Year 5	Extra proceeds on sale of business	110	40	180

Juliet would require a return of at least 12% from any project undertaken.

Assume that the cash flows arise at the end of each year and ignore cash flows arising after this five year period.

REQUIRED:

a) Calculate the payback period for each of the three options.

b) Calculate the accounting rate of return for each of the options if the average investment required for each option is as follows:

Extension	€140,000
Terrace	€70,000
New shop	€215,000

Depreciation would be charged on the straight-line basis on all of the projects.

c) Calculate the net present value for each of the options.

d) Interpret your findings for parts (a) to (c).

e) If Juliet would like to proceed with no more than one of the projects, advise her as to which of the options, if any, she should choose based on your appraisals. Discuss other factors that Juliet should take into account in her decision-making.

15.2 Bryd Ltd

Bryd Ltd runs a chain of five small supermarkets in Wales specializing in the sale of local produce. The supermarkets have been doing well in recent years, and the company has funds available to invest in a new project. The board of directors is considering three possible projects:

1. **Farmer support**

   This project would involve investing in local farmers by providing them with expert consultancy advice to enable them to produce food more efficiently. This would bring some benefits to Bryd Ltd as participating farms would offer a significant discount to the company on future supplies.

2. **Good-food café**

   This project would set-up cafés at two of the supermarkets, offering drinks and snacks to shoppers throughout the supermarkets' opening hours.

3. **Art and craft gallery**

   This project would involve setting up a gallery attached to Bryd's biggest supermarket, to sell paintings, ceramics, and other crafts made by Welsh artists.

The finance director has used some investment appraisal techniques on the figures, the results of which are shown in Table 15.13.

Table 15.13

	Payback period	ARR (%)	NPV (£'000)
Farmer support	5 years	8	78
Good-food café	3 years	15	150
Art and craft gallery	4 years	12	195

REQUIRED:

a) Explain what is meant by payback period, ARR, and NPV.

b) Advise the board of Bryd as to which of the projects they should consider proceeding with.

c) Outline other factors that they might consider.

DISCOUNT FACTOR TABLE

Table 15.14

Discount factor table									
	Discount rates								
Years	2%	5%	7%	10%	12%	15%	17%	20%	25%
1	0.98	0.95	0.93	0.91	0.89	0.87	0.85	0.83	0.80
2	0.96	0.91	0.87	0.83	0.80	0.76	0.73	0.69	0.64
3	0.94	0.86	0.82	0.75	0.71	0.66	0.62	0.58	0.51
4	0.92	0.82	0.76	0.68	0.64	0.57	0.53	0.48	0.41
5	0.91	0.78	0.71	0.62	0.57	0.50	0.46	0.40	0.33
6	0.89	0.75	0.67	0.56	0.51	0.43	0.39	0.33	0.26
7	0.87	0.71	0.62	0.51	0.45	0.38	0.33	0.28	0.21
8	0.85	0.68	0.58	0.47	0.40	0.33	0.28	0.23	0.17
9	0.84	0.64	0.54	0.42	0.36	0.28	0.24	0.19	0.13
10	0.82	0.61	0.51	0.39	0.32	0.25	0.21	0.16	0.11

Chapter Sixteen Performance Measurement

Smart success

Learning Objectives

At the end of this topic, you should be able to:

- consider how a business might set its long-term strategy
- assess the performance of a business using non-financial as well as financial measures
- consider the use of benchmarking to improve performance
- construct a balanced scorecard
- calculate customer profitability.

Introduction

As businesses become more complex, managers may look for more sophisticated methods to plan and control their operations. A budget can be used to assess performance in the short-term, often just for the year ahead. Long-term decisions such as capital investment need to be part of a wider and longer-term plan. Businesses need to consider their strategy over several years and look at a range of performance measures to assess how well they have done. These can include non-financial measures across all functions of the business.

Case Study
Smart drives on

Sam began his operation by printing team kits in his garage. Ten years on, he has built a successful multinational business, selling a wide range of products, manufacturing various types of sports equipment, and distributing them through a variety of channels. However, Sam is concerned that, as his business becomes more complex, he needs to understand more about how he should measure the performance of each product group, manufacturing operation, country, and distribution channel. Should his success merely be measured in financial terms? What other factors should he consider as he plans for the next five years?

Performance measurement: strategy and objectives

Many managers rely on their budgets to plan and control the financial operations and to measure the performance of their business. Through the budgeting process, managers can co-ordinate their activities and communicate their plans to each other. Senior management can authorize their employees to carry out certain responsibilities and can lay down limits on their expenditure. Reporting actual financial results against the budget gives managers useful information in taking corrective action where plans have not been successful. Budgets are often used to set targets for key managers and then used to pay rewards for good performance.

However, performance should not simply be measured against one set of financial plans, agreed at the beginning of the year. Budgets should form part of a wider corporate strategy, laid down by senior managers. This should include the long-term business strategy, which sets out the vision and mission of the organization. What are the business's objectives for the next five years? How will it set about achieving those objectives? To assess this, the management must analyse its internal strengths and weakness against the external environment. It can then determine what strategic options are available and what operational plans are needed to achieve these objectives. Measuring performance has to be done at several levels: against the high-level business strategy and against the low-level operational plans (see Figure 16.1). A budget can be a financial mechanism to ensure these top- and low-level plans are consistent and achievable.

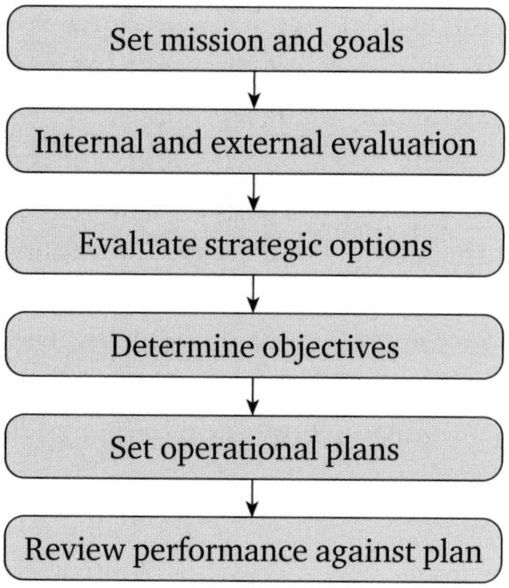

Figure 16.1 Corporate planning process

Ponder Point

Where do you think the Smart Group will be in five years' time? What should be its long-term business strategy?

Terminology

The corporate strategy of a business sets out its long-term plan, assessing its competitive advantage by matching its internal strengths to external opportunities.

The operational plan of a business translates the corporate strategy into sets of financial and non-financial objectives for managers in the short-term.

Financial and non-financial performance measurement

The performance of a business should not just be measured in financial terms. Think about a game of tennis. You can simply assess the performance by its result: Jamie beat Winston. Perhaps, that is all that matters, if the winner goes through to the next round of a tournament. Most people will ask *by how much* did Jamie beat Winston? Was it a full five-set match, or did Jamie win easily, rarely losing a game? The tennis points are rather like the profit (or loss) in a company. So we could say that the business simply made a profit.

However, you might want to know *why* Jamie beat Winston. Rather than looking just at the result in the number of points won, you can also ask for more operational data about the match. For example, how many first serves did Jamie get in? How many double faults did Winston serve? This data is often only useful when it is compared to something meaningful. In Jamie's case, it could be expressed as a percentage: what percentage of first serves did Jamie get in? Or it can be contrasted with a competitor: Winston served 20 double faults compared to Jamie's 3.

Some performance measures might not even relate to the match itself but are needed to explain why Jamie was successful. Winston might want to compare how many hours' training he did compared to Jamie in the weeks leading up to the match. Performance measurement is not simply about the result (such as profit in a business and points in a tennis match) but is also about understanding the situation as a whole.

Ponder Point

Choose a different sport. What performance indicators would you use to assess how a team has performed?

Key performance measures

As well as measuring their performance in financial terms, businesses will analyse a range of non-financial data to set targets and assess how well they are performing. The marketing director may consider that a target market share is the most appropriate way of setting his objectives. A production director may assess the efficiency of his factory by looking at how many products it produced per shift. A human resources director might assess the commitment of her staff by the number of days lost through sickness.

Good performance measurement is about asking pertinent questions to understand what is happening and finding the appropriate measures to explain why. These measures will change as the business faces new situations or takes on new challenges.

Demonstration Exercise 16.1

Sam has set-up a transport business, Smart Drive, to distribute sports equipment in the UK. It has been so successful that it now has its own customers as well as Sam's business. It has two warehouses that hold inventory: one in the south and one in the north of the UK. The sports equipment is delivered to retail outlets in vans. Sam suspects that the south warehouse is run in an inefficient way and is keen to assess its performance. So far he has gathered some financial and non-financial data about the costs of each warehouse, listed in Table 16.1.

Table 16.1

Smart Drive performance data		
	South warehouse	**North warehouse**
Total cost per warehouse per annum	£300,000	£120,000
Number of retail outlets	325	175
Number of vans	20	8
Total distance driven per annum	500,000 km	550,000 km
Number of deliveries per annum	4,000	2,100
Volume of sales per annum	280,000 units	150,000 units
Number of employees	35	20

Required:

a) Assess the performance of each warehouse by combining financial and non-financial data, and complete Table 16.2.

b) Discuss key issues arising from your answer to (a).

Table 16.2

Smart Drive warehouse performance		
	South warehouse **£**	**North warehouse** **£**
Cost per retail outlet	923 (£300,000 ÷ 325)	
Cost per van	15,000 (£300,000 ÷ 20)	
Cost per km		
Cost per delivery		
Cost per employee		
Cost per unit		

Demonstration Exercise 16.2

To understand whether the costs are being controlled effectively, the operational efficiency also needs to be assessed. For example, at Smart Drive it is important to keep van costs as low as possible by filling the van as much as possible. To do this, they can calculate the sales volumes per delivery. What other ratios would be useful? What other data would you like so as to make a full assessment of the relative performance of the two warehouses?

Ponder Point

Service industries have traditionally been measured by the three 'E's: economy, efficiency, and effectiveness. Economy is how cheaply a service can be provided. How might you measure the efficiency of a transport operation? How is this different from effectiveness?

Benchmarking

One way of assessing a business's performance is to measure it against other businesses. If you can discover the best practice in the industry and benchmark your business against it, you should be able improve your performance. By using non-financial measures as well as financial measures, it can be much easier to understand why another business performs better. Once key performance indicators have been compared, management need to understand the processes underlying them to see how they can be improved. The ideal comparison is with direct competitors, but this is unlikely to be feasible in a competitive business situation. One alternative is to find a similar operation in a different market. For example, a clothing retailer could compare its accounts department to that of a supermarket. They operate in different markets, but their processes of collecting cash, paying suppliers, and preparing accounts should be very similar. Another option is to compare similar operations within the same business, just as Smart Drive has done with its warehouses.

Ponder Point

What processes might you look at to explain why the south warehouse cost per employee is significantly higher than that of the north warehouse?

The balanced scorecard

Over the last three decades, the balanced scorecard has become a popular way of combining non-financial performance measures with financial data (see Figure 16.2). It is designed to be a comprehensive framework, linking a company's strategy and objectives to its performance measures. As it has a simple format, it limits the number of performance measures that can be assessed at a given time. Rather than measuring a large range of unconnected indicators, managers must choose which are most important and understand how they link together. They should be able to see the cause and effect of their decisions.

The original balanced scorecard, developed by Kaplan and Norton, has four perspectives: financial, customer, internal processes, and learning and growth. Some companies have developed other perspectives, such as stakeholders. For each perspective, objectives are set that link to the overall strategy of the company. Each objective must have a measure and a target, with some explanation of what actions need to be taken to achieve this, called initiatives.

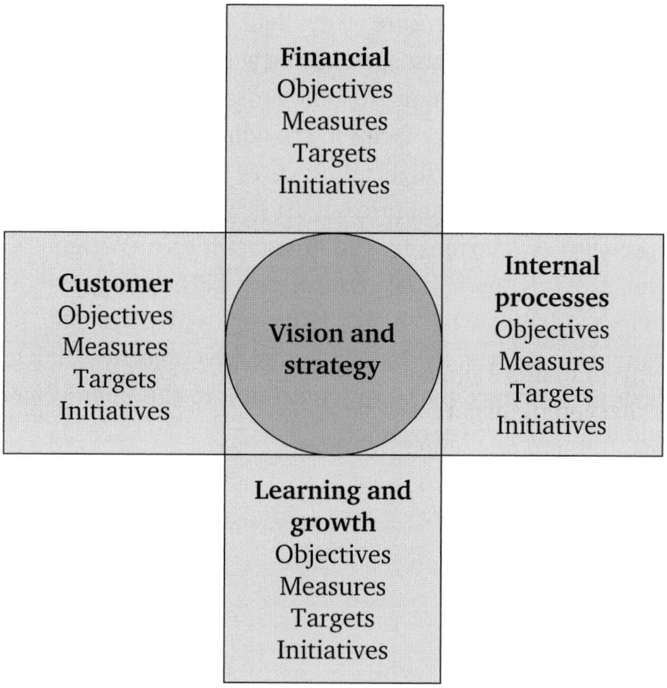

Figure 16.2 Balanced scorecard format
Adapted from Kaplan, R., and Norton, D. (2007).

Terminology

A balanced scorecard is a strategic management tool linking financial and non-financial performance measures between four business perspectives (financial, customer, internal processes, and learning and growth).

Benchmarking allows managers to compare the operational and financial performance of one business or operation against another by using key performance measures.

Demonstration Exercise 16.3

Consider how the balanced scorecard could be used in an airline industry (see Figure 16.3). As a commercial operation, an airline business is looking to maximize its return on investment. Keeping its operating costs to a minimum will be key to its long-term financial performance. Efficient use of its assets will also ensure a healthy return on investment. However, critical to the success of an airline is its reputation for safety, so a balance needs to be struck between the costs of maintaining the aircraft against the risk of mechanical failure. Maintenance staff must be highly trained to ensure every flight meets safety levels. To utilize its assets efficiently, the planes must spend as little time as possible on the ground (called 'turnaround time'), minimizing time for safety checks. This will also help to keep flights to schedule, a key factor in providing a good service to customers. To operate cost-effectively, the flights must carry as many passengers as possible (called the 'load factor'), so ticket prices must be set at competitive rates. This, in turn, puts pressure on maximizing the financial return. Without a committed workforce, much of this operational performance will be undermined. A balanced scorecard helps to identify what the key issues are with a business, linking strategy to operational measures. By understanding how objectives link together, we can see which performance measures contribute to the improvement of other measures and where objectives conflict.

Demonstration Exercise 16.3 – solution

Financial

Objective	Measure
Improve ROCE	ROCE %
Cut costs	Cost per flight

Customer

Objective	Measure
Set prices competitively	Average price per flight compared to industry
Punctuality of flight times	Number of flights on time

Internal processes

Objective	Measure
Improve turnaround time	Average time on ground between flights
Minimize delays through maintenance defects	Time lost through repairs

Learning and growth

Objective	Measure
Improve safety training	Number of employees attending training courses
Ensure workforce is satisfied	Staff turnover

Figure 16.3 Example of a balanced scorecard for an airline

Demonstration Exercise 16.4

From your understanding of financial measures, what do you consider to be the most appropriate financial objectives and measures for Smart Drive?

Leading and lagging indicators

Financial measures are usually relatively easy to measure and understand. But they often provide information too late for managers to take effective action. If your profit has decreased from last year, valuable time may have been lost in finding out what has gone wrong. These indicators are called 'lagging' indicators, as they report on past performance. Companies also need 'leading' indicators to give advance warning of what might happen in the future.

Ponder Point

What leading indicators could be used in a transport business?

Demonstration Exercise 16.5

Develop some customer objectives and measures that might give Smart Drive some warning about a future decline in profits. Think about what a customer might expect and whether these expectations are being met.

Strategy mapping

The scorecard is most useful when the cause and effect of measures can be seen by linking the different perspectives. The customer perspective will include objectives and measures that improve the company's relationship with its customers, including its quality of products and services. To ensure that the customer is satisfied, the internal processes of the business must ensure that the right product or service is delivered at the right time.

Demonstration Exercise 16.6

Take the customer objectives developed in Demonstration Exercise 16.5 for Smart Drive. What internal process objectives and measures would be appropriate to ensure that the needs of Smart Drive's customers are satisfied? What does the business also need to do internally to ensure it meets its profit targets?

Qualitative Measures

Not all the marks of success of a business can be measured precisely. Sometimes, good performance has to be a matter of judgement. For example, the quality of a product could be measured by the number of defects, which is a quantitative measure, but also by a customer's opinion of whether they like the product, which is a qualitative measure.

Demonstration Exercise 16.7

The fourth perspective of the balanced scorecard is 'learning and growth'. This includes all aspects concerning how a business looks to its future, such as developing new products or services and investing in its employees. What objectives and measures might be appropriate for assessing employee morale and development at Smart Drive? Which are quantitative and which are qualitative measures?

Customer profitability analysis

To compliment budgetary control within a company, management accounts may also include a product profitability schedule. This shows how much each product is contributing to the overall profit of the business. Depending on the method of allocating overheads used (see Chapter 11), this may show just a contribution to overheads, or a full allocation of all costs, including manufacturing and non-manufacturing overheads.

With the introduction of activity-based costing (see Chapter 11), customer profitability analysis has been used to assess the viability of a business's customer base. By costing out the activities involved, a business can understand what it costs to sell its goods to certain customer groups. For example, a clothing manufacturer can sell its products to retail outlets or by using the internet. By understanding all the processes in the different supply chains and then costing them out, a business can calculate its profit by customer or by distribution channel, and not just by product.

Terminology

Customer profitability analysis (CPA) often uses activity-based cost information to assess the profitability of different customers or different distribution channels.

Demonstration Exercise 16.8

Sam analyses the three ways in which he sells his team kits to his customers: directly to his customers, through a retailer, or over the internet. Selling products directly to customers involves visiting every customer to negotiate each contract separately, delivering kits using Smart Drive in small quantities, and then invoicing the customer for each delivery. Kits sold through retail outlets are delivered in large quantities by Smart Drive to a central warehouse. As the retailer negotiates a discount from the list price annually and is invoiced monthly, there are few customer visits. Internet sales from Smart4sport.com are growing rapidly and are delivered by post.

Table 16.3

Smart Drive customer profitability			
	Direct contracts	**Internet**	**Retail outlets**
Number of team kits	100,000	50,000	300,000
List price	£20	£18	£20
Discount	None	None	20%
Customer visits per year	400	None	50
Number of invoices per annum	3,000	15,000	4,000
Number of deliveries per annum	1,000	15,000	750
Average cost per delivery	£330	£7	£600

Table 16.4

Smart Drive ABC data	
Manufacturing cost per kit	£8
Cost per customer visit	£300
Cost of processing an invoice	£3.50

Required:

From the data in Tables 16.3 and 16.4, calculate the customer profitability for each distribution channel, and complete table 16.5. The solution for direct contracts has been given as an example.

Table 16.5

Smart Drive profitability by sales channel			
	Direct contracts £	Internet £	Retail outlets £
Gross revenue	2,000,000 (100,000 × £20)		
Discount	–		
Net revenue	2,000,000		
Manufacturing cost of kit	800,000		
Cost of customer visits	120,000		
Invoicing cost	10,500 (3,000 × £3.50)		
Delivery cost	330,000 (1,000 × £330)		
Contribution by distribution channel	739,500		
Contribution per kit	7.40		

Demonstration Exercise 16.9

Sam is now considering his future strategy. His ambition is to float the company on the stock exchange and go travelling. To do this, he needs to develop a five-year plan with a detailed strategy for profit growth. This will need to include product development, including possible acquisitions of other companies, building a wider customer base, and being able to manufacture and deliver the products and services to meet these expectations. Draw up a five-year strategy for the Smart Group, and design a balanced scorecard with detailed objectives and measures for each perspective to deliver this.

Case Study
Final words

Sam contemplates his success. He has built his business from printing team kits in his garage to a multi-product, global manufacturing operation. He has succeeded financially, but he has achieved so much more than just making a return on his initial investment. He has provided jobs and given his customers new and exciting products. He has worked hard to achieve his ambitions and looks back with pride. Moreover, in understanding how to run a business, he has also discovered the importance of understanding accounting.

Summary of Key Points

- The corporate strategy of a business sets out the long-term plans of a business by identifying its competitive advantage through analysing its internal strengths and external opportunities.
- The success (or failure) of a business can be measured by a range of financial and non-financial performance measures.
- Businesses can compare their performance against other businesses by benchmarking.
- A balanced scorecard is a performance measurement tool to translate strategy into management objectives, by understanding the cause-and-effect relationships between performance measures.
- Activity-based costing methods can be applied to assess the customer or distribution-channel profitability of a business.

Smart Questions: a wider perspective

1. How can the balanced scorecard contribute to the successful management of a business?
2. Why should non-accountants have an understanding of accounting?
3. Why should accountants have a sound understanding of business?
4. In what way can accountants contribute to setting corporate strategy?

Wider Reading

Ferreira, A., and Otley, D. (2009) 'The design and use of performance management systems: an extended framework for analysis', *Management Accounting Research*, Vol 20, pp. 263–282. This article provides detailed recommendations for performance measurement system requirements.

Kaplan, R., and Norton, D. (2007) 'Using the balanced scorecard as a strategic management system', *Harvard Business Review*, Vol 85 Issue 7/8, pp. 150–161. This is the latest in a series of articles from the authors of the balanced scorecard.

Practice Questions

16.1 Tarun's key performance measures

Tarun owns a small chain of middle-range hotels in the Netherlands and wishes to assess their relative performance. In addition to providing rooms, every hotel has a bar and a small restaurant. He has gathered some financial and non-financial data about each hotel (see Table 16.6). The hotels are open for 300 nights in a year and have an average of 1.5 guests per room per night.

Table 16.6

Tarun's hotel data			
	The Hague	**Amsterdam**	**Delft**
Total revenue per hotel per annum	€619,000	€708,000	€238,200
Total operating profit per hotel per annum	€69,400	€65,700	€20,540
Number of rooms	20	25	10
Average number of rooms occupied per night	17	21	6
Rate per room	€50	€60	€40
Total restaurant revenue	€294,000	€240,000	€151,200

REQUIRED:

a) Assess the performance of each hotel by combining financial and non-financial data.

b) Discuss key issues arising from the above answer.

16.2 Tarun's balanced scorecard

Draw up a list of additional objectives and performance measures for Tarun's hotel chain, and use them, with the performance measures in Practice Question 16.1, to design a balanced scorecard. For each, suggest whether they are qualitative or quantitative measures. Which are leading or lagging indicators for the financial and customer perspectives?

16.3 Jabu

Jabu, a brand manager in a South African confectionery manufacturer, reviews his product profitability sheets. His energy sweets are making an overall loss, but he needs to know whether this is true for both his customer groups: supermarkets and independent corner shops. He sells in bulk to supermarkets, who negotiate large discounts and expect delivery to their central warehouse. Sales to small independent owners of corner shops are time-consuming, but he can charge them full price. The average cost of visiting a customer is 6,000 rand.

REQUIRED:

Using the information in Table 16.7, calculate the profitability of the energy sweets by distribution channel, and advise Jabu on what he should do.

Table 16.7

Jabu customer profitability data		
	Supermarkets	**Corner shops**
Number of boxes of energy sweets supplied	1,200	700
List price per box	270 rand	270 rand
Discount	30%	none
Manufacturing cost per box	108 rand	108 rand
In-store promotion cost	40,000 rand	nil
Customer visits per year	3	12
Bad debts	nil	5% of sales value
Number of deliveries per annum	100	240
Average distance per delivery	250 km	150 km
Delivery cost per km	1.25 rand	1.25 rand

Management Accounting: Case Study
Orchid Products

Orchid is a personal products company manufacturing shampoo, conditioner, and liquid soap. As it faces tough competition in a static market with no price inflation, the managing director and his team are considering how best to improve its financial performance. They are considering a number of options. A review of the product profitability suggests that they should not be selling liquid soap, but the sales director is concerned that the management accounting information is misleading. He would prefer to increase sales volume by reducing the selling prices or by running a major advertising campaign. The operations director wishes to use the spare capacity on the manufacturing line by producing a shampoo for a supermarket chain under the supermarket's own label, while the marketing director would like to launch a new shower gel product.

Table MA.1

Current product data						
	Volume (000 bottles)	Selling price per bottle £	Direct costs per bottle £	Distribution cost per bottle £	Bottles per machine hour	Bottles per labour hour
Shampoo	2,000	1.50	0.6	0.20	2,600	14,000
Conditioner	1,500	1.75	0.5	0.20	3,100	6,700
Liquid soap	500	1.25	0.4	0.30	2,010	1,500

Note: Assume direct costs and distribution are 100% variable. The majority of direct costs are materials with a small proportion of direct labour.

Table MA.2

Factory indirect costs	£k
Supervisor salaries	94.3
Insurance	194.6
Depreciation: equipment	120.6
Power	274.9
Factory administration	142.3
Total manufacturing cost	**826.7**

Notes: Indirect costs are currently allocated on a direct labour hour basis.
Non-manufacturing costs include sales and marketing of £675,000, allocated on sales volume, and a head office charge of 10% of sales revenue.

Table MA.3

Current product profitability (allocations on labour hour basis)								
	Sales revenue £k	Direct costs £k	Indirect (overhead) £k	Gross margin £k	Distribution £k	Sales & marketing £k	Head office £k	Operating profit £k
Shampoo	3,000	1,200	169	1,631	400	338	300	593
Conditioner	2,625	750	264	1,611	300	253	263	795
Liquid soap	625	200	394	31	150	84	63	(266)
Total	**6,250**	**2,150**	**827**	**3,273**	**850**	**675**	**626**	**1,122**

Required:

a) Calculate an overhead rate based on the machine hours in Table MA.1, and use this to recalculate the current product profitability. Why would this be a more appropriate method of allocating overheads than shown in Table MA.3?

b) How would your revised product profitability affect your advice to the board about discontinuing the sales of liquid soap?

c) Assess the proposal of the sales director, by quantifying the impact of reducing prices by 10% and increasing volume by 15%. Would running an advertising campaign costing £250,000 to increase volume by the same amount but leaving the selling price unchanged be more cost effective?

d) Using the costing information in Table MA.1, assess the impact of agreeing to a contract to manufacture a supermarket's own-label shampoo. The operations director confirms that the contract would be for 500,000 bottles and be sold at a 20% discount on current selling prices. Direct costs would be the same, but there would be a bulk delivery charge of £85,000. What other factors should be taken into account?

e) The marketing director has given the management accountant some estimates on which to base her calculations for the launch of a shower gel (see Tables MA.4 and MA.5). She forecasts that they could sell 350,000 bottles in the first year, with growth of 10% per annum thereafter. She would expect to adopt a penetrating price strategy initially, with prices at £2 per bottle, but hopes to increase prices by 2% every year after that. She proposes to support the new shower gel with promotions costing £45,000 per year. Distribution costs are expected to be in line with existing products. By calculating the net present value over the next five years using a discount rate of 5%, advise the board whether they should invest £250,000 in equipment for this project. You should also outline the limitations and non-financial considerations that also need to be taken into account.

Table MA.4

Shower gel: raw material costs		
Per bottle	**Quantity**	**Cost**
Detergent	200 ml per bottle	£1.50 per litre
Perfume	50 ml per bottle	£20.00 per litre
Bottle	1 per bottle	£0.03 per bottle
Cap	1 per bottle	£0.01 per bottle

Table MA.5

Shower gel: assumptions		
Per 1,000 bottles	**Quantity**	**Cost**
Direct labour	10 hours	£10 per hour
Outer packaging	10 boxes	£15 per box

Answers to Demonstration Exercises and Practice Questions

Chapter 1

Demonstration Exercise solutions

1.2

Smart Sports				
Cash budget for the three months ended 30 June 2011				
	Apr 2011 £	May 2011 £	June 2011 £	Total 2nd quarter 2011 £
Receipts				
Capital				
Receipts from cash customers			5,000	5,000
Receipts from credit customers		2,400	4,000	6,400
Total receipts	**–**	**2,400**	**9,000**	**11,400**
Payments				
Printing machine		5,500		5,500
Payments to suppliers	1,500	2,000	4,000	7,500
Printer hire	100	100	100	300
Accountant's fees	125	125	125	375
Delivery	75	100	100	275
Telephone			375	375
Other expenses	300	400	400	1,100
Drawings	600	600	600	1,800
Total payments	**2,700**	**8,825**	**5,700**	**17,225**
Net receipts/(payments)	(2,700)	(6,425)	3,300	(5,825)
Balance brought forward	7,075	4,375	(2,050)	7,075
Balance carried forward	**4,375**	**(2,050)**	**1,250**	**1,250**

1.3

a) Football kits:

	Gross profit margin
Superstars	$1{,}800/6{,}000 \times 100 = 30.0\%$
United	$800/2{,}000 \times 100 = 40.0\%$
University	$1{,}350/3{,}000 \times 100 = 45.0\%$

b) The overall gross profit margin that would be made on the three football kits

$$= \frac{(1{,}800 + 800 + 1{,}350)}{(6{,}000 + 2{,}000 + 3{,}000)} \times 100\% = 35.9\%$$

c) Hockey kits:

	Gross profit margin
Rovers	900/2,400 × 100% = 37.5%
Tigers	2,000/4,000 × 100% = 50.0%
Panthers	1,000/5,000 × 100% = 20.0%

d) The overall gross profit margin on the three hockey kits

$$= \frac{(900 + 2{,}000 + 1{,}000)}{(2{,}400 + 4{,}000 + 5{,}000)} \times 100\% = 34.2\%$$

e) The profitability of the different contracts is very variable. The Tigers contract is expected to make a 50% gross profit margin, whereas the Panthers contract will make only a 20% margin. Overall, however, the gross profit margin expected to be made on selling football kits is 35.9%, which is only slightly more than the margin of 34.2% expected to be made on the hockey kits.

1.4

Smart Sports							
Cash budget for the six months ended 31 December 2011							
	July £	**August** £	**September** £	**October** £	**November** £	**December** £	**Total** £
Receipts							
From customers		2,400	2,400	3,000	3,000	3,400	**14,200**
Loan	12,000						**12,000**
Total receipts	**12,000**	**2,400**	**2,400**	**3,000**	**3,000**	**3,400**	**26,200**
Payments							
Payments to suppliers	–	3,440	1,440	1,800	1,800	2,040	**10,520**
Telephone			400			400	**800**
Electricity			650			650	**1,300**
Accountant's fees	125	125	125	125	125	125	**750**
Delivery costs	100	100	100				**300**
Other expenses	110	110	110	110	110	110	**660**
Van				10,000			**10,000**
Drawings	600	600	600	600	600	600	**3,600**
Total payments	**935**	**4,375**	**3,425**	**12,635**	**2,635**	**3,925**	**27,930**
Net receipts/ (payments)	**11,065**	**(1,975)**	**(1,025)**	(9,635)	365	(525)	(1,730)
Balance brought forward	1,250	12,315	10,340	9,315	(320)	45	**1,250**
Balance carried forward	**12,315**	**10,340**	**9,315**	**(320)**	**45**	**(480)**	**(480)**

Working to find payments to suppliers:

	Sales in month £		Cost of sales = purchases £	Purchases paid for
July	2,400	× 60%	1,440 plus £2,000 of inventory	August 2011
August	2,400	× 60%	1,440	September
September	3,000	× 60%	1,800	October
October	3,000	× 60%	1,800	November
November	3,400	× 60%	2,040	December
December	3,800	× 60%	2,280	January 2012

Practice Question solutions

P 1.1 Maris

a) Purchases are 75% of sales for the month, and so will be:

January	February	March	April	May	June
€3,000	€3,300	€3,750	€4,050	€4,200	€4,500

b) Cash received from sales will be:

	January	February	March	April	May	June
Sales	€4,000	€4,400	€5,000	€5,400	€5,600	€6,000
Immediate	€1,000	€1,100	€1,250	€1,350	€1,400	€1,500
1 month	0	€2,000	€2,200	€2,500	€2,700	€2,800
2 months	0	0	€1,000	€1,100	€1,250	€1,350
Total	**€1,000**	**€3,100**	**€4,450**	**€4,950**	**€5,350**	**€5,650**

c) Cash paid for purchases:

January	February	March	April	May	June
0	€3,000	€3,300	€3,750	€4,050	€4,200

P 1.2 Sue

a)

Oxford Cycles							
Cash budget for the six months ended 30 June 2012							
	January £	February £	March £	April £	May £	June £	Total £
Receipts							
Cash sales	8,000	6,000	5,000	5,000	5,000	8,000	37,000
Total receipts	**8,000**	**6,000**	**5,000**	**5,000**	**5,000**	**8,000**	**37,000**
Payments							
Petrol	200	200	200	200	200	200	1,200
Purchases	1,600	5,333	4,000	3,333	3,333	3,333	20,932
Shop rental	900			900			1,800
Wages	1,200	1,200	1,200	1,200	1,200	1,200	7,200
Van	4,200						4,200
Drawings	700	700	700	700	700	700	4,200
Electricity	400	400	400	400	400	400	2,400
Total payments	**9,200**	**7,833**	**6,500**	**6,733**	**5,833**	**5,833**	**41,932**
Net receipts/ (payments)	(1,200)	(1,833)	(1,500)	(1,733)	(833)	2,167	(4,932)
Balance brought forward	3,500	2,300	467	(1,033)	(2,766)	(3,599)	3,500
Balance carried forward	**2,300**	**467**	**(1,033)**	**(2,766)**	**(3,599)**	**(1,432)**	**(1,432)**

Working to find payments to suppliers:

	Sales in month £		Cost of sales = purchases £	Purchases paid for
January	8,000	× 66.67%	5,333	February
February	6,000	× 66.67%	4,000	March
March	5,000	× 66.67%	3,333	April
April	5,000	× 66.67%	3,333	May
May	5,000	× 66.67%	3,333	June
June	8,000	× 66.67%	5,333	July

b) The cash budget for Oxford Cycles shows that the business is expected to exceed its overdraft limit in April and May 2012. Sue could consider renegotiating her bank overdraft facility to see if it can be increased, or she can take steps to reduce her outgoings. She could consider the following courses of action:

(i) Take on one new member of staff rather than two. This would reduce outgoings by an estimated £600 per month and allow the business to stay within its overdraft facility.

(ii) Reduce the level of drawings she plans to make.

(iii) Defer purchasing the van and maybe use a delivery firm or rent a van when needed.

Chapter 2

Demonstration Exercise solutions

2.2

1. There would be no effect on profit, as sales and purchases are not affected.
2. The cash balance would go down by €30 as less cash would have come in from sales.

2.3

Many items could be accepted, including:

Assets
Computer.

Liabilities
Amounts Sam owes for goods purchased on credit.

Capital
Amount put into the business by Sam.

Income
Amounts from sales of team kits.

Expenses
Salaries.

Drawings
Money taken out by Sam for personal use.

2.4

	Capital or revenue expense
Printing machine	Capital
Computer	Capital
Purchases of goods for resale	Revenue
Accountant's fees	Revenue
Electricity	Revenue
Insurance	Revenue
Telephone	Revenue
Delivery expenses	Revenue
Sundry expenses (including postage, stationery)	Revenue
Drawings	Neither. A deduction from capital

2.5

		€	
1.	Opening inventory	30	
	Purchases	50	
		80	
	Closing inventory	20	
	Cans sold	60	
2.	Sales (60 × €3)		180
	Less: cost of sales		
	Opening inventory (30 × €2)	60	
	Add: purchases (50 × €2)	100	
		160	
	Less: closing inventory (20 × €2)	40	
			120
	Profit		60

2.6

Smart Sports		
Income statement for the year ended 31 December 2011 *(First draft – without any adjusting entries)*		
	£	£
Income (Sales)		51,000
Less: Cost of sales		
Opening inventories	0	
Purchases	34,500	
Less: closing inventories	2,700	
		31,800
		19,200
Gross profit		
Less: Expenses		
Electricity	1,920	
Insurance	1,750	
Telephone	1,500	
Sundry expenses	1,650	
Accountant's fees	1,500	
Delivery costs	1,200	
		9,520
Net profit		9,680

Practice Question solutions

P 2.1 Jo

a) Jo's cost of sales:

	S$
Opening inventories	–
Purchases	
1,700 × 50 cents	850
Closing inventories	
700 × 50 cents	350
Cost of sales	**500**

b) Jo's gross profit

Sales	1,200
Less: cost of sales	500
Gross profit	**700**

P 2.2 Sophie

Sophie			
Trial balance as at 31 December 2012			
	Debit €	**Credit** €	
Capital		15,000	Capital
Sales		35,000	Income
Wages	15,000		Expenditure
Hair products purchased	5,000		Expenditure
Rent of salon	6,000		Expenditure
Light and heat	1,500		Expenditure
Drawings	6,500		Drawings
Fixtures and fittings	7,000		Assets
Trade payables		250	Liabilities
Bank account	9,250		Assets
	50,250	**50,250**	

P 2.3 Helga

a) (Note: All items in ***bold italics*** represent revenue income and expenses.)

Helga		
Trial balance as at 30 November 2012		
	Debit €	**Credit €**
Capital		50,000
Loan (interest at 5%)		10,000
Sales		***235,700***
Wages	***25,200***	
Purchases	***182,400***	
Rent and rates	***15,900***	
Motor expenses	***3,600***	
Sundry expenses	***2,000***	
Interest on loan	***500***	
Light and heat	***1,800***	
Office expenses	***3,100***	
Drawings	12,000	
Motor vehicles	25,000	
Fixtures and fittings	18,000	
Trade receivables	11,800	10,500
Trade payables		
Bank account	4,900	
	306,200	**306,200**

b)

Helga		
Income statement for the year ended 30 November 2012		
	€	€
Sales		235,700
Less: Cost of sales:		
Purchases	182,400	
Less: closing inventory	15,000	
		167,400
Gross profit		**68,300**
Less: Expenses		
Wages	25,200	
Rent and rates	15,900	
Motor expenses	3,600	
Sundry expenses	2,000	
Interest	500	
Light and heat	1,800	
Office expenses	3,100	
		52,100
Net profit		**16,200**

c) The **trade receivables account** shows the amount owed by customers who have bought goods from the business on credit. Often, businesses allow 30–45 days credit, and so between the time the customer receives the goods and the time they pay for them, the amount due will be a trade receivable.

The **trade payables account** shows the amount owed to suppliers for goods they have supplied to the business on credit. Between the time the goods are delivered to the business and the time the amount owed for the goods is paid, the amount due will be a trade payable.

Chapter 3

Demonstration Exercise solutions

3.2

a) **Non-current assets**: printing machine and computer.

b) **Current assets**: inventory, trade receivables, and bank balance.

Current liabilities: trade payables.

c) Yes. The loan would be a non-current liability.

d)

Smart Sports		
Statement of financial position as at 31 December 2011 *(first draft without any adjusting entries)*		
	£	£
ASSETS		
Non-current assets		
Printing machine		5,500
Computer		3,500
		9,000
Current assets		
Inventory	2,700	
Trade receivables	4,100	
Bank balance	11,080	
		17,880
Total assets		**26,880**
CAPITAL AND LIABILITIES		
Capital at the beginning of the year		10,000
Add: Profit for the year		9,680
Less: Drawings		(7,200)
Capital at the end of the year		12,480
Non-current liabilities		
Loan		12,000
Current liabilities		
Trade payables		2,400
Total capital and liabilities		**26,880**

3.4

a) The amount of the insurance prepayment = £117 × 3 months = £351.

b) The actual total cost of insurance cover provided for Smart Sports during the year ended 31 December 2011 = £1,750 – £351 = £1,399.

c) The effect of adjusting for this prepayment is that the expenses figure will decrease and the profit for the year will increase.

3.5

Smart Sports		
Income statement for the year ended 31 December 2011 (after adjusting for accruals and prepayments)		
	£	£
Sales		51,000
Less: Cost of sales		
Purchases	34,500	
Less: closing inventory	2,700	
		31,800
Gross profit		19,200
Less: Expenses		
Electricity (1,920 + 480)	2,400	
Insurance (1,750 – 351)	1,399	
Telephone	1,500	
Accountant's fees	1,500	
Delivery costs	1,200	
Interest (12,000 × 6% × 6/12)	360	
Sundry expenses	1,650	
		10,009
Net profit		**9,191**

Smart Sports		
Statement of financial position as at 31 December 2011 (after adjusting for accruals and prepayments)		
	£	£
TOTAL ASSETS		
Non-current assets		
Printing machine		5,500
Computer		3,500
		9,000
Current assets		
Inventory	2,700	
Trade receivables	4,100	
Prepayment	351	
Bank balance	11,080	
		18,231
Total assets		**27,231**
CAPITAL AND LIABILITIES		
Capital at the beginning of the year		10,000
Add: Profit for the year		9,191
Less: Drawings		(7,200)
Capital at the end of the year		11,991
Non-current liabilities		
Loan		12,000
Current liabilities		
Trade payables	2,400	
Accruals (480 + 360)	840	
		3,240
Total capital and liabilities		**27,231**

Practice Question solutions

P 3.1 Nick's Office Supplies

a) A prepayment is an expense paid during one accounting year that relates to the following year. For example, where a business has a 31 December year-end, insurance premiums paid in December 2011, which provide cover for 2012, will represent a prepayment.

Where a prepayment has been made, it is necessary to:

(i) deduct the amount of the prepayment from the trial balance figure to arrive at the amount to include as an expense in the income statement

(ii) show the prepayment as a current asset on the statement of financial position.

b) An accrual is an expense incurred during one accounting year that is not paid until after the year-end. Hence, the amount is owing at the end of the year. For example, where a business has a 31 December year-end, electricity used in November and December 2011 but paid for in 2012 will need to be accrued for at the year-end.

Where an accrual has to be accounted for, it is necessary to:

(i) add the amount of the accrual to the trial balance figure to arrive at the amount to include as an expense in the income statement

(ii) show the accrual as a current liability on the statement of financial position.

c)

Nick's Office Supplies		
Income statement for the year ended 31 December 2011		
	£	£
Sales		477,600
Less: Cost of sales		
Opening inventories	27,440	
Purchases	322,400	
	349,840	
Less: closing inventory	38,600	
		311,240
Gross profit		166,360
Less: Expenses		
Wages	83,630	
Advertising	4,400	
Electricity (5,050 + 1,200)	6,250	
Insurance	16,080	
Interest (10,000 × 10%)	1,000	
		111,360
Net profit		55,000

d)

Nick's Office Supplies		
Statement of financial position as at 31 December 2011		
	£	£
ASSETS		
Non-current assets		
Premises		154,000
Office equipment		27,900
		181,900
Current assets		
Inventories	38,600	
Trade receivables	51,880	
Bank	37,700	
		128,180
Total assets		**310,080**
CAPITAL AND LIABILITIES		
Capital at the beginning of the year		208,160
Add: Profit for the year		55,000
Less: Drawings		(27,000)
Capital at the year-end		236,160
Non-current liabilities		
Loan		10,000
Current liabilities		
Trade payables	61,720	
Accruals (1,200 + 1,000)	2,200	
		63,920
Total capital and liabilities		**310,080**

P 3.2 Ming

a)

Ming		
Income statement for the year ended 31 March 2013		
	Yuan	**Yuan**
Sales		446,660
Less: Cost of sales		
Opening inventories	59,830	
Purchases	239,190	
	299,020	
Less: closing inventory	63,000	
		236,020
Gross profit		**210,640**
Less: Expenses		
Wages (173,850 + 5,750)	179,600	
Rent (18,500 – 3,480)	15,020	
Other expenses	23,230	
		217,850
Net loss		7,210

b) Ming's business actually made a small loss for the year ended 31 March 2013. Despite achieving a reasonable gross profit figure, the amount paid as wages to her sister was substantial and led to the overall loss for the year. Perhaps Ming could consider working on the stall herself for more time each week, so as to reduce the amount she has to pay out as wages.

Ming could be advised to review a breakdown of the items included in 'other expenses' to see if any of them could be reduced or avoided.

c)

Ming		
Statement of financial position as at 31 March 2013		
	Yuan	**Yuan**
ASSETS		
Non-current assets		
Motor vehicle		75,000
Current assets		
Inventories	63,000	
Trade receivables	5,270	
Prepayment	3,480	
		71,750
Total assets		**146,750**
CAPITAL AND LIABILITIES		
Capital at the beginning of the year		252,800
Less: Loss for the year		(7,210)
Less: Drawings		(105,130)
Capital at the year-end		140,460
Current liabilities		
Bank overdraft	540	
Accrual	5,750	
		6,290
Total capital and liabilities		**146,750**

Chapter 4

Demonstration Exercise solutions

4.2

a) At the rate of 25% per annum.

b) £5,500 × 25% = £1,375.

c)

At the first accounting year-end, 31 December 2011			
	Cost £	**Accumulated depreciation** £	**Net book value** £
Printing machine	5,500	1,375	4,125

At the second accounting year-end, 31 December 2012			
	Cost **£**	**Accumulated depreciation** **£**	**Net book value** **£**
Printing machine	5,500	2,750	2,750

At the third accounting year-end, 31 December 2013			
	Cost **£**	**Accumulated depreciation** **£**	**Net book value** **£**
Printing machine	5,500	4,125	1,375

At the fourth accounting year-end, 31 December 2014			
	Cost **£**	**Accumulated depreciation** **£**	**Net book value** **£**
Printing machine	5,500	5,500	–

4.3

a)

	£
Cost of the computer	3,500
1st year's depreciation charge (40% × 3,500)	1,400
Net book value at 31 December 2011	2,100
2nd year's depreciation charge (40% × 2,100)	840
Net book value at 31 December 2012	1,260
3rd year's depreciation charge (40% × 1,260)	504
Net book value at 31 December 2013	756

b)

At the first year-end, 31 December 2011			
	Cost **£**	**Accumulated depreciation** **£**	**Net book value** **£**
Computer	3,500	1,400	2,100

At the second year-end, 31 December 2012			
	Cost £	**Accumulated depreciation** £	**Net book value** £
Computer	3,500	2,240	1,260
At the third year-end, 31 December 2013			
	Cost £	**Accumulated depreciation** £	**Net book value** £
Computer	3,500	2,744	756

4.4

Smart Sports		
Income statement for the year ended 31 December 2011 (Final version)		
	£	£
Sales		51,000
Less: Cost of sales		
Purchases	34,500	
Less closing inventory	2,700	
		31,800
Gross profit		19,200
Less: Expenses		
Electricity (1,920 + 480)	2,400	
Insurance (1,750 – 351)	1,399	
Telephone	1,500	
Sundry expenses	1,650	
Accountant's fees	1,500	
Interest (12,000 × 6% × 6/12)	360	
Delivery costs	1,200	
Depreciation charge on printing machine (5,500 × 25%)	1,375	
Depreciation charge on computer (3,500 × 40%)	1,400	
Bad debt	820	
		13,604
Net profit		5,596

Smart Sports			
Statement of financial position as at 31 December 2011 (Final version)			
	Cost	**Accum. depn**	**Net book value**
ASSETS			
Non-current assets			
Printing machine	5,500	1,375	4,125
Computer	3,500	1,400	2,100
	9,000	2,775	6,225
Current assets			
Inventory		2,700	
Trade receivables (4,100 – 820)		3,280	
Prepayment		351	
Bank balance		11,080	
			17,411
Total assets			**23,636**
CAPITAL AND LIABILITIES			
Capital at the beginning of the year			10,000
Add: Profit for the year			5,596
Less: Drawings			(7,200)
Capital at the year-end			8,396
Non-current liabilities			
Loan			12,000
Current liabilities			
Trade payables		2,400	
Accruals (480 + 360)		840	
			3,240
Total capital and liabilities			**23,636**

Practice Question solutions

P 4.1 Douggen

a) Depreciation is provided in order to gradually charge the cost of non-current assets to the income statement over the life of those assets. Non-current assets have a finite useful life, and they will be used in the business to help generate profits over that period.

b) Plant and machinery depreciation charge for 2012 and 2013

$$= \frac{\text{cost} - \text{residual value}}{\text{estimated useful life}}$$

$$= \frac{£80{,}000 - 8{,}000}{4}$$

$$= £18{,}000$$

When the straight-line method of providing for depreciation is used, the depreciation charge is the same for each year of the asset's life.

c) Plant and equipment is to be depreciated at the rate of 22.5% per annum on the straight-line basis.

The rate is found from:

$$\frac{\text{depreciation charge for the year}}{\text{cost of the asset}} \times 100$$

$$= \frac{£18{,}000}{£80{,}000} \times 100\%$$

$$= 22.5\%$$

d) To answer these questions, the depreciation charges arising need to be calculated using each of the two methods of providing for depreciation on motor vehicles:

(i) Depreciation charge on the straight-line basis for 2012 and 2013

$= £24{,}000 \times 25\% = £6{,}000$

Depreciation charge on the reducing-balance basis for 2012

$= £24{,}000 \times 35\% = £8{,}400$

Depreciation charge on the reducing-balance basis for 2013

$= (£24{,}000 - £8{,}400) \times 35\% = £5{,}460$

(a) The straight-line basis gives the smallest depreciation charge for the year ended 31 December 2012.

(b) The reducing-balance basis gives the smallest depreciation charge for the year ended 31 December 2013.

(c) The straight-line method gives the smallest depreciation charges for both years combined.

(ii) If Douggen wishes to maximize profits over the first two years, the business should choose the straight-line method for depreciating motor vehicles, as this gives the smallest charge for depreciation on motor vehicles.

e) Extract from the statement of financial position as at 31 December 2012:

Non-current assets	Cost £	Accumulated depreciation £	NBV £
Plant and machinery	80,000	18,000	62,000
Motor vehicles	24,000	6,000	18,000
	104,000	**24,000**	**80,000**

P 4.2 Russells

Russells		
Income statement for the year ended 31 December 2012		
	€	**€**
Sales		**220,360**
Less: Cost of sales		
Opening inventories	7,800	
Add: Purchases	92,000	
	99,800	
Less: Closing inventories	8,200	
		91,600
Gross profit		**128,760**
Less: Expenses		
Wages (43,600 + 4,800)	48,400	
Electricity (8,000 + 1,200)	9,200	
Motor expenses	4,450	
Other business expenses	3,050	
Bad debts	110	
Increase in provision for doubtful debts (4% × 11,750)	470	
Depreciation charge on plant and equipment	11,700	
Depreciation charge on fixtures and fittings	3,000	
		80,380
Net profit		**48,380**

P 4.2 cont.

Russells			
Statement of financial position as at 31 December 2012			
	Cost €	Accum. depn €	NBV €
ASSETS			
NON-CURRENT ASSETS			
Freehold premises	67,500	–	67,500
Plant and equipment	39,000	11,700	27,300
Fixtures and fittings	15,000	3,000	12,000
	121,500	14,700	106,800
CURRENT ASSETS			
Inventory		8,200	
Trade receivables	11,750		
Less: provision	470		
		11,280	
Bank balance		4,200	
			23,680
Total assets			130,480
CAPITAL AND LIABILITIES			
Capital			
Capital at 1 January 2012			85,000
Add: profit for the year			48,380
			133,380
Less: drawings			24,000
Capital at 31 December 2012			109,380
CURRENT LIABILITIES			
Trade payables		15,100	
Accruals (electricity + wages)		6,000	
			21,100
Total capital and liabilities			130,480

P 4.3 Poppy

a) Sales income for the year:

(10 clients × €250 × 12 months) + (2 clients × €250 × 6 months)

= €30,000 + €3,000 = €33,000.

b) Bank balance at 30 June 2012:

Cash received

Capital €8,000

From customers: sales revenues less receivables = €33,000 – €1,250 = €31,750

Total cash paid into bank = €39,750

Cash paid out

Non-current assets €8,000

Consumables €1,500

Session costs (€5 × 1,320* sessions) = €6,600

Drawings €24,000

Total cash paid out = €40,100

Bank overdraft at the year-end = €39,750 – €40,100 = €350.

*Number of training sessions = (10 clients × 10 sessions × 12 months) + (2 clients × 10 sessions × 6 months) = 1,320 sessions during the year.

c)

Poppy		
Income statement for the year ended 30 June 2012		
	€	€
Sales		33,000
Less: Expense		
Session costs	6,600	
Consumables	1,500	
Depreciation charge on non-current assets (€8,000 × 20%)	1,600	
		9,700
Net profit		**23,300**

Note: The non-current assets have been depreciated on the straight-line basis.

Poppy			
Statement of financial position as at 30 June 2012			
	Cost €	Accum. depn €	NBV €
ASSETS			
Non-current assets			
Sports equipment	8,000	1,600	6,400
Current assets			
Trade receivables			1,250
Total assets			7,650
CAPITAL AND LIABILITIES			
Capital introduced			8,000
Add: Profit for the year			23,300
Less: Drawings			(24,000)
Capital at the end of the year			7,300
Current liabilities			
Bank overdraft			350
Total capital and liabilities			7,650

d) Poppy made a profit of €23,300 in her first year of trading, and the drawings she made exceeded this amount.

e) If Poppy were to employ an assistant, it would cost the business an additional €7,200 (€600 × 12 months) per annum in wages. The business would still make a profit, but Poppy would need to be prepared to take a much smaller level of drawings in order for the business to expand in the future.

If, as a result of employing the assistant, Poppy could take on additional clients, then it would make employing an assistant a far more viable solution.

Chapter 5

Demonstration Exercise solutions

5.2

a) Offering 50,000 shares of £1 nominal value would mean that the shareholders could buy and sell smaller amounts of shares. This would enable smaller investors to take a stake in the company and hopefully attract more potential investors.

b) Shares would hopefully be issued at a price in excess of the nominal value when the business has been trading successfully for some time.

c) Benefits of share ownership include:
- Betty will be investing in Sam's business to enable it to grow and expand.
- She will possibly achieve a capital gain on the shares held if their value increases.
- She might receive dividends from the company.

Drawbacks include:
- Her money will be tied up and inaccessible for some time.
- The amount she has invested could be lost if the company fails.
- When she decides to sell her shares, it may not be straightforward to do so.

d) When Betty wishes to sell her shares, she could possibly find a buyer by offering them to Sam or one of the other shareholders. She could approach other family or friends who know the business.

5.3

a) Venture capital finance would enable the business to grow and expand. Venture capitalists usually appoint a representative onto the board of directors bringing wider experience to the board.

b) Venture capitalists would be interested in the past, current, and particularly the future expected profitability of the business. They would also want to know details about the assets and liabilities of the business. Other than financial information, they would be interested in knowing about:
- the business's products or services, its main customers, and its markets
- the business's strategy for the next few years
- the directors and managers of the business, their qualifications, and their experience
- competitors, suppliers, employees, etc.
- what it plans to do with the funds raised.

c) Having obtained venture capital finance, the board, including Sam, would have to consider the demands of a greater variety of investors. The venture capitalists would expect regular briefings, and they would be able to influence board decisions.

d) Venture capitalists would usually acquire an equity stake. They would expect to make a capital gain from that investment arising from an increase in the share price. In some instances, they might also expect dividend payments. Occasionally, they may purchase some debt in the company. They would expect to receive interest on loans made and the loan repaid when due.

5.4

a) Sam, Dot, Dan, and Betty will be the shareholders and hence the owners of the company.

b) No.

c) Once the company is formed, Sam will be able to receive a salary to reward him for working for the business. He might also receive dividends to reward him for his investment in the business.

d) Green Bank will expect to receive interest on the amount loaned.

e) This would place a greater burden on Smart Sports Ltd in terms of having to meet higher interest obligations and also having to repay a bigger loan in five years' time. However, as interest payments are tax allowable, this would reduce the tax liability of the company.

f) If Betty sells her shares at a profit in two years' time, it will have no effect on the profits made by Smart Sports Ltd. The gain made would belong to Betty.

g) Profits that are retained enable the company to re-invest and grow in the future.

Practice Question solutions

P 5.1 Monk Ltd

a)

Option 1 Debenture interest = £300,000 × 6% = £18,000.
Option 2 Preference dividend = £400,000 × 5% = £20,000
Debenture interest = £200,000 × 6% = £12,000.
Option 3 Debenture interest = £500,000 × 7% = £35,000.

b)

	Option 1	Option 2	Option 3
First year	£	£	£
Profit	40,000	40,000	40,000
Debenture interest	18,000	12,000	35,000
Preference dividend	______	20,000	______
Profits available to ordinary shareholders	**22,000**	**8,000**	**5,000**

	Option 1	Option 2	Option 3
Second year	£	£	£
Profit	95,000	95,000	95,000
Debenture interest	18,000	12,000	35,000
Preference dividend	______	20,000	______
Profits available to ordinary shareholders	**77,000**	**63,000**	**60,000**

c)

	Option 1	Option 2	Option 3
First year	£	£	£
Profits available to ordinary shareholders	**22,000**	**8,000**	**5,000**
Number of ordinary shares	70,000	40,000	50,000
Profit per share	**31.4 pence**	**20 pence**	**10 pence**

	Option 1	Option 2	Option 3
Second year	£	£	£
Profits available to ordinary shareholders	77,000	63,000	60,000
Number of ordinary shares	70,000	40,000	50,000
Profit per share	**110 pence**	**158 pence**	**120 pence**

d) Factors Chris should consider:

- Chris should be made aware that the interest payments would have to be made but that the preference dividends do not have to be paid each year. Most preference shares are cumulative, so that dividends not paid in one year are payable in later years.
- Option 3 would be the most risky one to take. In the first year when expected profits are £40,000, option 3 would leave the company with only £5,000 left after interest obligations have been met. If profits were to fall below the expected level, the business would still have to meet those interest obligations. There would be the risk that it might struggle to do so.
- Options 1 and 2 would be less risky options as the interest obligations are significantly lower. The disadvantage of option 1 is that it leads to a greater number of shareholders invested in the business, and as a result, future profits will be spread across a greater number of shares.
- With option 2, preference dividends would have to be met before any ordinary dividends could be paid. However, once the interest and preference dividends obligations have been met, the resulting profits will benefit a smaller number of shares.
- If Chris is going to hold a certain number of the ordinary shares, then he will end up with a higher proportion of the share capital in option 2, where fewer ordinary shares will be issued. Depending on how many ordinary shares he intends to buy, this might mean that he has control of the voting shares.

P 5.2 Herring

a) **Sole trader**

Advantages

- The simple business structure would allow Jorge to start trading more quickly.
- There would be no need to register the business.
- There would be no need to comply with company law and various reporting requirements.

Disadvantages

- There would be no limited liability provided to Jorge, the owner.
- Ulrika would not be able to become a part owner of the business. She would probably make a loan to the business.
- It is usually more difficult for a sole trader to raise funds.

b) **Limited company**

Advantages

- Shareholders, including Jorge, would be protected by limited liability.
- It is usually easier for companies to raise funds.

- Ulrika could be offered shares in the company, enabling her to become an owner.
- Companies are seen as having an improved status.

Disadvantages

- The company would need to comply with company law and various reporting requirements.
- Financial information has to be filed and made publicly accessible.
- Annual returns have to be filed giving a variety of information, including details of the directors.

Chapter 6

Demonstration Exercise solutions

6.3

a) No loan interest is owing at the year-end, as the total interest liability for the year would have been 7% × £18,000 = £1,260. This is the amount that has been paid according to the trial balance.

b) There is no figure for retained profits at the beginning of the year, because this is the first year that the company has traded.

c)

Smart Sports Ltd			
Statement of financial position as at 31 December 2012			
	Cost £	**Accum. dep'n £**	**NBV £**
ASSETS			
Non-current assets			
Printing machine	24,000	6,000	18,000
Motor vehicle	28,000	7,000	21,000
Computer	6,700	2,680	4,020
	58,700	15,680	43,020
Current assets			
Inventory		20,200	
Trade receivables and prepayments		21,090	
Bank		11,440	
			52,730
Total assets			95,750

	Cost £	Accum. depn £	NBV £
EQUITY AND LIABILITIES			
Equity			
Ordinary shares of £1 each			50,000
Retained profits			7,590
Total equity			**57,590**
Non-current liabilities			
Loan (2017)			18,000
Current liabilities			
Trade payables and accruals		15,510	
Taxation due		4,650	
			20,160
Total equity and liabilities			**95,750**

6.4

a) The nominal value of each share is €10.

b) The number of ordinary shares issued was 10,000 (10,000 shares with a nominal value of €10 each would increase the share capital account by €100,000).

c) The share issue would have raised €600,000.

(Increase in share capital + increase in share premium = €100,000 + €500,000 = €600,000).

d) The valuation placed on the property = €1,850,000 + €650,000 = €2,500,000.

e) Total dividend paid = €2 × 30,000 shares = €60,000.

f)

Zippy shirts SA					
Statement of changes in equity for the year ended 30 June 2012					
	Ordinary share capital €'000	**Share premium €'000**	**Revaluation reserve €'000**	**Retained profits €'000**	**Total equity €'000**
At 1 July 2011	200	600	–	1,200	2,000
Share issue	100	500			600
Total comprehensive income			650	574	1,224
Dividends paid				(60)	(60)
At 30 June 2012	**300**	**1,100**	**650**	**1,714**	**3,764**

Practice Question solutions

P 6.1 Adiga Ltd

a)

Adiga Ltd					
Statement of changes in equity for the year ended 31 December 2012					
	Ordinary share capital £'000	**Preference share capital £'000**	**Share premium £'000**	**Retained profits £'000**	**Total equity £'000**
At 1 January 2012	1,100	400	260	120	1,880
Profit for the year				151	151
Dividends paid (£28,000 + £44,000)				(72)	(72)
At 30 June 2012	**1,100**	**400**	**260**	**199**	**1,959**

b)

Adiga Ltd		
Statement of financial position as at 31 December 2012		
	£'000	**£'000**
ASSETS		
Non-current assets		
At net book value		1,500
Current assets		
Inventory	430	
Trade receivables	329	
Prepayments	59	
Bank	190	
		1,008
Total assets		**2,508**
EQUITY AND LIABILITIES		
Equity		
Ordinary shares of £1 each		1,100
7% preference shares		400
Share premium		260
Retained profits		199
Total equity		**1,959**

(cont.)

	£'000	£'000
Non-current liabilities		
6% debenture (2018)		300
Current liabilities		
Trade payables	205	
Accruals	44	
		249
Total equity and liabilities		2,508

c) The amount of preference dividends for the year is fixed. As they are 7% preference shares, this means that each preference shareholder will always receive a total dividend of 7 pence per £1 share each year, if a preference dividend is paid. The preference dividend has to be paid in full before an ordinary dividend can be paid.

The level of ordinary dividends is not fixed, and the total ordinary dividend for this year is only four pence per share. This seems low to Deepak, but the directors have to decide on a level of dividends that will leave sufficient retained profits in the business to allow the business to grow in the future. From a profit for the year of £151,000, dividends paid in total amount to £72,000, leaving retained profits for the year of £79,000. This seems a reasonable balance.

Deepak needs to consider that, as well as dividends, his shares will hopefully increase in value if the business continues to increase in size and profitability in the future. The dividends reinvested should enable the business to do just this.

P 6.2 Sacha SA

a) When the property revaluation is recorded, then:

- the value of the property will be shown at €2,000,000 on the statement of financial position at the year-end
- the increase in the property value will be recorded in a revaluation reserve and is not included as part of the profit for the year
- the revaluation gain will be shown as 'other comprehensive income'.

b)

Sacha SA	
Statement of comprehensive income for the year ended 31 March 2013	
	€'000
Profit for the year	199
Other comprehensive income: Gain on property revaluation	360
Total comprehensive income for the year	559

c)

Sacha SA					
Statement of changes in equity for the year ended 31 March 2013					
	Ordinary share capital €'000	Share premium €'000	Revaluation reserve €'000	Retained profits €'000	Total equity €'000
At 1 April 2012	1,000	150	–	780	1,930
Profit for the year				199	199
Other comprehensive income (revaluation gain)			360		360
Dividends paid				(60)	(60)
At 31 March 2013	**1,000**	**150**	**360**	**919**	**2,429**

d)

Sacha SA		
Statement of financial position as at 31 March 2013		
	€'000	**€'000**
ASSETS		
Non-current assets		
Property, at valuation		2,000
Plant and equipment, at net book value		353
		2,353
Current assets		
Inventory	734	
Trade receivables	516	
Bank	30	
		1,280
Total assets		**3,633**
Equity and liabilities		
Equity		
Ordinary shares		1,000
Share premium		150
Revaluation reserve		360
Retained profits		919
Total equity		**2,429**
Non-current liabilities		
5% debenture (2020)		600
Current liabilities		
Trade payables and accruals		604
Total equity and liabilities		**3,633**

P 6.3 Meditor

a) Yes, the company did make a profit. Retained earnings increased by €366,000 to €2,308 k at 30 September 2013, which represents the profit retained during the year.

b) The property is Meditor's most significant asset. At €3.5 million, its value on the statement of financial position is much greater than other assets.

c) During the year ended 30 September 2013, Meditor raised €900,000 from an issue of ordinary shares and repaid a €600,000 loan.

Share capital increased by €300,000, and share premium increased by €600,000, revealing that the share issue raised €900,000.

The loan was on the 2012 statement of financial position but is not on the 2013 one. It must have been repaid.

d) The company did not buy any new properties.

The difference between the 2013 and 2012 property figures is €1,260,000, (€3,500,000 – €2,240,000). This is the same as the amount that has been added to the revaluation reserve, which reveals that the property has been revalued during the year. No new properties were purchased.

e) The plant and equipment that Meditor owns has on average been owned for a number of years. This can be deduced from the fact that these assets have been heavily depreciated.

f) At 30 September 2012, the company had an overdraft of €111,000, but at 30 September 2013, the company had a positive cash balance of €640,000. While it is a good sign that the overdraft has been eliminated, the current cash balance is rather high. Meditor may plan to invest the funds in the next financial year, perhaps in new plant and equipment.

Chapter 7

Demonstration Exercise solutions

7.2

a) Financing cash flow.

b) Investing cash flow.

c) Investing cash flow.

d) Operating cash flow.

e) Financing cash flow.

7.4

a) The business has an overdraft at 31 December 2013 because of the significant expenditure on property, plant, and equipment (£96,000) and the large increase in inventories during the year (£18,800).

b) Sam could consider some of the following actions:
   - Raise additional long-term funding, for example, by taking out another loan.
   - Reduce the value of inventory held, or at least minimize any increase in inventory held.
   - If additional non-current assets are needed, consider hiring or leasing them.
   - Arrange longer credit terms from suppliers.

7.5

a) The proceeds from the shares issued to Raja should be shown as a cash inflow from financing activities.

b) Betty's sale of her shares during the year will not result in any cash flowing into the company, and there will be no effect on the statement of cash flows.

c)

Smart Sports Ltd	
Statement of cash flows for the year ended 31 December 2014	
	£
Cash flows from operating activities	
Operating profit	62,555
Add: Depreciation	30,605
	93,160
Working capital movements	
Less: Increase in inventories	(18,600)
Less: Increase in trade receivables and prepayments	(9,300)
Add: Increase in trade payables and accruals	31,040
Cash generated from operations	96,300
Interest paid	(1,100)
Net cash from operations	**95,200**
Cash flows from investing activities	
Purchase of property, plant, and equipment	(60,100)
Cash flows from financing activities	
Proceeds of share issue	30,000
Repayment of loan	(20,000)
Dividends paid	(17,500)
Net decrease in cash	27,600
Cash balances at 1 January 2014	(10,430)
Cash balances at 31 December 2014	**17,170**

7.6

Smart Sports Ltd's statement of cash flows for the year ended 31 December 2014 allows users to see how that business has funded its operations during the year and how liquid the business is at the year-end. Points to note include the following:

1. Smart Sports' cash balances have increased significantly over the course of the year such that the large overdraft of £10,430 at the beginning of the year has been replaced by a large positive bank balance of £17,170 by the year-end.

2. Cash generated from operations of £95,200 could easily cover the dividends of £17,500 and interest of £1,100 that were paid.
3. Overall, long-term funding raised £10,000 during 2014. The company raised £30,000 from the shares issued to Raja, while £20,000 was used to repay loans during the year.
4. Smart Sports Ltd made a significant investment in non-current assets during 2014 by spending £60,100 on new non-current assets. The funding for this expenditure could easily be covered by the funds generated from operations, which amounted to £95,200 in 2014.
5. Although inventories and trade receivables have increased over the year, trade payables have increased by far more, enabling Smart Sports Ltd to rely more heavily on the short-term funding provided by credit suppliers.
6. The cash balance at 31 December 2014 is £17,170, which seems high and is certainly likely to be adequate to allow the business to operate on a day-to-day basis in the following year. The company may plan to use those funds in the near future.

Practice Question solutions

P 7.1 Rory's Newsmart

a)

Rory's Newsmart Ltd	
Statement of cash flows for the year ended 31 March 2014	
	£
Cash flows from operating activities	
Operating profit	69,000
Add: Depreciation.	16,000
	85,000
Working capital movements	
Less: Increase in inventories	(91,400)
Less: Increase in trade receivables	(60,600)
Less: Decrease in trade payables and accruals	(11,600)
Cash generated from operations	(78,600)
Less: Tax paid	(21,000)
Net cash from operating activities	(99,600)
Cash flows from investing activities	
Purchase of property, plant, and equipment	(224,000)
Cash flows from financing activities	
Proceeds of share issue	120,000
Net decrease in cash	(203,600)
Cash balances at 1 April 2013	133,600
Cash balances at 31 March 2014	**(70,000)**

b) The above reconciliation shows why, despite making a profit for the year of £48,000 and making a share issue that raised £120,000, the company had an overdraft of £70,000 at the year-end. The main reasons were as follows:

1. £224,000 was spent on purchases of non-current asset during the year: £120,000 on property and £104,000 on equipment. This was probably mainly due to expenditures made to acquire and equip the new branch opened during the year.
2. Only £120,000 was raised from the share issue, and £99,600 was the net cash generated from operations. These long-term sources of funds total £219,600, which is almost enough to cover the significant expenditure on the new branch and its fixtures.
3. During the year, inventories increased markedly (by £91,400), probably as a result of stocking the new branch.
4. Trade receivables also rose sharply, which was possibly due to the new branch or possibly caused by poor credit control. A newsagent would not be expected to have significant trade receivables.
5. At a time of rising inventories and trade receivables, trade payables fell, which further increased the overdraft. Perhaps suppliers are demanding faster payment or the company is paying its suppliers too quickly.

To summarize, although the business was profitable, it has obviously undergone a significant expansion during the year with the addition of the new branch. This has resulted in significant investment in property, equipment, and working capital. The share issue did not raise sufficient extra long-term funding, when taken with the funds from operations, to cover this expansion. The control of inventories, trade receivables, and trade payables may need further investigation to ensure that control of these items is adequate.

Rory's concerns regarding the possibility of theft having led to the overdraft are probably misguided. The overdraft was caused by the factors explained above.

P 7.2 Biscuit Barrels

The statement of cash flows reveals that the company made a profit of $126,500 during 2011, but after adjusting for working capital movements this was reduced to $113,510 cash from operations.

The lower cash from operations figure was mainly caused by a large increase in inventories held. Although trade payables increased by $4,040, trade receivables increased by a much larger amount, leading to funds flowing out of the business to fund working capital.

A $50,000 loan was repaid during the year using funds from operations as no additional long-term funding was raised. Funds from operations also funded the $31,000 dividend paid during the year.

In addition to repaying the loan, the business spent a significant sum—$72,000—on new equipment. Older equipment sold raised the sum of $18,770, a fraction of the amount spent on the new equipment. The new equipment was funded from the cash left from operations, plus it used all the cash in the bank account and caused it to move into overdraft.

Overall, the negative movement in the bank balance was caused by the large loan repayment, the amount spent on purchases of equipment, and the dividend paid in a year when no extra long-term funding was raised.

To improve its cash flow in the future, Biscuit Barrels should consider one or more of the following options:

- Reduce the levels of inventory held.
- Pay a smaller dividend or no dividend at all.
- Spend less on purchases of non-current assets.
- If additional non-current assets are to be purchased, extra long-term funding should be raised.
- If further loans have to be repaid, consider raising extra long-term funding.
- Keep working capital levels to a minimum.

Chapter 8

Demonstration Exercise solutions

8.1

Profitability

- Current and future investors.
- Long-term lenders.

Liquidity

- Banks and other lenders, particularly short-term lenders.
- Trade payables.

Efficiency

- Management.
- Trade payables.

Management would be interested in all of the above ratios.

8.2

a)

	Delhi	**Mumbai**
ROCE	300/1,900 × 100 = 16%	120/600 × 100 = 20%
Gross profit margin	2,700/6,500 × 100 = 42%	840/2,700 × 100 = 31%
Net profit margin	300/6,500 × 100 = 4.6%	120/2,700 × 100 = 4.4%
Use of assets	6,500/1,900 = 3.4 times	2,700/600 = 4.5 times.

b) The Mumbai branch is generating a greater return on capital employed, showing that it is using the funds at its disposal more effectively than Delhi. For every rupee of long-term funds in Mumbai, the branch is making a profit of 0.2 rupees, compared to 0.16 rupees at the Delhi branch.

The greater gross profit margin at Delhi shows that the branch is achieving a better margin on sales made. One possible reason for this is that Mumbai, being a new shopping arcade, may have to price its goods more competitively to attract a new customer base.

Despite the higher gross profit margin at Delhi, both branches achieved almost the same operating profit margin. This is because, relative to sales, Delhi is incurring more overheads than Mumbai. From the income statement it can be seen that Delhi's expenses are much greater than those of the Mumbai branch. A review of expenses to sales can be undertaken.

	Delhi	Mumbai
Expenses to sales	0.36	0.27
Wages:sales	0.14	0.15
Depreciation:sales	0.07	0.015
Rent:sales	0.05	0.06
Other expenses: sales	0.11	0.037

This reveals that Delhi has a greater level of expenses relative to sales. Further analysis shows that 'other expenses relative to sales' are much greater in Delhi. A more detailed investigation of the 'other expenses' would be required to gain further insight into the difference in levels of expenditure.

The use of assets ratio reveals that Mumbai is using its assets more effectively to generate sales.

8.4

	2015	2014
Current ratio	1.12:1 55/49	1.54:1 54/35
Acid test ratio	0.16:1 (55 – 47)/49	0.4:1 (54 – 40)/35
Inventory days	57 days (47/303 × 365)	52 days (40/280 × 365)
Trade receivable days (10% of sales on credit)	75 days (8/38.8 × 365)	51 days (5/36 × 365)
Trade payable days	45 days (38/310 × 365)	42 days (35/300 × 365)

Points for discussion with Running Fast Ltd:

- The short-term and very short-term liquidity of the company has declined sharply in 2015.
- As a retailer, you would expect the current and the acid test ratio to be low, but the acid test ratio of 0.16 is extremely low.
- Working capital does not seem to have been managed effectively.
- Inventory days and trade receivable days both increased, showing that, relatively, more money is tied up in these assets in 2015 than in 2014.
- The trade payable payment period is 45 days, suggesting that on average Sam Sports would have to wait 45 days to receive payment from Running Fast Ltd.
- Overall, advise not to supply Running Fast Ltd on credit because of their very poor liquidity position.
- Offer to supply goods for cash.

Practice Question solutions

P 8.1 TC Ltd

a) False: On average, TC Ltd's trade receivables are taking less time to pay in 2013 than 2012.

b) True: The inventory days have increased by six days.

c) Trade receivable days might decrease if the company was better at collecting their debts by chasing up overdue amounts, or the company could have offered a discount for prompt payment, encouraging customers to settle their debts earlier. Inventory days might increase if the company is having difficulty selling their inventory.

P 8.2 DogsRUs

a)

	DogsRUs	**Fido**	**Happy Dog Foods**
Gross profit margin	29.30%	26.00%	33.10%
Trade payable days	99 days	58 days	58 days
Trade receivable days	99 days	60 days	114 days
Inventory days	115 days	70 days	55 days

b) DogsRUs and Fido need to improve margins achieved by raising prices and/or buying more keenly, because compared to Happy Dog Foods' gross profit margin, those of DogsRUs and Fido are lower.

Fido has lower trade receivable days compared to those of DogsRUs and Happy Dog Foods. DogsRUs and Happy Dog Foods need to improve credit control procedures—by watching bad debts, monitoring credit limits, chasing late payers, offering prompt payment discounts, etc. This would improve trade receivable days.

DogsRUs takes much longer to pay its suppliers, with trade payable days of 99 compared to 58 for both DogsRUs and Happy Dog Foods. Could Fido and Happy Dog Foods extend the credit that they take from suppliers? Has DogsRUs perhaps had some cash flow problems?

DogsRUs holds far more inventory than the others at 115 days—is this necessary? Could it reduce the funds tied up in inventory?

c)

(i) If Happy Dog Foods had had an exceptionally high turnover in December 2012, then the trade receivable days figure will have been distorted upwards as a result of the extra sales made on credit in the final month of the year.

(ii) If DogsRUs made a large amount of purchases in December 2012, then the trade payable days figure will have been distorted upwards as a result of the extra purchase made on credit in December 2012.

In addition, the inventory holding period will show up as a longer period because the amount held in inventory at the year-end (31 December 2012) will be greater than usual.

Chapter 9

Demonstration Exercise solutions

9.1

a) Gearing proportions for the alternative funding methods:

Financed by share issue: (20 + 130)/(250 + 200 + 500) × 100 = 16%

Financed by gearing: (20 + 330 + 200)/(50 + 500) × 100 = 100%

b)

	Sam Sports Ltd finance raised by share issue £	Sam Sports Ltd finance raised by gearing up £
Profit before interest and dividends	50,000	50,000
Less: Interest on loan	1,000	1,000
Less: Interest on debentures		26,400
Less: Preference dividend	13,000	20,000
Profits available to ordinary shareholders	36,000	2,600
Number of ordinary shares	250,000	50,000
Profit available per ordinary share	14.4p	5.2p

c) If Sam Sports is financed by a share issue, it will still pay interest on the loan but will not have interest to pay on debentures, so its overall interest payments will be much lower. If Sam Smart Sports' profits are less than £47,400 and the company was financed by gearing, then there would be no profits available to ordinary shareholders, as the profits would all be used to cover the interest on the loan and the interest on the debentures (totalling £47,400). Therefore, if the profits are likely to be less than £50,000, Sam would be advised to fund his expansion by shares.

d)

	Sam Sports Ltd finance raised by share issue £	Sam Sports Ltd finance raised by gearing up £
Profit before interest and dividends	400,000	400,000
Less: Interest on loan	1,000	1,000
Less: Interest on debentures		26,400
Less: Preference dividend	13,000	20,000
Profits available to ordinary shareholders	386,000	352,600
Number of ordinary shares	250,000	50,000
Profit available per ordinary share	£1.54	£7.05

e) When much greater profits are made, it would be much better for shareholders in the company if the expansion had been financed by gearing. Once fixed interest and dividend obligations have been covered, the remaining profits are divided between a smaller number of ordinary shares in the highly geared company.

HIGH GEARING = high risk at low levels of profitability

= high returns at higher levels of profitability

9.2

	Rick's Boards	Peter's Snowsports
Earnings per share	210/800 × 100 = 26.25 cents	2,260/6,000 × 100 = 37.7 cents
Price to earnings	$1.8/0.2625 = 7 times	$2.3/0.377 = 6 times
Dividend yield	4 cents/$1.80 × 100 = 2.2%	6 cents/$2.3 × 100 = 2.6%
Dividend cover	26.25/4 = 6.56 times	37.7/6 = 6.28 times
Interest cover	(270 + 28)/28 = 11 times	(2,300 + 168)/168 = 15 times

Rick's Boards showed a rise in its earnings per share (EPS) between 2013 and 2014 and since then has shown a downward trend. This is compared to Peter's Snowsports, which has shown a steady increase in its EPS.

The PE ratio for Rick's Boards is seven times compared to six times for Peter's Snowsports. This is a measure of what the market is anticipating in terms of growth, and both are relatively low PEs. However, it would appear that the market is expecting slightly better growth from Rick's Boards. The consumer/discretionary sector in Australia shows average PEs of around 9.

Dividend yield for both companies sits at around 2–3%, a relatively low yield for investors.

Both companies can easily cover their dividend payments and their interest payments with their profits, and are both low-risk companies. This is reflected in the returns that they are showing.

Dan has chosen these companies because of his passion for snowboarding and for the fact that they have good corporate and social responsibility. They are both low-risk investments but are showing relatively low returns by way of dividends. Rick's Boards is showing a slightly higher PE ratio; Peter's Snowsports has a trend of improving EPS, and Dan should therefore consider investing in Peter's Snowsports.

Practice Question solutions

P 9.1 Dee Ltd

a) Gearing measures the extent to which a business is financed by debt rather than equity capital.

b)

Dee Ltd's gearing ratio

80/(90 + 65 + 45) × 100 = 40%

c) The risks to a company of having a high level of gearing are that they may not be able to meet their interest obligations and capital repayments when due. If a company cannot meet these obligations, it may be forced into bankruptcy/liquidation.

P 9.2 Joisa plc

a)

	2010	2011	2012
Earnings per share	15 pence £0.9m/6m	22 pence £1.3m/6m	43 pence £2.6m/6m
Price to earnings ratio	7.3 times £1.1/0.15	5.5 times £1.2/0.22	4.3 times £1.85/0.43
Dividend yield	7.3% (0.5m/6m)/1.1 × 100	9.7% (0.7m/6m)/1.2 × 100	8.1% (0.9m/6m)/1.85 × 100
Dividend cover	15 pence/8.3 pence 1.8 times	22 pence/11.6 pence 1.9 times	43 pence/15 pence 2.9 times

b) Earnings per share has increased over the period 2010–2012, showing that fundamentally the company has been improving its profitability over the period considered. However, the price to earnings ratio has fallen, perhaps suggesting less confidence from the market in the future prospects for the company.

Dividend yield has fallen, with shareholders receiving a smaller yield. However, Joisa plc can easily cover its dividend payments.

Chapter 10

Demonstration Exercise solutions

10.2

a)

- Hire of the machine — Fixed
- Material costs — Variable
- Labour costs — Variable

b)

Variable costs		
Material	£8.50	
Staff		
Racquet framing	£2.25	(£9 ÷ 4 racquets)
Racquet-stringing	£4.50	(£9 ÷ 2 racquets)
	6.75	
Total	**£15.25**	

c) Rent of machine: £550 × 12 = £6,600 per annum

10.3

Per racquet	
Sales price	£25.00
Variable costs, as calculated	£15.25
Contribution per racquet	£9.75

10.4

a) Fixed costs:

Hire of football pitch	£100
Coaches 2 × 160 =	£320
Total	£420

b) Variable costs per player:

Cost of the printed T shirt £6

c) Contribution per player:

Sales price	£25
Variable cost	£6
Contribution	£19

d) Break-even number of players:

$$\frac{\text{Fixed costs}}{\text{Contribution}} \quad \frac{£420}{£19} = 23 \text{ players}$$

e) Profit made with 40 players:

Contribution 40 × £19 =	£760
Less fixed costs	£420
Profit	£340

10.5

a) Fixed costs:

	£
Rental of boats	5,000
Maintenance (£100 × 10)	1,000
Kiosk	3,000
Boating staff – fixed costs	
(10 boating staff × £7 × 6 hrs × 5 days × 20 wks)	42,000
Advertising	1,250
Mooring	2,600
Uniforms	600
	55,450

b) Variable costs per trip:

	£
Hamper	35
Historical book	12
Boating staff – variable costs (£3 × 3 hrs)	9
	56

c) Break-even point:

Contribution per trip = 150 – 56 = £94
Break-even point = 55,450 / 94
= 590 trips

d) Profit – 10 trips per day:

	£
Total contribution = 94 × 10 × 5 × 20 =	94,000
Less fixed costs	= 55,450
Profit	38,550

10.6

1.

Margin of safety = (1,000 – 590)/1,000 × 100%
= 41%

This project has a large margin of safety (MOS). With an MOS of 41%, then the expected output can drop by up to 41% before the break-even point is reached. Hence this would not be a very risky project.

2. Given the nature of this business (dependence on weather, etc.), 41% is a reasonable margin of safety.

3. Owing to the acceptable margin of safety, it would seem reasonable to undertake the business.

10.7

a)

$$\frac{\text{Fixed costs}}{\text{Contribution per unit}} = \frac{£6{,}600}{£9.75} = 677 \text{ racquets}$$

b)

Contribution from sales 1,100 × £9.75 =	£10,725
Less fixed costs	£6,600
Profit	£4,125

c) Margin of safety 1,100 – 677 = 423 racquets

423/1,100 × 100 = 38%

This project is relatively low risk, as Sam can misjudge it by 38% before he would start making a loss.

d)

Sales	Cost per unit
600	£26.25
700	£24.68
800	£23.50
900	£22.58
1000	£21.85

Cost per unit is shown to decrease as the fixed costs are spread over more units.

Practice Question solutions

P 10.1 Pippa

a)

Fixed costs	Per annum £
Rent	12,000
Photographers	44,000
Technician	6,240
Advertising	550
Electricity	1,100
Drawings	16,000
Depreciation	2,560
Total	**82,450**

b) Fixed costs are very high (£82,450), while variable costs are minimal. The only variable cost is electricity of £4 per client hour. In order for this business to be viable, Pippa must be confident of achieving a sufficient level of business to cover all the fixed costs, otherwise it is a highly risky venture.

It would be better if the photographers and the technician could be paid by the hour worked rather than salaried. This would significantly reduce fixed costs as they would be paid only according to the number of customers the studio has.

c) $\text{Break-even point} = \dfrac{82{,}450}{(80-8)} = 1{,}145 \text{ sittings}$

$\text{Margin of safety} = \dfrac{1{,}300 - 1{,}145}{1{,}300} \times 100 = 12\%$

P 10.2 Wanda

a)

Fixed costs	Variable costs
Drawings—Wanda's salary	Petrol
Van depreciation	Electricity
Van expenses	Detergent
	Casual labour
	Washing machine depreciation

b)

Variable cost	Per bag £
Petrol (£2/2 bags)	1.00
Electricity	1.00
Detergent	0.50
Casual labour	8.00
Machine depreciation	0.20
	10.70

c)

Fixed costs	Per annum £
Drawings—Wanda's salary	22,000
Delivery van depreciation	4,000
Van expenses	2,000
	28,000

d) Wanda has far lower fixed costs, and more of her costs are variable. This makes it easier to control costs, and the venture is less risky than Pippa's. Even if no customers want portraits taken one day, Pippa will still have to pay her photographers and cover her other fixed costs. In Wanda's business, the casual labour is paid only when there is work that needs doing.

Chapter 11

Demonstration Exercise solutions

11.1

Product cost per unit calculated using blanket rate			
	Team kits £	Tennis racquets £	Badminton racquets £
Direct materials	3.00	10.00	8.00
Direct labour	2.50	7.50	12.50
Overheads	3.70 85,100/(15,000 + 6,000 + 2,000)	3.70	3.70
Total manufacturing cost per unit	**9.20**	**21.20**	**24.20**

11.2

Sam estimates that the business will make 30,000 units in total and will incur £90,000 in actual costs. The blanket rate is 90,000/30,000 = £3 per unit.

a) If the business actually made 30,000 units and incurred £100,000 in overheads costs, it will recover £3 × 30,000, or £90,000. But this is £10,000 less than it spent. It will have under recovered its overhead and will need to charge the accounts with £10,000 more, thus reducing the profit.

b) If the business actually made 35,000 units and incurred £90,000 in overheads costs, it will have recovered £105,000 (£3 × 35,000), but as it spent only £90,000, it will have over recovered its overhead by £15,000. It will need to increase the profit by £15,000.

c) If the business actually made 35,000 units and incurred £100,000 in overheads costs, it will have recovered £105,000, or £5,000 more than its actual overhead. It will need to increase the profit by £5,000.

11.3

a)

STAGES 1 & 2: Allocate and apportion indirect costs					
	Team kit-printing £	Frame-making £	Racquet-stringing £	Maintenance £	Total £
Hire of machinery	4,000	6,600			10,600
Supervisor salary	30,000 × 50% = 15,000	30,000 × 25% = 7,500	7,500		30,000
Rent	5,000/10,000 × 40,000 = 20,000	3,000/10,000 × 40,000 = 12,000	4,000	4,000	40,000
Depreciation	12,000/30,000 × 3,000 = 1,200	16,000/30,000 × 3,000 = 1,600	200		3,000
Electricity	20,000/30,000 × 1,500 = 1,000	8,000/30,000 × 1,500 = 400	100		1,500
Total for each department	**41,200**	**28,100**	**11,800**	**4,000**	**85,100**

b)

STAGE 3: Re-apportion service (maintenance) department costs					
	Team kit-printing £	Frame-making £	Racquet-stringing £	Maintenance £	Total £
Total department	41,200	28,100	11,800	4,000	85,100
Re-apportion maintenance	3,000/5,000 × 4,000 = 2,400	2,000/5,000 × 4,000 = 1,600		(4,000)	–
Total manufacturing department costs	**43,600**	**29,700**	**11,800**	–	**85,100**

11.4

a) Team kit rate = £43,600/15,000 kits = £2.91 per kit.

b)

Total estimated frame-machine and racquet-stringing labour hours			
	Tennis racquet hours	Badminton racquet hours	Total hours
Frame-machine hours	0.25 × 6,000 = 1,500	0.25 × 2,000 = 500	2,000
Racquet-stringing labour hours	0.5 × 6,000 = 3,000	1.0 × 2,000 = 2,000	5,000

c)

STAGE 4: Calculate departmental rate		
	Frame-making department	**Racquet-stringing department**
Total departmental cost	29,700	11,800
Frame-machine hours	2,000	
Racquet-labour hours		5,000
Rate	£14.85 per machine hour (£29,700/2,000)	£2.36 per labour hour (£11,800/5,000)

d)

STAGE 5: Apply departmental rates to calculate product cost per unit			
Cost per unit	**Team kit £**	**Tennis racquet £**	**Badminton racquet £**
Direct materials	3.00	10.00	8.00
Direct labour	2.50	7.50	12.50
Overhead: team kit framing stringing	 2.91	 3.71 (0.25 × £14.85) 1.18 (0.5 × £2.36)	 3.71 (0.25 × £14.85) 2.36 (1 × £2.36)
Total manufacturing cost per unit	**8.41**	**22.39**	**26.57**
If a blanket rate were used (Demo. Ex. 11.1), total manufacturing cost per unit would be:	9.20	21.20	24.20

Absorption costing produces a more accurate full cost than the blanket rate, as the former reflects the characteristics of each department and does not average costs across all manufacturing departments. In this case, the cost of the team kits reduces, while the cost of the racquets increases. While the kit department's total overhead cost of £43,600 is about equal to that of the racquets' £41,500 (£29,700 + £11,800), there are twice as many team kits compared to racquets. The overhead cost per kit is therefore significantly cheaper. A badminton racquet is now even more expensive than a tennis racquet as the former takes twice as long to string, which is reflected in its overhead cost per racquet.

11.5

Shuttlecock departmental costs and rates			
	Cork base €	**Feather** €	**Canteen** €
Depreciation (allocated)	45,000	12,000	5,000
Rent apportioned on floor space (square m)	17,500 (35,000/90,000 × €45,000)	22,500	5,000
Insurance apportioned on floor space (square m)	3,500 (35,000/90,000 × €9,000)	4,500	1,000
Supervisor costs apportioned on time	10,000 (10/40 × €40,000)	30,000	
Inspection costs apportioned on time	3,200 (40/100 × €8,000)	4,800	
Total department cost	79,200	73,800	11,000
Re-apportion canteen on employees	3,667 (15/45 × €11,000)	7,333	(11,000)
Total production cost	82,867	81,133	
Rate per machine hour	69.06 (82,867/1,200)		
Rate per direct labour		54.09 (81,133/1,500)	

Shuttlecock product cost per unit	
	Cost per box (€)
Direct materials: cork base	0.83
Direct materials: feathers	2.59
Direct labour: cork-base machine	0.45
Direct labour: feathering	1.53
Cork-base overhead (100 boxes per hour)	0.69
Feather overhead (25 boxes per hour)	2.16
Total cost per box	**8.25**

11.6

a)

Cost per driver for each activity			
Activity	**Cost pool £ per annum**	**Cost driver**	**Cost per driver**
Writing a specification for each type of racquet	1,000	20 specifications	£50 per specification
Placing a purchase order for materials	3,000	500 purchase orders	£6 per purchase order
Frame machine set-up	2,000	30 set-ups	£66.67 per set-up
Frame manufacture	18,624	1,687 machine hours	£11.04 per machine hour
Racquet-stringing	11,800	3,750 labour hours	£3.15 per labour hour
Delivery cost	5,000	270 deliveries	£18.52 per delivery

b)

Total activity-based costs for standard and customized tennis racquets		
	Standard tennis racquet £	**Customized tennis racquet £**
Specification	250	750
Purchase orders	2,100 (350 × £6)	900
Frame machine set-up	1,000 (15 × £66.67)	1,000
Frame manufacture	16,560 (6,000 × 0.25 × £11.04)	2,070
Racquet-stringing	9,450 (6,000 × 0.5 × £3.15)	2,362
Total manufacturing costs	29,360	7,082
Delivery costs	2,222 (120 × £18.52)	2,778
Total manufacturing & delivery cost	**31,582**	**9,860**

c)

Unit cost per tennis racquet		
	Standard tennis racquet £	**Customized tennis racquet £**
Direct materials	10.00	12.00
Direct labour	7.50	15.00
ABC manufacturing cost	4.89 (£29,360/6,000)	9.44 (£7,082/750)
ABC delivery cost	0.37	3.70
Total manufacturing and delivery cost	**22.76**	**40.14**

d) Sam estimates that he could sell these racquets for £30. Sam would have marketed the customized racquets based on the standard manufacturing and delivery cost of £22.76. He will now have to reconsider whether to make the customized racquets or increase his prices to cover the additional manufacturing and delivery costs.

Practice Question solutions

P 11.1 Elixir

The blanket rate can be calculated as £562,500/450,000 = £1.25. This can be applied to the actual number of bars of soap sold and compared to the actual overhead costs incurred.

a) Actual overheads of £583,750 and sales of 460,000 bars of soap would result in an under recovery of £8,750 (£1.25 × 460,000 – £583,750). This would require an adjustment to reduce the profit in the accounts.

b) Actual overheads of £525,450 and sales of 430,000 bars of soap result in an over recovery of £12,050 (£1.25 × 430,000 – £525,450). This would require an adjustment to increase the profit in the accounts.

c) Actual overheads of £533,550 and sales of 460,000 bars of soap result in an over recovery of £41,450 (£1.25 × 460,000 – £533,550). This would require an adjustment to increase the profit in the accounts.

d) Actual overheads of £595,250 and sales of 445,000 bars of soap result in an under recovery of £39,000 (£1.25 × 445,000 – £595,250). This would require a charge to reduce the profit in the accounts.

P 11.2 Bambino

a)

Allocate and apportion manufacturing department costs			
	Packet department €	**Jar department** €	**Canteen** €
Supervisor salaries	50,000	56,000	30,000
Cleaning apportioned on number of cleaning times per annum	2,000 (€6,000 × 40/120)	4,000	–
Depreciation apportioned on net book value of equipment	22,910 (€458,200/€1,142,900 × £57,145)	32,615	1,620
Factory administration apportioned on personnel per department	4,480 (€9,240 × 16/33)	3,360	1,400
Total departmental cost	**79,390**	**95,975**	**33,020**

b)

Re-apportion service department and calculate rate			
	Packet department	**Jar department**	**Canteen**
Re-apportion canteen on employees	€18,869 (16/28 × €33,020)	€14,151	€(33,020)
Total manufacturing department cost	€98,259	€110,126	–
Machine hours	1,600 hours	1,245 hours	
Rate per machine hour	€61.41	€88.45	

P 11.3 Shamrock

a) Calculation of bakery rate: €75,000/2,227,000 = €33.68 per 1,000 pizzas.

Note: As both types of pizza use the same base, a rate per pizza is an appropriate measure. Had they required different bases, then a rate per machine hour could have been calculated (€75,000/1,670 hours = €44.91 per bakery machine hour).

b)

Calculation of topping rate: Total hours = (5 × 1,345,000) + (6 × 882,000) ÷ 1,000
= 12,017 labour hours.

Rate per labour topping hour = €87,000/12,017
= €7.24.

c)

Unit cost per pizza (€)		
Per 1,000 pizzas	**Margherita**	**Pepperoni**
Pizza-base cost	120.00	120.00
Topping-ingredient cost	345.00	479.00
Topping direct labour cost	45.00	57.00
Packaging cost	22.00	22.00
Bakery overhead	33.68	33.68
Topping overhead	36.20 (7.24 × 5)	43.44
Total cost	**601.88**	**755.12**

Chapter 12

Demonstration Exercise solutions

12.1

a)

2019 budget: sales revenue and units				
	Team kits	Tennis racquets	Badminton racquets	Total
Sales units	16,000	10,000	5,000	31,000
Sales price per unit	£15	£33	£35	
Total sales revenue	**£240,000**	**£330,000**	**£175,000**	**£745,000**

b)

2019 budget: raw material usage				
	Numbers of unprinted team kits	Aluminium (kg)	String (metres)	Accessory kits
Team kits	16,000 × 1 = 16,000 kits			
Tennis racquets		6,000 (10,000 × 0.6 kg)	36,000 (10,000 × 3.6 m)	10,000 (10,000 × 1 accessory kit)
Badminton racquets		2,500	15,000	5,000
Total	**16,000 kits**	**8,500 kg**	**51,000 metres**	**15,000 kits**

c)

2019 budget: raw material cost per unit					
	Team kits @ £3.50 per kit	Aluminium @ £12 per kg	String @ £0.50 per metre	Accessory kits @ £2 per kit	Total material cost per unit
Cost per team kit	1 kit @ £3.50				£3.50
Cost per tennis racquet		£7.20 (£12 × 0.6 kg)	£1.80 (£0.5 × 3.6 m)	£2.00 (£2 × 1)	£11.00
Cost per badminton racquet		£6.00	£1.50	£2.00	£9.50

12.2

a)

2019 budget: raw material purchases (units and cost)				
	Unprinted team kits	**Aluminium (kg)**	**String (m)**	**Accessory kits**
Production requirement: units	16,000	8,500	51,000	15,000
Opening raw material inventory: units	(1,600)	(850)	(5,100)	(1,500)
Closing raw material inventory: units	1,700	800	5,500	1,400
Purchase requirements: units	16,100	8,450	51,400	14,900
Purchase cost Total: £213,250	£56,350 (16,100 × £3.50)	£101,400 (8,450 × £12)	£25,700 (51,400 × £0.50)	£29,800 (14,900 × £2)

12.3

2019 budget: direct labour			
	Kit	**Tennis**	**Badminton**
Cost per unit	£2.50 (£10 × 0.25)	£7.50 (£10 × (0.25 + 0.5))	£12.50 (£10 × (0.25 + 1.0))
Units	16,000	10,000	5,000
Direct labour cost Total: £177,500	£40,000	£75,000	£62,500

12.4

2019 budget: factory expenditure			
	2018 expenditure £	**2019 assumptions**	**2019 budget £**
Hire of machinery	10,600	Same as 2018	10,600
Supervisor salary	30,000	Increase by 5%	31,500
Rent	40,000	Increase by 3%	41,200
Factory depreciation	3,000	Same as 2018	3,000
Electricity	1,500	Increase by 10%	1,650
Total			**87,950**

Blanket rate = £87,950/31,000 units = £2.84 per unit.

12.5

a)

2019 budget: unit cost per product			
	Team Kit **£**	**Tennis racquet** **£**	**Badminton racquet** **£**
Materials (from Ex. 12.1(c))	3.50	11.00	9.50
Direct labour (from Ex. 12.3)	2.50	7.50	12.50
Overhead (from Ex. 12.4)	2.84	2.84	2.84
Total cost of sales per unit	**8.84**	**21.34**	**24.84**

b)

2019 budget: cost of sales				
Number of units—sales	16,000	10,000	5,000	
Total cost of sales	**£141,440** (16,000 × £8.84)	**£213,400**	**£124,200**	**£479,040**

c)

2019 budget: income statement	
	£
Sales (from Ex. 12.1(a))	745,000
Cost of sales (from Ex. 12.5(b))	479,040
Gross profit	265,960
Expenses (£98,000 + £23,000 + £67,250)	188,250
Operating profit	77,710

12.6

a)

Furniture budget: total sales revenue			
	Chairs	**Tables**	**Total**
Sales revenue (kuna)	1,250,000 (12,500 × 100)	1,600,000 (4,000 × 400)	2,850,000

Furniture budget: total sales and production units		
	Chairs	**Tables**
Sales	12,500	4,000
Opening inventory	(1,200)	(230)
Closing inventory	1,000	320
Production	12,300	4,090

b)

Furniture budget: raw material purchases in quantity and cost				
	Chairs	**Tables**	**Total**	**Total cost kuna**
Raw material: kg plastic	36,900 (3 × 12,300)	20,450	57,350	516,150 (57,350 × 9)
Raw material: kg aluminium	18,450 (1.5 × 12,300)	16,360	34,810	104,430 (34,810 × 3)
Raw material: number of bolts	98,400 (8 × 12,300)	65,440	163,840	81,920 (163,840 × 50/100)

c)

Furniture budget: direct labour in cost and hours			
	Chairs	**Tables**	**Total**
Hours	2,050 (12,300/6)	1,022.5	3,072.5
Kuna	123,000 (2,050 × 60)	61,350	184,350

d) Overhead = 65,800 + 3,500 + 115,300 + 42,600 = 227,200 kuna

227,200 kuna/3,072 labour hours = 73.96 kuna per labour hour

Furniture budget: product cost per unit		
	Chairs kuna	**Tables kuna**
Plastic	27.00 (9 × 3)	45.00
Aluminium	4.50 (3 × 1.5)	12.00
Bolt	4.00 (50/100 × 8)	8.00
Direct labour	10.00 (60/6)	15.00
Overhead	12.33 (73.96/6)	18.49
Total per unit	57.83	98.49

e) Cost of sales kuna

Chair cost of sales = 57.83 kuna × 12,500 units = 722,875

Table cost of sales = 98.49 kuna × 4,000 units = 393,960

Total cost of sales = 1,116,835

f)

Furniture budget: income statement in kuna	
Sales (from Ex. 12.6(a))	2,850,000
Cost of sales (from Ex. 12.6(e))	1,116,835
Gross profit	1,733,165
Expenses (730,000 + 457,800)	1,187,800
Operating profit	545,365

12.7

Badminton racquet variance analysis Jan–July 2019					
	2019 budget	**2019 actual**	**Variance**	**2019 flexed budget**	**Flexed variance**
Badminton racquet units	3,000	2,500	(500)	2,500	
Sales (£)	105,000	90,000	(15,000)	87,500	2,500
Variable costs (£)	66,000	60,000	6,000	55,000	(5,000)
Contribution (£)	39,000	30,000	(9,000)	32,500	(2,500)

The sales manager's performance has been weak, with sales volume less than budget by 500 units. However, against a flexed budget taking into account the reduced volume, sales pricing has been above budget, with a favourable variance of £2,500. On the other hand, the production manager has not made sufficient variable cost savings after taking into account the lower sales volumes.

12.8

As the direct labour rate was £10.50 compared to a budget of £10 per hour, there was an adverse labour rate variance of £4,200 for tennis racquets and £3,750 for badminton racquets. In the case of tennis racquets, this was offset by a favourable variance in labour usage, possibly suggesting that better trained staff worked more efficiently, even if they were paid more. However, this was not matched with the badminton racquets. This could be due to staff not achieving target hours per racquet as they got used to a new product.

Practice Question solutions

P 12.1 Renata

a)

Sales and production budget in units			
	Strawberry units	**Raspberry units**	**Kiwi units**
Sales	178,000	236,000	53,000
Opening inventory	(16,300)	(25,000)	(4,200)
Closing inventory	14,240	18,880	4,240
Production	175,940	229,880	53,040

b)

Raw material usage budget				
	Strawberry	**Raspberry**	**Kiwi**	**Total**
Fruit (kg)	105,564	114,940	63,648	
Sugar (kg)	70,376	114,940	53,040	238,356
Jars	175,940	229,880	53,040	458,860
Lids	175,940	229,880	53,040	458,860
Labels	351,880	459,760	106,080	917,720

c) & d)

Total raw material budget costs and cost per jar			
	Strawberry €	Raspberry €	Kiwi €
Fruit	139,344	179,306	146,390
Sugar	14,075	22,988	10,608
Jar	21,113	27,586	6,365
Lid	5,278	6,896	1,591
Labels	7,038	9,195	2,122
Total cost	**186,848**	**245,971**	**167,076**
Cost per jar	1.06	1.07	3.15

Total raw material cost budget is €599,895.

P 12.2 Turkish teddies

Labour budget		
	Standard teddy	Dressed teddy
Cost of manufacturing time per teddy in lira	5.00 (10.00 lira × 0.5 hours)	7.50
Cost of packaging time per teddy in lira	0.13 (8 lira per hour / 60 teddies per hour)	0.13
Total direct labour cost per teddy in lira	5.13	7.63
Total number of teddies	50,000	15,000
Total direct labour cost in lira	256,500	114,450

Total direct labour budget is 370,950 lira.

P 12.3 Sole

By calculating the percentage increases in certain cost categories, comparisons can be made with other data to see whether the assumptions are realistic. For example, a sales price increase can be compared to general inflation, volume growth to market expectation, and material cost increases to volume growth and selling price increases. The board should be challenging the management accountant on a number of issues, including:

1. Is the selling price inflation of 4% (average price of a shoe £36.40 in budget compared to £35 actual price) per annum realistic when general inflation is 2%?
2. How is the volume growth of 5% per annum going to be generated, given the market is competitive, with no increase in marketing expenditure? (Volume for budget 89,670 units compared to 85,400 actual units.)

3. Material costs increase only by volume (5%),[1] with no allowance for cost inflation.
4. Direct labour costs increase only by 2%[2] in line with inflation. How is the labour force structured? Would sales volume increases result in an increase in the number of direct labour hours?
5. Has the rent been checked to the current rent agreement? When is the next rent review due?
6. How have the cost savings in factory administration been calculated? Are they based on realistic assumptions?
7. The head office charge has been kept at current levels, despite an increase in revenue. They should be calculated at 10% of sales revenue.

Notes:
[1] (1,345,050 – 1,281,000)/1,281,000 × 100 = 5%
[2] (696,864 – 683,200)/683,200 × 100 = 2%

Chapter 13

Demonstration Exercise solutions

13.1

The new selling price will be:

a) £28.60 (£22 × 1.3)

b) £27.50 (£22/0.8).

13.2

The cost of sales must be:

a) £27 (£45 × (1 – 0.4))

b) £26.47 (£45/1.7).

13.3

a) The selling price will be £17 (£20 × (1 – 0.15)).

b) Smart Sports' selling price to the retailer will be £33 (£60 × 0.55).

c) The final selling price of each racquet to the badminton player is £85 (£51/0.6).

13.5

Indoor-hockey T-shirts: special price	
Costs per unit	**£**
Material	8.00
Temporary labour	3.00 (£3,000/1,000)
Delivery	0.5
Total cost per unit	**11.50—minimum price**

Note: The cost of the permanent workforce is not included, as this will not change as a result of the decision to accept the contract.

13.7

Badminton racquets optimum price			
Number of badminton racquets	**Selling price per racquet**	**Contribution per racquet**	**Total contribution**
5,000	£30	£6 (£30 – £24)	£30,000
4,000	£35	£11	£44,000
3,000	£40	£16	£48,000
2,000	£45	£21	£42,000

The optimum price would be £40, in order to maximize total contribution.

13.8

a) If the UK division has spare capacity, the transfer price to India should be at least the variable cost of the products in the UK or £2.50 per team kit (£1,250/500).

b) If the UK division is working at full capacity, the transfer price should be the market price of £2,400.

c) If India has found an alternative local supplier who would sell them a design at an equivalent cost of £3.75 per team kit, they should agree to buy from the UK if it is prepared to sell the design for less than £1,875 (£3.75 × 500). If the UK has spare capacity, they would probably be willing to do so.

Practice Question solutions

P 13.1 Tatiana

Tatiana's selling price of her outfits would be:

a) 1,000 rubles

b) 2,100 rubles

c) 1,560 rubles.

Timur's selling price to Tatiana will be:

d) 900 rubles

e) 550 rubles

f) 700 rubles.

P 13.2 Nickolai

Nickolai's cost of sales will be:

a) 3,030 rubles

b) 960 rubles.

Nickolai and Boris' negotiations:

c) 510 rubles

d) 1,125 rubles.

P 13.3 St Pierre

St Pierre contribution analysis		
	Total for 500,000 cans C$'000	**Total for one million cans C$'000**
Contract price	350.0	630.0
Tuna	90.0	180.0
Additional materials	10.0	20.0
Can	7.5	15.0
Label	2.5	5.0
Direct labour	52.5	105.0
Total variable costs	162.5	325.0
Distribution	35.0	50.0
Contribution	152.5	255.0
Label machine	200.0	200.0
Net contribution	(47.5)	55.0

It would be unadvisable for St Pierre to accept the contract for 500,000 cans, as it will not make any contribution, but it could consider the one-million can contract. However, in the long-term, it must estimate what impact this pricing might have on its existing customers, who might demand more competitive prices. Production overheads are not taken into account when calculating the contribution, as these will not change in the short-term, whether or not the contract is accepted.

Chapter 14

Demonstration Exercise solutions

14.2

Olympic contract: assessing relevant costs			
Revenue/ Cost	**Detail**	**Relevant/ non-relevant**	**Total relevant revenue/(costs) £**
Revenue	Contract value of supplying football team kits	Relevant	75,000
Cost	Tennis kit contract	Opportunity	(15,200)
	Samples provided to secure contract	Sunk	Nil
	Hire of logo machine	Relevant	(3,400)
	Cost of basic kits (20 × £1,575)	Relevant	(31,500)
	Cost of logo materials (20 × £50)	Relevant	(1,000)
	Depreciation on printing machine	Non-relevant	Nil
	Temporary labour	Relevant	(15,700)
	Supervisor	Non-relevant	Nil
	Allocated office costs	Non-relevant	Nil
Net benefit			8,200

As relevant revenues exceed relevant costs, they should go ahead with the Olympic contract.

14.4

a)

Specialist IT manager or buy-in consultancy advice		
	Employ specialist £	**Buy-in IT services £**
Salary & pension	65,000	
Training	1,500	
Telephone and travel	700	
IT contract savings	(11,500)	
Contract consultant: 34 weeks × 35 hours per week @ £50 per hour		**59,500**
Total	**55,700**	**59,500**

They should consider employing an in-house IT specialist, but the costs are so close that they must consider other factors too.

b) What other considerations need to be taken into account?

If they employ a specialist, they may not be able to terminate the employment contract easily without incurring significant other costs such as redundancy. On the other hand, they will gain from the continuity of experience of having one employee who consistently works with Smart Sports, rather than using consultants who may change frequently. If they contract out IT, they will lose much specialist knowledge from the company. Sam may be more likely to be able to control salary increases than IT contract hour price rises. He would also need to consider how accurate his estimate is of the consultancy hours. Should they be reduced, savings could be made by hiring a consultant.

14.6

String: limiting factor			
	Tennis racquet	**Badminton racquet**	**Squash racquet**
Sales demand for next month	1,250 racquets	600 racquets	500 racquets
Contribution per unit	£12.50	£14.00	£19.50
String required per racquet	3.6 metres	3.0 metres	2.8 metres
Contribution per metre	£3.47	£ 4.67	£6.96
Production priority	3	2	1
String usage	3,000 metres (6,200 – 1,800 – 1,400)	1,800 metres	1,400 metres
Optimum number of racquets	833	600	500

14.8

Lee's cutting equipment

Saving per garment can be calculated from:

1 minute per garment/60 minutes per hour × £8.50 labour cost per hour = 14.17 pence

$$\frac{\text{Fixed (tool cost)}}{\text{Savings per garment}} = \frac{£750}{£0.142} = 5{,}282 \text{ garments}$$

Lee will need to cut at least 5,282 garments in his first year in order to break-even on the cost of the new machine.

14.10

Rather than looking at a profitability analysis of his drinks, Danni needs to reformat it as a contribution statement and compare it to the savings that would be made by discontinuing the energy product range.

Danni's Drinks contribution analysis				
	Original €	**Energy** €	**Sugar-free** €	**Total** €
Sales revenue	252,500	56,320	130,260	439,080
Cost of goods sold	101,000	34,918	58,617	194,535
Contribution	151,500	21,402	71,643	244,545

Cost savings from discontinuing energy drinks:

	€
Utility	5,230
Supervisory	13,450
Advertising	3,250
Total	21,930

While energy drinks make a contribution to overheads, once the incremental savings have been taken into account, it would still be advisable for Danni to discontinue them. The savings from discontinuing the energy drinks, €21,930, are still more than their contribution of €21,402.

Practice Question solutions

P 14.1 Brookes

Analysis of relevant revenues and costs of a market research contract			
			£
Relevant revenue	Fee	Relevant	75,000
Relevant costs	£5,000 × 6 months market researcher salary	Relevant	(30,000)
	Specialist software	Relevant	(15,000)
	Processing costs	Relevant	(8,000)
Opportunity cost	Existing staff		(14,000)
Sunk cost	£10,000 initial research	Non-relevant	Nil
Committed cost	£5,000 market researcher salary	Non-relevant	Nil
Allocate cost	10% of fee	Non-relevant	Nil
Net benefit			8,000

The project should go ahead, as relevant revenues of £75,000 exceed relevant costs of £67,000 by £8,000.

P 14.2 Carlos

New frozen products: make or buy analysis			
	Yogurt €	Boxes of chocolates €	Sorbet €
Bought-in price per 100 units	95	150	60
Raw materials per 100 units	30	50	20
Variable labour costs per 100 units	20	50	10
Distribution per 100 units	15	30	11.75
Equipment cost per 100 units	25	28	6.25
Made-in cost	90	158	48
	MAKE	BUY	MAKE

Carlos should make the yogurt and the sorbet himself but buy-in the boxes of chocolate. The overhead allocation of 10% sales should not be taken into account, as it is not a relevant cost, since the overhead cost will remain unchanged regardless of whether Carlos makes or buys in these products.

P 14.3 Fleur

Book product group: product profitability			
	Adult £	Children £	Educational £
Sales revenue	746,000	568,000	342,000
Cost of goods sold	373,000	430,800	102,600
Rent of shop	148,659	113,187	68,154
Shop staff	33,786	25,724	15,490
Promotional expenses	22,500	42,500	10,200
Profit	168,055	(44,211)	145,556

While a product profitability report would suggest that children's books should be discontinued, this can be reformatted as a contribution statement.

Book product group: product contribution			
	Adult £	Children £	Educational £
Sales revenue	746,000	568,000	342,000
Cost of goods sold	373,000	430,800	102,600
Promotional expenses	22,500	42,500	10,200
Contribution	350,500	94,700	229,200

The children's product group should not be discontinued even if it looks as if it makes a loss from the product profitability. The contribution made by the children's books is more than the savings that would be made from the rent and staff if it were to be discontinued (£50,000 rent + £25,000 salaries = £75,000).

Chapter 15

Demonstration Exercise solutions

15.2

To find the average annual operating profit, the depreciation charge must be computed. If depreciation is charged on the straight-line basis:

$$\text{Depreciation per annum} = \frac{\text{Cost less residual value}}{\text{Estimated useful life}}$$

$$= \frac{(£1{,}500 - 200) - £100}{4\text{ years}}$$

$$= £300\text{k}$$

The average annual profit will then be:

Year 1	Operating profit after depreciation (£360k – £300k)	£60k
Year 2	Operating profit after depreciation (£550k – £300k)	£250k
Year 3	Operating profit after depreciation (£710k – £300k)	£410k
Year 4	Operating profit after depreciation (£340k – £300k)	£40k
	Average for the 4 years (60k + 250k + 410k + 40k)/4	**£190k**

$$\text{The average amount invested in the project} = \frac{\text{Cost of project} + \text{residual value}}{2}$$

$$= \frac{(£1{,}300\text{k} + £100\text{k})}{2}$$

$$= £700\text{k}$$

Accounting rate of return (ARR) = 190/700 × 100% = 27%

Note that the amount of £40k that has already been spent by Danni and Sam while researching the venture is not a relevant cost.

An ARR of 27% is a better rate of return than they currently achieve in their existing businesses. Based on ARR alone, they should consider proceeding further with this project.

15.4

To find the payback period:

	Cash inflow/ (outflow) £'000	Cumulative cash flow £'000	
At start	(1,300)	(1,300)	
After one year	360	(940)	(1,300) + 360
After two years	550	(390)	(940) + 550
After three years	710	320	(390) + 710
After four years	440	760	320 + 440

The payback period will be between two and three years:

$$\text{Payback period} = 2 \text{ years} + \frac{390}{710} \times 12 \text{ months} = 2 \text{ years and } 7 \text{ months}$$

The payback period for the project is less than the target of three years, and they should therefore consider proceeding with this project.

15.5

a) To find the NPV:

Time		Cash flows £'000	Discount factor (15%)	PV £'000
At start	Initial costs	(1,300)	1	(1,300)
After one year	Net cash flow	360	0.87	313
After two years	Net cash flow	550	0.76	418
After three years	Net cash flow	710	0.66	469
After four years	Net cash flow	440	0.57	251
Net present value				**£151k**

b) To find the IRR:

The IRR is clearly above 15%. If we calculate the NPV using a discount rate of 20%:

Time		Cash flows £'000	Discount factor (20%)	PV £'000
At start	Initial costs	(1,300)	1	(1,300)
After one year	Net cash flow	360	0.83	299
After two years	Net cash flow	550	0.69	380
After three years	Net cash flow	710	0.58	412
After four years	Net cash flow	440	0.48	211
Net present value				**£2k**

The IRR of the project is therefore 20% as the NPV is very close to zero when that discount rate is used.

c) Danni and Sam should consider proceeding with this project, as it yields a positive NPV using the discount rate of 15%. If the required return was 20%, then it would not be worthwhile for them to proceed, as the NPV of the project is minimal using that discount rate.

15.6

To find the payback period:

	Cash inflow/ (outflow) £'000	Cumulative cash flow £'000	
At start	(254)	(254)	
After one year	40	(214)	(254) + 40
After two years	70	(144)	(214) + 70
After three years	140	(4)	(144) + 140
After four years	120	116	(4) + 120

The payback period is three years.

To find the NPV at 10%:

Time		Cash flows £'000	Discount factor (10%)	PV £'000
At start	Initial costs (250 + 4)	(254)	1	(254)
After one year	Net cash flow	40	0.91	36
After two years	Net cash flow	70	0.83	58
After three years	Net cash flow	140	0.75	105
After four years	Net cash flow	120	0.68	82
Net present value				**£27k**

To find the NPV at 15%:

Time		Cash flows £'000	Discount factor (15%)	PV £'000
At start	Initial costs	(254)	1	(254)
After one year	Net cash flow	40	0.87	35
After two years	Net cash flow	70	0.76	53
After three years	Net cash flow	140	0.66	92
After four years	Net cash flow	120	0.57	68
Net present value				**(£6k)**

The payback period is reached three years into the four-year project, which would indicate that it is quite a risky venture. Using a discount rate of 10%, a positive NPV of £27k is calculated, but with the higher discount rate of 15%, a small negative NPV of £6k is found.

The IRR will be 15%.

Advice:
Based purely on the above, it would seem to be unwise for Smart Sports to consider proceeding with this project. As it would be using a new technology and offering an untried product, the company should require the project to generate expected returns of 15%, at the higher end of its required returns.

There could, of course, be other factors that might influence the decision:

- Will the venture raise the profile of Smart Sports to a new audience?
- Is the venture likely to attract some good publicity for the business?
- Is it likely that the licence would be extended after the four years?

Practice Question solutions

P 15.1 Juliet

a)

Payback period for extension = 3 years
Payback period for the terrace = 2 years + 26/44 × 12 months
= 2 years and 7 months
Payback period for the new shop = 3 years + 50/78 × 12 months
= 3 years and 8 months

b)

Accounting rate of return—extension		
Depreciation per annum = (€168k – €110k) / 5 = €11.6k		
Year 1	Operating profit after depreciation (€51k – €11.6k)	€39.4k
Year 2	Operating profit after depreciation (€56k – €11.6k)	€44.4k
Year 3	Operating profit after depreciation (€61k – €11.6k)	€49.4k
Year 4	Operating profit after depreciation (€63k – €11.6k)	€51.4k
Year 5	Operating profit after depreciation (€68k – €11.6k)	€56.4k
	Average for the five years	**€48.2k**

For extension:

Accounting rate of return (ARR) = 48.2/140 × 100% = 34%

Accounting rate of return—terrace		
Depreciation per annum = (€96k – €40k) / 5 = €11.2k		
Year 1	Operating profit after depreciation (€30k – €11.2k)	€18.8k
Year 2	Operating profit after depreciation (€40k – €11.2k)	€28.8k
Year 3	Operating profit after depreciation (€44k – €11.2k)	€32.8k
Year 4	Operating profit after depreciation (€46k – €11.2k)	€34.8k
Year 5	Operating profit after depreciation (€50k – €11.2k)	€38.8k
	Average for the five years	**€30.8k**

For terrace:

Accounting rate of return (ARR) = 30.8/70 × 100% = 44%

Accounting rate of return—new shop		
Depreciation per annum = (€247k – €180k) / 5 = €13.4k		
Year 1	Operating profit after depreciation (€60k – €13.4k)	€46.6k
Year 2	Operating profit after depreciation (€65k – €13.4k)	€51.6k
Year 3	Operating profit after depreciation (€72k – €13.4k)	€58.6k
Year 4	Operating profit after depreciation (€78k – €13.4k)	€64.6k
Year 5	Operating profit after depreciation (€80k – €13.4k)	€66.6k
	Average for the five years	**€57.6k**

For new shop:

Accounting rate of return (ARR) = 57.6/215 × 100% = 27%

c)

NPV calculation—extension				
Time		**Cash flows €'000**	**Discount factor (12%)**	**Present value €'000**
At start	Cash outflow	(168)	1	(168.0)
Year 1	Cash inflow	51	0.89	45.4
Year 2	Cash inflow	56	0.80	44.8
Year 3	Cash inflow	61	0.71	43.3
Year 4	Cash inflow	63	0.64	40.3
Year 5	Cash inflows (68 + 110)	178	0.57	101.5
Net present value				**€107.3k**

NPV calculation—terrace				
Time		Cash flows €'000	Discount factor (12%)	Present value €'000
At start	Cash outflow	(96)	1	(96.0)
Year 1	Cash inflow	30	0.89	26.7
Year 2	Cash inflow	40	0.80	32.0
Year 3	Cash inflow	44	0.71	31.2
Year 4	Cash inflow	46	0.64	29.4
Year 5	Cash inflows (50 + 40)	90	0.57	51.3
Net present value				**€74.6k**

NPV calculation—new shop				
Time		Cash flows €'000	Discount factor (12%)	Present value €'000
At start	Cash outflow	(247)	1	(247.0)
Year 1	Cash inflow	60	0.89	53.4
Year 2	Cash inflow	65	0.80	52.0
Year 3	Cash inflow	72	0.71	51.1
Year 4	Cash inflow	78	0.64	49.9
Year 5	Cash inflows (80 + 180)	260	0.57	148.2
Net present value				**€107.6k**

d)

To summarize:

	Payback period	ARR	NPV
Extension	3 years	34%	€107.3k
Terrace	2 years & 7 months	44%	€74.6k
New shop	3 years & 8 months	27%	€107.6k

- The terrace project has the shortest payback period, which means that the business would recoup its cash outlay more quickly than with the other projects.
- The terrace would also give the highest ARR, which means that it gives the best overall return when measured in terms of the accounting profits that will flow from the project.
- Options 1 and 3, the extension and the new shop, give the highest NPV, which is the most meaningful appraisal technique. The difference between the two projects is insignificant.

- Although the payback period is shorter and the ARR is higher for option 2 than for the other options, NPV is a better measure to use for deciding between the alternative projects. NPV does take account of all the cash flows, and it recognizes and adjusts for the time value of money.

e) Based on the above, Juliet should consider proceeding with the extension or the new shop. The extension involves a smaller initial outlay, which might make it more attractive to Juliet, it would yield a higher ARR than the new shop and it has a shorter payback period than the new shop.

Other factors Juliet might consider:

- How reliable are the various cash flow projections? The figures could be reworked with a range of forecasts to see how the payback period, ARR, and NPV would vary.
- Would the terrace make the restaurant more visible to passing traffic and as a result bring extra customers into the existing restaurant?
- Would building the terrace or building the extension disrupt the existing business?
- If the new restaurant is to be considered, presumably Juliet would need to ensure that she could manage both sites or find another manager for the new restaurant.

P 15.2

a) **The payback period** is the length of time that it will take for the cash inflows from a project to cover the initial cash outlays. The shorter the payback period, the better.

ARR measures the profitability of a project given the sums invested in it. The higher the ARR, the better.

NPV is an investment appraisal technique that calculates the net present values of all the cash flows associated with a project. It takes account of the time value of money and is the most meaningful way of assessing competing projects. The higher the NPV, the better.

b) Based purely on the figures calculated for each of the appraisal techniques:

The art and craft gallery will yield the highest NPV, which is the most meaningful investment appraisal technique as it takes account of all the cash flows associated with a project. In addition, it takes account of the time value of money. This project has a long payback period of four years, which makes it rather risky.

The café project would give the shortest payback period, making it the least risky one. It also yields the highest ARR, but this technique is a cruder measure of the project's return compared to NPV.

c) Other factors that they may wish to consider:

The farmer support project would not be chosen, based purely on the appraisal results, but it may have other merits. Perhaps it would generate good publicity for the firm and enhance its profile in the region. Such a project may be in keeping with the philosophy of the firm.

The art and craft gallery would be supporting local artists and may, similarly, generate goodwill for the firm. Enhancing the standing of the firm may bring in increased sales and profits in the future.

Chapter 16

Demonstration Exercise solutions

16.1

a)

Smart Drive warehouse performance		
	South warehouse £	North warehouse £
Cost per retail outlet	923	686
Cost per van	15,000	15,000
Cost per km	0.60	0.22
Cost per delivery	75	57
Cost per unit	1.07	0.80
Cost per employee	8,571	6,000

b) It is costing 35% more to service a retail store in the south than the north (£923 compared to £686). The cost to deliver each sales unit is higher in the south (£1.07 compared to £0.80). Costs per km are three times as high (60p compared to 22p), whereas costs per employee are nearly 50% higher in the south warehouse compared to the north. (£8,751 compared to £6,000). This would suggest that the south is more inefficient, but more operational data would be useful to assess why this is.

16.2

Smart Drive warehouse operational performance		
	South warehouse	North warehouse
Sales volume per van	14,000	18,750
Sales volume per outlet	862	857
Km per van	25,000	68,750
Outlets per van	16.25	21.9
Sales volume per delivery	70	71

As the sales volume per delivery and per outlet is similar in both warehouses, it is of concern that the sales volume per van is so much lower in the south warehouse. Each van is travelling significantly fewer kilometres, which suggests that they are operating too many vans for the size of the business. Each van in the south is delivering to fewer stores than in the north. (This is likely to account for the higher cost of south warehouse employees, some of whom will be driving the vans.)

What other data would you like to have to make a full assessment of the relative performance of the two warehouses?

It would be useful to have other performance information, such as percentage of deliveries on time and percentage of correct goods delivered, to make a full assessment of the warehouses' performance. More qualitative data could include customers' opinions on the service provided, assessed by means of a customer satisfaction survey.

16.4

Financial perspective—possible measures	
Objective	**Measure**
Improve ROCE	ROCE % compared to previous year
Improve profit per warehouse	Profit/sales % by warehouse
Increase revenue	Revenue per delivery compared to previous year
Make cost savings	Cost saving % by warehouse from previous year

16.5

Customer perspective—possible measures	
Objective	**Measure**
Ensure competitive pricing	Price per km compared to competitor
Improve customer satisfaction	Rating in questionnaire compared to previous year
Improve customer loyalty	% customers returning for more business

16.6

Internal processes—link to customer perspective		
Customer objective	**Measure**	**Internal processes**
Ensure competitive pricing	Price per km compared to competitor	Better route planning
Improve customer satisfaction	Rating in questionnaire compared to previous year	Reduce breakages
Improve customer loyalty	% customers returning for more business	Improve promptness of deliveries

Internal process objective	Measure
Better route planning	Average km per delivery
Reduce breakages	% damaged goods
Improve prompt deliveries	% deliveries on time
Efficient utilization of vans	% capacity used
Efficiency of employees	Number of boxes handled per employee

16.7

Learning and growth—possible measures		
Objective	**Measure**	**Quantitative/Qualitative**
Encourage stability of the workforce	Staff turnover	Quantitative
Improve employee morale	Staff satisfaction survey	Qualitative
Fully trained workforce	Average days training per staff member	Quantitative
Improvement ideas	Number of feasible ideas per employee	Quantitative Qualitative—what is a feasible project?

16.8

Smart Drive customer profitability			
£	**Direct contracts** £	**Internet** £	**Retail outlets** £
Gross revenue	2,000,000 (100,000 × £20)	900,000	6,000,000
Discount	–	–	1,200,000
Net revenue	2,000,000	900,000	4,800,000
Manufacturing cost of kit	800,000	400,000	2,400,000
Cost of customer visits	120,000	–	15,000
Invoicing cost	10,500	52,500	14,000
Delivery cost	330,000	105,000	450,000
Contribution by distribution channel	739,500	342,500	1,921,000
Contribution per unit	£7.40	£6.85	£6.40

16.9

The following are criteria you could use to assess a good balanced scorecard:

- A sensible but imaginative strategy based on the history of Smart Sports:

  for example, new products, new geographical areas of sale (exports), more efficient production (e.g. moving manufacturing to Far East).

- Specific objectives by each of four categories to match strategy:

  not simply increase market share but specific plans, for example, launch specific new products, increase volume of certain products, increase new customers by a specific marketing campaign, attract wider customer base.

- Measures must be linked to objectives and be realistic, specific and measurable:

  For example not 'better-quality products' but % number of defects.
- A good balanced scorecard shows links between objectives and measures in the four categories:

  For example, ideas for number of research projects (learning and growth) will lead to number of new products launched (customer), which will lead to improved profitability (finance).

Practice Question solutions

P 16.1 Tarun's key performance measures

a)

Tarun's hotels			
	The Hague	**Amsterdam**	**Delft**
Operating profit per room	€3,470 (€69,400/20)	€2,628	€2,054
Operating profit %	11.2%	9.3%	8.6%
Occupancy %	85%	84%	60%
Revenue from rooms	€255,000 (17 × 300 × €50)	€378,000	€72,000
Revenue from rooms/total revenue %	41.2%	53.4%	30.2%
Number of guests	7,650 (17 × 1.5 × 300)	9,450	2,700
Restaurant revenue per guest	€38.43	€25.40	€56.00

b) The hotel in Delft is the least profitable within the hotel chain, both in terms of operating profit per room and in terms of operating profit as a percentage of revenue. This is likely to be because of a lower occupancy rate. However, Delft is generating a significantly higher restaurant revenue per guest than the other two hotels. The hotel in The Hague is outperforming Amsterdam in terms of profitability, despite a similar occupancy rate. This would suggest that the higher restaurant revenue per guest results in significantly improved profitability. Tarun could therefore look at improving his restaurant facilities in Amsterdam as well as increasing the occupancy rates in Delft.

P 16.2 Tarun's balanced scorecard

Financial

Objectives	**Measures**	**Comment**
Increase profitability of each hotel	Operating profit % per hotel	Quantitative lagging
Improve occupancy rates	Average occupancy per hotel compared to previous year	Quantitative lagging

Customer

Objectives	Measures	Comment
Improve customer satisfaction	Guest satisfaction ratings	Qualitative leading
Improve customer loyalty	Number of repeat customers	Quantitative leading

Internal process

Objectives	Measures	Comment
Improve operational efficiency of room cleaning	Time to clean room	Quantitative
Improve quality of service	Number of customer complaints Analysis of types of complaints	Quantitative Qualitative

Learning and growth

Objectives	Measures	Comment
Ensure staff morale is high	Employee satisfaction	Qualitative
Ensure high quality staff service levels	Staff absence levels	Quantitative

P 16.3 Jabu

Jabu's customer profitability data		
	Supermarkets rand '000	**Corner shops rand '000**
Gross revenue	324.0 (270 × 1,200/1,000)	189.0
Discount	97.2	–
Manufacturing cost	129.6 (108 × 1,200/1,000)	75.6
In-store promotion	40.0	nil
Cost of customer visits	18.0 (3 × 6,000/1,000)	72.0
Bad debts	–	9.5
Delivery cost per annum	31.25 (100 × 1.25 × 250/1,000)	45.0
Total profit	**7.95**	**(13.1)**

Jabu should discontinue his business with the corner shops or renegotiate his prices unless he can make operational savings elsewhere. If the corner shops are not prepared for a price increase, then Jabu should consider reducing the number of customer visits and having fewer deliveries with larger quantities of boxes of sweets. Customer visits to corner shops are costing 103 rand per box compared to 15 rand per box for the supermarkets. The delivery cost per box of sweets to the corner shops is 64 rand, compared to 26 rand for the supermarkets.

Glossary

Absorption costing is a management accounting technique where indirect or overhead costs are spread fairly across the range of products made by the business.

Accounting is the recording and communicating of financial information to both internal and external users.

Accounting rate of return (ARR) is an investment appraisal technique to calculate the average profit from a project given as a percentage of the average investment in the project.

Accruals arise where an expense has been incurred but not paid for by the date when the statement of financial position is prepared.

Accumulated depreciation is the total depreciation that has been charged on an asset since it was purchased. This is deducted from the cost of an asset to arrive at its net book value.

Activity-based costing (ABC) is a costing method that analyses the processes or activities needed to make a product. By understanding the cause (or driver) of those activities, it links the cause and effect of costs on a product.

Allocated costs are those indirect costs that are directly associated with a manufacturing department, such as a production supervisor working for one particular department.

Apportioned costs are those indirect manufacturing costs that cannot be directly associated with a department and need to be shared between departments on a fair basis, such as rent.

Assets are things that the business owns that will bring financial benefits to the business in the future.

Bad debts arise when a customer who owes money to the business for goods or services received on credit becomes unable to pay the amount due. At that time the bad debt should no longer be included in the trade receivables figure, as it does not represent an asset.

Balanced scorecards are a strategic management tool linking financial and non-financial performance measures between four business perspectives (financial, customer, internal processes, and learning and growth).

Benchmarking allows managers to compare the operational and financial performance of one business or operation against another by using key performance measures.

Bottom-up budgets are built up from detail provided by each manager responsible for a budget, with targets being agreed by all involved.

Break-even points are situations in which neither a profit nor a loss is made.

Budgets are financial plans prepared and approved by management, usually for the year ahead.

Capital is the amount the owner has invested in a business.

Capital expenditure refers to expenditure where the business will benefit from it for more than one accounting period, for example, the purchase of a delivery van or building.

Capital income includes money invested by the owner of the business and loans from third parties.

Cash flows from financing activities are cash flows that alter the long-term financing of the company. These include the proceeds of share issues or the amount paid out to redeem a loan.

Cash flows from investing activities include the amounts paid out to purchase non-current assets and the proceeds received from selling non-current assets.

Cash flows from operating activities are cash flows that arise from the normal trading activities of the business.

Cash purchases are those purchases for which cash payment will be made at the same time as the goods or services are received.

Cash sales are made when the cash is received at the same time as the goods or services are delivered.

Committed costs are ones that have to be paid for, whether or not management make a specific decision. They are a non-relevant cost.

Contribution is defined as the difference between the selling price of a product and the variable costs incurred in producing that product.

A **contribution analysis** looks at what each sector of the business contributes to the overheads. This excludes any allocated fixed costs.

The **corporate strategy** of a business sets out its long-term plan, assessing its competitive advantage by matching its internal strengths to external opportunities.

A **cost driver** is the factor that causes the cost of the activity to change, such as the number of set-ups.

The **cost of sales** is the cost of goods sold in a period, taking into account movements in inventories.

Cost-plus pricing is where the product is priced to achieve a standard mark-up.

A **cost pool** is the total estimated cost of one activity, such as machine set-up.

Credit purchases are those purchases where the goods or services have been received by the business but for which payment is made at a date after the goods have been delivered.

Credit sales are made when the payment is received after the goods or services have been delivered.

Current assets are assets that will be held by the business for less than one year, including inventory held for resale and cash balances.

Current liabilities are amounts that are due to be paid within a year, including amounts owed to suppliers.

Customer profitability analysis (CPA) often uses activity-based cost information to assess the profitability of different customers or different distribution channels.

Debentures are long-term loans raised by a company where security is usually provided for the loan.

The **depreciation charge** is the amount charged to the income statement so as to spread the cost of non-current assets over the life of those assets. Non-current assets have a finite useful life, and they will be used in the business to help generate profits over that period.

Direct costs are those costs directly associated with a product, such as material and labour costs.

Directors are those employees elected by the shareholders to run the company. Every limited company must have at least one director.

A **dividend** is a payment made to a company's shareholders to reward them for investing.

Dividend cover considers the extent to which available profits can meet dividend payments.

Dividend yield compares the dividend received from a share with the market price of a share.

The **double-entry book-keeping system** is the method of recording the two entries for each and every transaction.

Drawings are the amount taken out of the business for the owner's personal use.

Earnings per share (a fundamental ratio) shows how much profit is being made for each share.

Elastic prices are those where customers are sensitive to how high or low a selling price is set.

The **entity concept** recognizes that the transactions of a business should be recorded separately from the transactions of its owner. This principle should be followed even if the business is not a separate legal entity.

The **equity of a company** comprises the ordinary share capital and all the reserves, including the share premium and retained profits.

Estimated useful life is the expected length of time that a non-current asset will be used in the business.

Expenses are the costs incurred by the business or organization to enable the business to trade.

A **favourable variance** occurs when sales value is more, or expenditure is less, than budgeted. This will result in a profit higher than budgeted.

Financial accounting is the provision of financial information to external users.

Fixed costs are those costs that remain the same whatever the level of output (over a limited range of output). For example, rent payable will be unchanged regardless of the number of units produced.

Full costing takes into account both direct costs and indirect costs associated with the manufacturing of a product.

A **functional budget** is the individual departmental budget, for example of the sales, production, and finance departments.

Gearing measures the extent to which a business is financed by debt rather than equity capital.

The **going concern concept** means that, when producing accounts, there is an assumption that the business will continue to operate for the foreseeable future unless there is any evidence to suggest that it will not.

Gross profit is calculated as the difference between sales revenues and the cost of goods sold.

The **historic cost concept** requires transactions to be recorded at their original cost to the business, and as a result, the assets of a business are included at their historic cost on the statement of financial position.

The **income statement** shows the revenue income less the revenue expenditure for a financial period and computes the profit or loss generated.

An **incremental budget** is calculated by taking the previous year's actual figures and adjusting for changes such as price inflation.

Indirect costs are those costs that cannot be directly associated with a product, such as rent and depreciation. They are often called overheads.

Inelastic prices are those where customers are not sensitive to how high or low a selling price is set.

An **intangible asset** is an asset without any physical substance. Examples include goodwill and brand names.

Interest cover considers the number of times that operating profit covers the interest expense.

Internal rate of return (IRR) is the discount rate that, when applied to a project's cash flows, will yield a net present value of zero.

Inventories (stock) are goods for resale held in stock by the business.

A **liability** is an amount owed by the business where the business has an obligation to make a payment.

Life-cycle costing considers the costs throughout the life of the product, including the pre-manufacturing, manufacturing, and post-manufacturing costs.

Limited liability means that, should the company be wound up, shareholders stand to lose only the amount that they have invested in the business. (This assumes that their shares have been fully paid for.)

The **limiting factor** is the constraint that will limit the business's growth in the following year. For example, the expected level of sales often determines how a business should start to plan its operations.

Liquidity means the level of cash, bank, and other liquid assets available to the business. The liquidity of a business must be sufficient to allow the company to meet its liabilities as they fall due. Liquidity is a measure of the ability of a business to pay its debts as they fall due.

Management accounting is the provision of information to internal managers for planning, decision-making, and control.

Margin pricing is where the product is priced to achieve a standard margin based on the selling price.

Marginal costing is a method which only takes into account variable costs and ignores fixed costs. It can also be called variable costing.

A **master budget** is the overall business financial plan, made up of a budgeted income statement, cash budget, and budgeted statement of financial position.

The **matching concept** requires expenses to be matched to the revenue that they have generated, in order to arrive at the profit for the year.

The **net book value (NBV)** is found by taking the cost of an asset and deducting the accumulated depreciation that has been charged on that asset since it was purchased. This is the value of the asset shown on the statement of financial position.

Net present value (NPV) is an investment appraisal technique to calculate the present values of all the cash flows associated with a project and, by totalling them, calculate the net present value that a project would be expected to yield.

Net profit is the profit calculated after all the business's expenses have been deducted.

The **nominal value** of shares represents their face value and is nearly always the amount at which the shares are issued when the company is formed.

Non-current assets are assets intended for long-term use in the business.

Non-current liabilities are amounts that are due to be paid after a year, including long-term loans.

Non-relevant revenue or costs are those that remain unchanged following a specific management decision.

Operating profit is the profit arrived at after all operating expenses have been charged but before any interest has been charged.

The **operational plan** of a business translates the corporate strategy into sets of financial and non-financial objectives for managers in the short-term.

An **opportunity cost** is the amount of benefit lost when a certain course of action is taken. This is a relevant cost for decision-making purposes.

Ordinary shares entitle their owner to receive an ordinary dividend from the company. Ordinary shareholders are the owners of the company and are entitled to vote at general meetings, which gives them control over the business.

Overhead costs are the indirect costs of a business that cannot be associated directly with a product.

The **over recovery** of overheads occurs after an absorption rate has been applied throughout the year and products have been charged with *more* than the actual overhead incurred by the year-end.

The **payback period** is the length of time that the cash inflows from a project will take to cover the initial cash outlays.

A **penetrating price** strategy is often used where prices are elastic, setting prices low to take advantage of customers being sensitive to prices.

A **public company** can offer its shares for sale to the general public.

Purchases are the costs incurred by the business or organization in buying the goods it plans to sell to its customers. A purchase is made when the goods or services are received from the supplier.

Preference shares entitle their owners to receive dividends at a fixed rate before the ordinary dividend can be paid. Preference shareholders are not generally entitled to vote at general meetings.

A **prepayment** arises where an expense has been paid before the statement of financial position date but the benefit of that expense will be obtained in the following financial year.

Present value (PV) is the value today of an amount that will be received in the future. To find the present value of a future cash flow, it has to be discounted using an appropriate discount rate.

A **price-skimming** strategy is often used where prices are inelastic, setting prices high to take advantage of customers not being sensitive to prices.

The **price-to-earnings (PE)** ratio compares the market price of a share with the profit earned per share. It is therefore a reflection of the market's expectations for the company's shares.

A **price variance** is the difference between budget and actual price multiplied by the actual sales volume.

The same principle can be applied to material costs or labour rate variances.

A **private company** is restricted from issuing its shares to the general public.

A **profitability analysis** looks at the profitability of a sector of the business, such as its products or operations. This usually includes an allocation of shared costs.

The **profit for the year** is the profit that a company has made after taxation. This profit can be either used to pay dividends to shareholders or retained by the business.

The **provision for doubtful debts** is an amount deducted from trade receivables to recognize the fact that a proportion of those amounts will eventually not be received by the business.

The **prudence concept** requires that, when accounts are being prepared, income should never be anticipated but all possible costs should be taken into account. That means that a cautious, but realistic, approach should be taken to ensure that profits are not overestimated.

A **public company** can offer its shares for sale to the general public.

Ratio analysis can be used to highlight underlying trends not always immediately obvious from the figures themselves.

Re-apportioned costs are the indirect costs of a service department (such as the canteen or maintenance departments) that are shared out between manufacturing departments on a fair basis.

The **reducing-balance method** of providing for depreciation applies the depreciation rate to the net book value of the asset, so that the depreciation expense is greatest in the first year of ownership and falls every year thereafter.

A **relevant cost** is one that results from a specific management decision and will affect the future cash position of the business by incurring incremental costs.

A **relevant revenue** is one that results from a specific management decision and will affect the future cash position of the business by the receipt of incremental revenue.

Residual value is the estimated amount that a non-current asset will be worth at the end of its useful life.

Retained profit is the profit that remains once taxation and dividends have been deducted, and retained profits enable the company to fund future growth.

Revenue expenditure relates to expenditure on day-to-day expenses, for example, telephone or staff salary costs.

Revenue income will be mainly income from sales. Other examples are rent received and interest received.

Sales are the income earned from selling goods or services. A sale is made when the goods or services are invoiced to the customer, which is usually at the point the goods or services are delivered to the customer.

Semi-variable costs are costs that contain both a fixed and variable element. For example, telephone charges include a fixed rental cost-plus a charge linked to telephone usage.

Shareholders' equity is the share capital and reserves of the company. The main reserve is usually the company's retained profits.

The **share premium** is a reserve that records the premium amounts raised when a company makes a share issue. The premium is the difference between the issue price and the nominal value of the shares issued.

Step-fixed costs are costs that will remain fixed as output increases until the activity reaches a level where the costs have to increase sharply. One example is supervision costs where an additional supervisor is required once a certain level of output is exceeded.

A **stock exchange** is a market where new capital can be raised and existing shares can be bought and sold.

The **straight-line method** of providing for depreciation charges an equal annual amount as an expense so that the asset falls in value evenly throughout its useful life.

A **sunk cost** is one that has already been spent and is not a relevant cost as it will not change as a result of a management decision.

Target costing compares the selling price less the desired profit to the costed specification of the product before it is manufactured.

A **top-down budget** is imposed by management from above, with little discussion about how targets are set.

Trade payables are the amounts owed to suppliers of the business who, having supplied goods or services on credit, have not yet been paid by the business.

Trade receivables are the amounts owed by customers of the business who, having been sold goods or services on credit, have not yet paid the business.

A **transfer price** is the internal price set for the sale of goods from one division of a business to another. This can be a market-based price, set in line with the external market prices, or a cost-based price, calculated from the internal costs of the business.

The **trial balance** is a record of all account balances at a point in time and is used to prepare the final accounts.

The **under recovery** of overheads occurs after an absorption rate has been applied throughout the year and products have been charged with *less* than the actual overhead incurred by the year-end.

An **unfavourable variance** occurs when sales value is less, or expenditure is greater, than budgeted. This will result in a profit lower than budgeted.

Variable costs vary directly with the number of units produced. For example, the cost of materials in making a product would be a variable cost.

A **variance** is the difference between budget and actual sales or expenditure.

Venture capital is long-term funding, usually equity capital, provided to small and medium-sized businesses to enable them to grow.

A **volume variance** is the difference between the budgeted and actual volume, multiplied by the budget selling price. A similar principle applies to material usage and labour efficiency variances.

Working capital is the amount invested in the short-term assets of a business. It is represented by inventories, short-term receivables, and cash balances less short-term liabilities. It is defined as the current assets less the current liabilities of a business.

A **zero-based budget** starts from first principles and calculates every number from scratch.

Index

References are to page numbers.

D

E

F

G

H

I

K

L

M

N

O

P

Q

R